WindFall

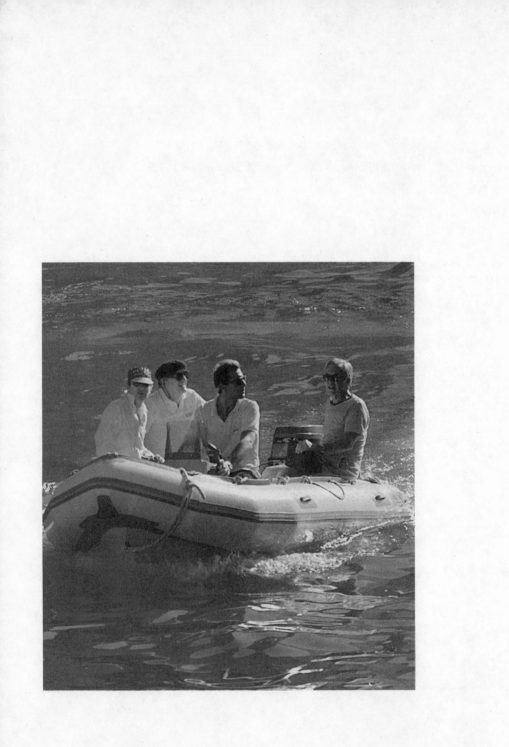

WindFall

THE END OF THE AFFAIR

William F. Buckley, Jr.

Photographs by Christopher Little

HarperPerennial

A Division of HarperCollinsPublishers

Grateful acknowledgment is made to the following for permission to reprint previously published material:

LITTLE, BROWN & COMPANY, INC.: Excerpts from *Admiral of the Ocean Sea: A Life of Christopher Columbus* by Samuel Eliot Morison. Copyright 1942 by Samuel Eliot Morison. Copyright renewed 1970 by Samuel Eliot Morison. Reprinted by permission of Little, Brown & Company, Inc.

THE NEW YORK TIMES: "2 Buckleys Become Best Sellers" by Edwin McDowell, April 16, 1986. Copyright © 1986 by The New York Times Company. Reprinted by permission of *The New York Times*.

RANDOM HOUSE, INC., AND FABER AND FABER LIMITED: Excerpt from "In Memory of Sigmund Freud" from *Collected Poems of W. H. Auden*. Copyright 1940 by W. H. Auden. Copyright renewed 1968 by W. H. Auden. Rights throughout the world excluding the United States are controlled by Faber and Faber Limited. Reprinted by permission of Random House, Inc., and Faber and Faber Limited.

A hardcover edition of this book was published in 1992 by Random House, Inc. It is here reprinted by arrangement with Random House, Inc.

HarperCollins books may be purchased for educational, business, or sales promotional use. For information please write: Special Markets Department, HarperCollins Publishers, Inc., 10 East 53rd Street, New York, NY 10022.

First HarperPerennial edition published 1993.

LIBRARY OF CONGRESS CATALOG CARD NUMBER 92-54848

ISBN 0-06-097551-2

93 94 95 96 97 CC/RRD 10 9 8 7 6 5 4 3 2 1

FOR BILL AND CAROL SIMON

CONTENTS

INTRODUCTION
AND ACKNOWLEDGMENTS

No acknowledgment can measure my indebtednesses, made manifold throughout this book. Most specifically to my companions at sea, for their companionship of course. Moreover, when I cross an ocean under sail (this is my fourth time) it is my habit to ask my crew to keep journals. Mostly they are cooperative (those who haven't been, in the past, have always had very good reasons. For instance, they had to cope with whales, or their right hand was disabled by the winch handle, or the most recent blow brought on *total* aphasia). But on Ocean4 everyone kept journals, of greater or lesser length, and on these I have gleefully leaned. Whatever your view of the book, please do not, in my presence, criticize their contributions to it.

And how does one thank the late Samuel Eliot Morison? He was a professor of history at Harvard; at one point an admiral in the fighting navy; the scholar put in charge of drawing together a naval history of the Second World War. But through it all he was fascinated by Columbus, and wrote extensively in several volumes about him and his adventures. The most popular of his Columbus books was *Admiral of the Ocean Sea*, for which he won a Pulitzer Prize. I quote here and there from Professor Morison, and from these quotations one can reconstruct a picture of this lively man with his lively mind and gifted pen. It is a pity he is not around, in 1992, to take a role in the celebration of the five-hundredth anniversary of Columbus's crossing. And to take care of Columbus's critics, a diabolical cult.

I have never given the impression, publicly or privately, that it was my intention to "celebrate" the crossing of Columbus. It is true that as we pursued more or less the route he followed, back in September–October of 1492, we were now and then engrossed by the knowledge that, aboard our vessel, we were seeing and experiencing some of the identical things Columbus did. That reflection gave us a keener appreciation of what he accomplished in that brazen voyage in search of the Indies.

No, this is not a volume about Columbus's crossing, and not, in any clinical sense, even a volume about our own Atlantic crossing. The ocean passage serves as a spinal column, but the book is primarily a tribute to people and to institutions that have nourished me, done so for many years; so many years that now I speak of the end of the affair, not knowing whether I will set out again to cross an ocean; knowing that I will never again serve, as I did for so long, as editor in chief of the journal I engendered, and love; increasingly aware of mortality (Reggie Stoops, you will see, is no longer with us) and of the fragility of even the most intimate associations. The book is about how I see the world, and how I see the world is the only way I know to react to the world.

I gave my manuscript to my companions to read, and happily report that none of them vetoed the use of any of the material I had gathered up. I am grateful to professors Thomas Wendel and Chester Wolford for their critical reading, as also Charles Wallen, Jr., and Father Kevin Fitzpatrick.

Frances Bronson, my assistant, guided the project through to completion with her inimitable savoir faire and spirit. Tony Savage typed the manuscript and gave useful suggestions. The first draft was typed by Catherine Ratzburg in Switzerland, to whom my thanks. My friend Joseph Isola, with his expert eye, has at this point expertly proofread twenty-six of my books. Chaucy Bennetts is coincidentally mentioned in the text of the book. I am infinitely obliged to her for consenting to emerge from retirement to copy-edit yet one more of my books. To be sure, she had little choice: I threatened suicide. As ever, my primary

PETER ROSEN PRODUCTIONS

(Admiral) (Professor) (Historian) Samuel Eliot Morison

reliance has been on Samuel S. Vaughan, my editor. The main reason socialism can't work is that there is no way in which equality can be generated because, you see, there is only one Sam Vaughan.

And of course this book is really a joint effort with Christopher Little. His shrewd photographer's eye lights up the book, lights up the sea, and life at sea. And if the subjects of his photography seem especially pleased and appealing, it is because they are being photographed by one of the gentlest spirits on earth. I hasten to add that two amateur photographers also collaborated in the venture: we have pictures here—taken after Christopher's departure in the Canary Islands—by Douglas Bernon and Tony Leggett. They are very, very good, and among other things dramatize the special virtues of professionalism.

I don't know whether any other writers have thought explicitly to acknowledge the sea. If not, let me be the first to say that without the sea, I would be—among other things—without a boat. It's true that true seasoned sailors know the sea as the enemy, because they know—I guess by now I can say we know—what it can do to you. A true soldier can think of a rifle as the enemy, for the same reason. But a rifle has also served as man's friend and, after the usual beloved priorities, the sea is my best friend.

W.F.B.
Stamford, Connecticut
November 1991

PROLOGUE

It was Sunday night, I had arrived in Raleigh in midafternoon, and I was alone in a large suite at a hotel, tired. It wasn't so much that I needed sleep—I was tired of going over yet again the tougher passages in the two harpsichord pieces I would perform, one of them a concerto with the North Carolina Symphony, the second a solo. The rehearsal would be the day after tomorrow, the performance, the following day.

It would be a crowded week: three *Firing Line* television programs would be taped right after the Tuesday rehearsal, and on Thursday, after the concert, back to New York to preside over a meeting of the *National Review* Advisory Council (directors of the magazine, plus substantial contributors to it). And then, on Friday, the Thirty-fifth Anniversary celebration of the magazine I had founded in 1955, following an extended rehearsal that afternoon of the fifty-minute-long documentary I had written for the occasion, which required the coordination of live voice-over, music, and slides. I would need to find the time to write out my farewell remarks (I would be announcing my retirement).

Why not now? A dismaying thought, but if not tonight, when?

I pulled out of one of my briefcases my Toshiba laptop. (Why do I use a Toshiba? is a question I am occasionally asked, to which I give the answer, "Because it tells you if there is a submarine underneath you"—a frivolous wisecrack, evoking the charges that had been filed against Toshiba two years ago, when it was ascertained by our counterespionage forces that a subsidiary of Toshiba, Inc., had sold to the Soviet Union the super-secret devices by which our Navy had succeeded in establishing whether an enemy submarine was below, within striking distance.) . . . What exactly to say at my final appearance as editor in chief? I was at that moment the senior editor in the United States, defined as having spent more years than anyone else as executive editor of a periodical publication. The party would be at the Waldorf-Astoria Grand Ballroom, all my colleagues there and eight hundred friends and supporters of the magazine. I had given the subject of what to say zero thought, but now, sitting down to write, I knew that at farewell addresses a little sentiment is not only tolerated, it is probably in order. I recalled with amusement the contrariness of John L. Lewis, the dyspeptic labor leader. When *he* resigned (pulling the UMW away from the AFL-CIO) he did so by writing out on an envelope and sending over to William Green, the head of the joint organization, his goodbye: "Green: We disaffiliate, /s/ Lewis." But he was being theatrical. I didn't want that.

I typed it out, about fifteen minutes of talk, and was finished well before midnight, leaving me time for one more go with the *Presto* movement of Bach's F Minor Concerto.

I began my talk by making those personal acknowledgments that seemed absolutely necessary. I'd be preceded by Tom Selleck (the master of ceremonies) and by Jack Kemp (the world's foremost enthusiast), by Tom Wolfe (who, I guessed correctly, would be witty and generous), and by George F. Will (*National Review*'s most illustrious alumnus, the reach of whose generosity about the magazine and me, on Friday night, would throw me off balance). I wrote a few dithyrambic paragraphs about the magazine and my colleagues. I acknowledged the role it had played in preparing a thinking movement in America to receive an *NR* subscriber, Ronald Reagan, as Chief Executive. I divulged my plans as sole stockholder to look after the magazine's future, in retirement, paying tribute to the new publisher and the new editor.

And then to a conclusion more deeply personal. "Since you were so kind as to ask about my personal plans"—this would bring an indulgent

JAN LUKAS

"Since you were so kind to ask after my personal plans"

laugh, since no one had asked after my personal plans; indeed no one
knew that the subject would come up, since my retirement came as a
surprise—"I disclose that I intend to continue to be active on other
fronts. Early this week"—I felt entirely confident in writing these
words even though I hadn't yet appeared with the symphony and
couldn't therefore anticipate exactly how well or poorly I'd do—"I
performed a harpsichord concerto with the North Carolina Symphony,
after which I resolved—with the enthusiastic acquiescence, I am certain, of the orchestra and the audience—that I will not devote my
remaining years to performing on the keyboard."

And I spoke of my immediate plans. "One month from today I will
set out with my companions on a small sailboat from Lisbon, headed
toward Barbados via Madeira, the Canaries, and Cape Verde, forty-
four hundred miles of decompression at sea, the cradle of God. But on
reaching the Caribbean, unlike the flying Dutchman, I will jump ship
to get on with other work."

Yes, another transoceanic passage, and one I was hugely looking forward to. My first time across the ocean in my own boat had been in 1975. It was a glorious success, and I decided to cross again east-bound in 1980. Another fine experience, so that in 1983, looking forward to 1985, I made elaborate plans to sail across the Pacific. In 1988 I hadn't made up my mind to give up the editorial reins of *National Review*, but did decide that even if I didn't, I would again take a month's leave to sail across the ocean, but this time I would travel with the trade winds. Travel the route of Christopher Columbus. I didn't know how exactly I would be imitating his route: I wouldn't discover that until our first landfall in Madeira. But that trade-wind passage had a special allure for me. It was as simple as this: That was the route by which, until the advent of power, traffic reached the New World from the Old. The great superhighway at sea, with the steady—well, usually steady—winds more or less astern pretty much all the way.

But I needed to say no more, and didn't, than that I'd be making that sail, and returning to work after its completion, though not to my desk at *National Review*.

I didn't feel, though, that I could end my formal career as magazine editor without attempting to communicate just something of the work-aday flavor of it, even as, in writing about the sea, one feels every now and then the compulsion to linger, even if nervously, over a little detail—to attempt perhaps the exact description of the feel of the hemp as you winch it in, to compose an intimate line or two about the feel of the helm as the wind quickens abeam, or even describe one of those concentrated engagements with calculations, bent over a plotting sheet. I would invite the audience to share with me the closing moments of an issue of the magazine—something of the ritual, the tension, something of the frolic, of the little exultations. . . .

And of course the act of closing will always crowd my own memory. Over nine hundred fortnightly issues of *National Review*. The hour is late, nearing five in the afternoon of press day, and the printer's messenger is already there waiting, so we move into the conference room, the only room at *National Review* in which more than four people can fit, and Priscilla reads out the editorial lengths, and I mark them down on the paleolithic calculator I bought in Switzerland in 1955, and Linda checks to see that I have got the right count. We have 1259 lines of

editorial copy but space for only 718. We absolutely need to run something on the subject of Judge Souter's testimony, but I see we can't afford
the seventy-eight-line editorial I processed earlier in the day. "Rick,
would you shorten this?"

"To what?" he asks, as a tailor might ask what the new waistline is to be.

The copy is spread about the room, occupying every level surface, and
you walk about counterclockwise, turning face down any editorial that
can wait a fortnight to appear and subtracting on your little calculator
its line count from the rogue total. I need to cut 541 lines. First your
eyes pass by the editorials and paragraphs that deal with domestic issues,
Priscilla having grouped them together; then those that deal with foreign
countries or foreign policy; then the offbeat material. You look down at
the calculator, having made the complete circle of the room, returning
to where you began: it shows 854 lines, and so you start the second
counterclockwise circuit, the killer instinct necessarily aroused: You have
got to cut another 136 lines. "Jeff, shrink this one by ten lines, okay?"
At *National Review* the editors always say okay, when a deadline looms.

So it is done, down to line length. And then you ask yourself, *Which
paragraph is just right for the lead?* The rule: It has to be funny, directly
or obliquely topical, engaging. I remember one from years and years ago:
"The attempted assassination of Sukarno last week had all the earmarks
of a CIA operation. Everyone in the room was killed except Sukarno."
And, during the days we feuded almost full time, "Gerald Johnson of
The New Republic wonders what a football would think about football
if a football could think. Very interesting, but not as interesting as, What
would a *New Republic* reader think of *The New Republic* if a *New
Republic* reader could think?"

Last week there wasn't anything absolutely, obviously preeminent, but
ever since it came up on the dumbwaiter from Tim Wheeler's fortnightly package, this one about colors had burrowed in the mind.
. . . Time is very short now. Okay, we'll lead with it. It reads:

> ■ Iraq and the budget are as nothing compared to
> the firestorm following the retirement of maize, raw
> umber, lemon yellow, blue grey, violet blue, green
> blue, orange red, and orange yellow, and their re-
> placement by vivid tangerine, wild strawberry,
> fuschia, teal blue, cerulean, royal purple, jungle
> green, and dandelion, by the makers of Crayola cray-
> ons.

Nice, no? Orson Bean used to say that the most euphonious word combinations in the language were "Yucca Flats" and "Fernando Llamas," though Whittaker Chambers, along with Gertrude Stein, preferred "Toasted Suzie is my ice cream."

And then you need the bottom eye-catcher, the end paragraph, traditionally very offbeat, usually nonpolitical but not necessarily. You knew which would be the end paragraph the moment you laid eyes on it, early in the day—another by Tim, whose reserves of mischief are reliable—and now you find it and designate it as such. It reads:

> ■ This week's invention is a sort of miniaturized bug zapper, battery-powered, to be inserted in the cervix for contraception and, the inventor hopes, prophylaxis. If you aren't shocked by this, you will be.

The editorials are now in order, and the line count is confirmed.

Odd, but for all the experience I have had speaking in public, I wasn't sure whether that brief description of the closing five minutes of labor before the birth of every new issue of the magazine would especially interest the assembly. But I had told them I was resigning, and that news came as a surprise, and for that reason they were especially attentive. And of course I did know, from experience—anyone would have known, even without experience—that a coda was needed. Brief, brief, but expressive of what I felt about the end of my very long affair with a journal I was so much devoted to, that had been central to my professional life. I would have to assimilate that loss, among others. I needed to say something special, however brief, after so long a countdown. . . .

> Another issue of *National Review* has gone to bed; and you acknowledge—the thought has ever so slowly distilled in your mind—that the time comes for us all to go to bed, and I judge that mine has come, and I leave owing to my staff, my colleagues—my successors—my friends, my muses, my God, an unrequitable debt for having given me so much, for so long. Good night, and thanks.

I had an awful premonition I wouldn't get through that last sentence without a break in my voice, and I was disastrously right—I didn't, and I was embarrassed.

· · · ·

Legend has it that when you retire from your principal activity it is psychologically important that you have something immediately to look forward to, in the absence of which you might be hit over the head by falling acedia. I did have two experiences to look forward to: the first, one more go with the harpsichord, this time with the Yale Symphony Orchestra; the second, the ocean passage I have described. In the talk, I touched on the therapeutic nature of it—that 4400 miles of decompression, the sea, "the cradle of God." I knew there would be agonizing moments in those thirty days ahead, moments of boredom, of frustration, of irritation, of near-despair; these are as inevitable to long ocean passages as pain is to learning, despondency to writing, loneliness to love. But the rewards outdistance the sacrifices. And the rule is, or ought to be in my judgment, that an effort should be made at requital. With me that effort is in composing a book in tribute to what the sea does—not all by itself; I would not bother to read a book about the sea that transcribed only what it was seen to do by a camera at satellite distance. Antoine de Saint-Exupéry confined to the subject of air travel makes my point. It is what the sea does to my friends and to me that incurs in me this felt obligation to let others in on it all, hoping that they might feel some of the balm my friends and I came home with.

BOOK

One

· CHAPTER ONE ·
Arriving in Lisbon

I elected to fly alone to Lisbon. For one thing there was no need to bring in another member of the crew a day early: they are all busy people, as am I, with this or that variable affecting our mobility. I work for myself in that I own the company (*National Review*) that is my primary employer. On the other hand, I also work for a newspaper syndicate (Universal Press), and have fixed obligations to it, three times per week. And then I work for a company (*Firing Line*) to which I am committed for forty-six programs per year; these, however, are conveniently scheduled. Since my columns can be written wherever I happen to be, so long as they can reach New York and then Kansas City (Universal Press's place of business) on time, I feel no tether there.

Nor does Van Galbraith (age sixty-one) who is a senior partner in Morgan Stanley and a director of two or three companies including Moët & Chandon and Club Med. His duties for Morgan Stanley are self-imposed, so that he is free so long as he does not run into an obstacle of his own making. There are directors' meetings of his other affiliations, but he had plenty of time to affect the scheduling of these so as to permit him the month of November off duty. His next fixed date is December 7 and, true, for a (very) few days at sea we would be worrying about that. Van's means of worrying is wonderfully entertaining but he does manage to generate a little tension. Five years earlier,

Van Galbraith

Dick Clurman

Christopher Little

when as ambassador to France he was scheduled to entertain the Vice President of the United States on July 4, we were sailing in the Pacific, and our goal, New Guinea, was still miles and miles away. There was some anxiety, but we made it to his chartered plane, though doing so was, well, exhausting. We punished him by giving him twenty-seven of our suitcases to take on the leg from Kavieng to Port Moresby, where he made his jet connection, arriving at the residence in Paris a comfortable two hours before the Vice President.

Dick Clurman (sixty-eight) is the world's most organized man. About three times a year, during the twenty-five years I've known him, he reminds me that he is Jewish, to which I reply that I will take his word for this (he does not practice his religion—or, rather, his ethnicity), but his conscience is that of a Calvinist. Although he is robust and convivial and hyper-lively, he always has his eye set on any obligation he has charted. For a generation, his responsibilities were to direct and look after every foreign and domestic correspondent who worked for *Time* and *Life* magazines; moreover to do so during the period when the greatest Calvinist of them all was in charge of the magazines he had founded. Some time after Henry Luce died, Dick felt the call to public service and joined the Lindsay administration in New York City as Commissioner of Parks, Recreation, and Culture. After that he was a private consultant, and then turned to writing books, his first being a vivid account of the libel trials of General Sharon (vs. Time Inc.), and General Westmoreland (vs. CBS)—a valuable volume, *Beyond Malice—The Media's Years of Reckoning,* which was a *succès d'estime* owing largely to Dick's ruthless fair-mindedness. I have often thought of him as someone who would do absolutely anything at all for a friend provided while doing so it was understood that he would be free to tell you what a damn fool you had been. He is working on a book about the implications of the merger of Time and Warner, and on that account very nearly declined my invitation to sail with us at all, but finally reordered his schedule, which involved sacrificing his Christmas vacation, so as to be able to join us for Leg One, Lisbon to the Canaries.

Christopher Little (forty-one) is able to justify the time off because he is the official photographer for the trip. The first time I crossed the ocean, in 1975 on my own schooner *Cyrano,* I generated *Airborne.* The pictures in that book were taken by my son Christopher, and one or

two by me. They were okay; in fact there is something to be said for
amateur photography. But the second trip, in 1980 (*Atlantic High*,
1982), used photographs taken by Christopher Little and they were so
dazzlingly good I thought it simply unfair not to use so striking a talent
when I went, in 1985, on the Pacific passage (*Racing Through Paradise*,
1987). If it had happened that Christopher Little had forgotten photography, or developed an allergy to film, I'd have asked him to join
us anyway, such pleasure do we get from his company (he is always
laughing, Van makes everyone laugh, and all that goes very well with
the lapping of the waves). But the pre-Christmas season is heavy with
professional obligations for a successful photographer, and Christopher
Little could sign on for only the first fortnight.

Tony Leggett (thirty-two) and Danny Merritt (forty) are the nearest
thing—and quite right, at their age—to formally indentured white-
collar types. Tony was introduced to me by author Louis Auchincloss
after Louis had read my first sailing book. I really should get to know
(wrote Mr. Auchincloss) his young friend who had just graduated from
Harvard, was an Olympic sailor, loved nothing more than blue-water
outings. We met, and have logged probably fifteen thousand miles of
sailing together. Since he works in New York he is readily available for
my impromptu overnight sails (Friday evenings). He was working for
an Italian-owned, New York–based financial house. His journal reads:

> While I had received permission from the head office back in Septem-
> ber, I was nervous, in view of three impending transactions on my plate,
> that Giorgi would suddenly say that I could not go. By Thursday Steve
> was saying I was stupid even to *consider* not going, and Gianni was
> calling me "Popeye the sailor man" with his Italian accent.

Tony, like Van, would stay the course, all the way to Barbados.

Danny Merritt's was an amusing case. He is in a way a godson, or
at least an adopted godson, because at about age twelve he began to
materialize in our household as a neighbor and best friend of my then
eleven-year-old son. He crewed on my yawl and by age sixteen was
acting as its skipper on charters. His father sent him to Switzerland to
get a little foreign experience and learning, which consisted primarily
in skiing with my wife and me—we ourselves winter not far from where

Dan Merritt

Tony Leggett

Captain Allan Jouning

he allegedly did his schoolwork. From there he did time at Regis College in Denver where he got his B.A. but during the summers he was home, sailing with my son, Christo, and me. He undertook, just after graduating, to help the captain prepare *Cyrano* for our Atlantic crossing, contracted a marriage that didn't work out, had a little girl who spends summers and vacations with him and his second wife, an industrious family therapist who is charming, notwithstanding that she concludes that anybody who finishes an entire beer is an alcoholic. They have two enchanting little boys. Suddenly, early this year, Dan was without a job, having crossed swords with a skilled but very demanding magazine publisher. I have from time to time concluded that if one wants a definitive insight into the depths of the human condition, one has merely to imagine a situation in which Dan Merritt couldn't get along with—anybody. If he, with his consummate good nature and humor, couldn't get along with somebody, should we wonder that Hitler couldn't get along with Stalin, or Arafat with Shamir?

What then happened was that while I was sailing off Yugoslavia in the early summer I learned that the publisher and associate publisher of *National Review* had offered Dan a job as marketing director (advertising sales was what he had done for his previous employer). And this, incredibly, without so much as consulting me, Danny's old friend and the proprietor of the magazine! I was both delighted and apprehensive, lest his skills not lie in the direction necessary for selling ads for *National Review*. (Danny doesn't know the difference between Adam Smith and Adam and Eve.) But lo! in the first few months he turned in a splendid performance, easily out-earning his salary. Now I greatly wanted Dan for the whole trip, since there is nobody his age who is better company, but nothing hurts a junior more in any organization than to have the top gun throw his weight around for the junior's benefit; and so, disconsolately, Danny and I agreed that he would be with us only for Leg One; a bit of sadness, but ocean trips give you a bit of sadness of every kind, and I knew this, as do all of us who have made transoceanic passages on sailboats.

On the uncomfortable flight I thought back on what had been a heady week. On Sunday I had performed with the Yale Symphony Orchestra, an experience that would intrigue me for years. The following day, almost exactly thirty-five years after I closed the first issue, I edited the last issue of *National Review* for which I would be directly responsible. The next day I taped three *Firing Line* episodes and wrote two columns, leaving only three more to write before my official two-week vacation which would begin halfway into our trip. Tomorrow morning I would first sleep—in my hotel room, for three hours: I am frequently eastbound on those terrible night flights that get you to Europe in the morning at about the time you would normally be going to bed, thoroughly dislocating you for a day or two after your arrival. This will be inevitable tomorrow. . . .

It was grand to see Captain Allan Jouning at the airport, where I handed him my allocated ration of missing parts for *Sealestial,* the ketch I had chartered for this voyage. We would meet for lunch, after my sleep, and go over the dire situation. As usual (the same kind of thing had happened in 1980 and in 1985), our ketch had more or less imploded during the preceding week. When *Sealestial* sailed over to Lisbon from Marbella, the captain had had to pour gallon after gallon of oil into the engine which, examined in Lisbon, was pronounced all but dead. Allan Jouning, resourceful as ever, contrived to concert all of Portugal, it seemed, so that an engine could be rebuilt and operating in time for our scheduled departure on Sunday. But to do this required me to bring one set of parts and Danny another set tomorrow. It also required that we persuade the mechanics to work on, notwithstanding a seemingly ceaseless string of holidays. You see, November 1 is, of course, All Saints' Day and, in Portugal, a legal holiday. The day after All Saints' Day is All Souls' Day, treated reverentially, in the manner of Boxing Day in England, which comes the day after Christmas and comfortingly prolongs that holiday. The day following that was a Saturday, when of course no Portuguese with any sense of pride is supposed to work; and the following day, Sunday, we were scheduled to leave.

What all this meant was that Captain Jouning consented to pay the men the black market sum of fourteen dollars per hour, which is about a third of what they'd be paid on a normal day in America, plus 25 percent overtime, which is one fourth of what they'd have charged in America for overtime. But all of this was hypothetical, Allan warned at our short airport session, negotiations having yet to be final. Given that Allan Jouning's preternatural calm makes the Doldrums turbulent by contrast, I caught an edge in his voice over the matter of our scheduled 11 A.M. Sunday departure. We agreed to go over it all at lunch.

It was only left to me to check in at the Hotel Ritz with my dozen pieces of gear. At the counter I had two surprises. The first was a genial voice from a middle-aged man in tweedy dress wearing a jaunty plaid fedora.

"Hello, Bill, I'm Jack Paar."

Jack Paar.

Funny how those things happen. I hadn't laid eyes on him since appearing on his program in 1962, back when he was the Johnny Carson of the day. He had been hyper-scornful of me and my politics and so overdid his inhospitality as to get "zinged"—his word—by hundreds of telegrams of protest, causing him the following day to bring on Gore Vidal to back him up and heap a little more compost on me and my works. I left the following day for Switzerland, and there I devoted the better part of a week to writing an extensive essay called "An Evening with Jack Paar." I cherish the long essay, in which I pinned down the extravagances of Mr. Paar and his guests, done at my expense and others'.

Before he was counseled by his producer to drop the subject of Buckley the Anti-Humanitarian, Paar had told his audience how genuine his worries were. "I am, however, more—more than ever—leaving Mr. Buckley out of it—["it" was Mr. Paar's indictment of the radical right] worried about what is called the 'radical right' after what happened over the weekend in California. There were the bombings of two ministers' homes out there by what they call the 'radical right wing,' and that's a shocking thing to me . . . almost killed a baby in a crib."

HUGH DOWNS (his regular mate at the time): "I think—wouldn't it be fair also, Jack, to say that Mr. Buckley would certainly not be a party ever to the bombing of somebody's home? You know, that's . . ."

PAAR: "Oh, I can't *believe* he would . . . But this climate of mistrust that's sprung up in this country by the now extreme right really frightens me. It does. The same as it did with the left, only more so because the right—they're now throwing bombs and that scares the hell out of me. I don't know how you feel about it."

That was *twenty-eight* years before. And now,
"How you doin', Bill?"
"Well fine, Jack. How are you?"
"Good, just coming back from a safari. Say, that last novel of yours—*Mongoose* was it?—was real good, real good. And your son Christopher's book *The White House*? . . . *The White House* . . ."
"*Mess?*"
"Yeah. *The White House Mess.* Terrific! Laughed my head off."
I thanked him cordially, we shook hands, and he went off.

Handed the key to my suite, which would be the center of Operation Ocean4 for the next forty-eight hours, I spotted the price on the hotel voucher: $952 dollars per day.
"What," I asked, pointing to the figure, "is this?"
"It is our presidential suite, sir."
"Ah, yes. Please give me a nonpresidential suite."
I pause to remark that the Ritz Hotel, with its superb service and food, is as expensive as any I have come across in any country, including countries that pay their mechanics more than fourteen dollars per hour for working on non-holidays. But I was tired, and it doesn't pay to concern yourself with cash-out-of-pocket husbandry before undertaking an ocean voyage: The experiences aren't congruent, the ocean begs the mind to think of infinity, the pocketbook being quite the opposite, the oppressive, unbending particularizer. I yearned now to sleep, and looked forward to talking with Allan in a few hours.

Over pizza, Allan recited to me the problems with *Sealestial*, principal among them the engine, but also the generator, which needed reassembling with fresh mufflers. We ticked off the long list of items discussed by phone and fax, including icemaker, fans, stowage space, air conditioning, spinnaker, the bimini (so to speak, the cockpit's parasol), the fiddles (they are ledges that prevent plates from sliding off dining surfaces) for the tables. . . . Then Allan said, "It will all be done,

WFB

The yacht FREEDOM

.pretty sure of that, when those parts come in tomorrow. Except for the autopilot—don't think that will work."

I had last sailed with Allan three months earlier, as a guest aboard the *Freedom*, the magnificent 127-foot ketch owned by William Simon, whom Allan serves as captain. I take satisfaction that it was I who introduced Allan to Bill Simon, having myself met Allan in 1978, when he was skippering *Sealestial* for its owners. Twice I had persuaded him to take time off to accompany me on ocean voyages, the first across the Atlantic in 1980, next across the Pacific in 1985. Our friendship is long-standing and this side of Triton, who could blow his wreathed horn and command the seas to quieten, I'd rather have him in reserve than any professional sailor I can think of.

But there is such a thing as being too fatalistic, and here was a case in point, his skepticism about any possibility of getting the autopilot to work. I remember how amusedly relaxed he was last August when, seeking to move north at Kalmar on the Swedish coast, Allan reckoned that the bridge we would need to pass under was four inches lower than the *Freedom*'s mast, which meant we would need to turn around and make a ninety-mile detour up the other end of Öland Island. Now that's the kind of thing that drives me *nuts,* though I doubt I'd have used my authority, had it been mine that afternoon on the *Freedom,* to launch the 100-horsepower dinghy and fasten the ship's halyard to its broadside, straining for four inches of heel just long enough to slide under the bridge. . . . But I *might* have.

What I was *not* going to take calmly was any possibility of proceeding across 4,400 miles of ocean without a functioning autopilot.

I pause here, without any promise not to pause again over the subject: I simply cannot understand professional sailors, or for that matter seasoned amateurs, who are indifferent to the availability of an autopilot. Three captains ago, the *Sealestial*'s autopilot was *not once used* in the long passage between Tahiti (where I had used it) and Hawaii, when I took over the boat to begin the Pacific passage. The captain simply *hadn't bothered* to turn it on and it was rotting away from disuse. I spent a heated day in Hawaii superintending its revival.

Now I told Allan that I simply did not want to start out without a functioning autopilot. I had set up a watch system that called for only two men to be on duty at any given time. Roughly 60 percent of the time when under sail, and 100 percent of the time when under power, a yacht with an autopilot can be mechanically steered, which leaves the relieved helmsman with time to read *Moby-Dick,* tie knots, write a book, or varnish the coaming. It is sheer affectation to suppose that time at sea is only prudently or enjoyably spent when someone is personally at the wheel. The ultimate professionals, the skippers who man their sailboats single-handedly, are entirely relieved of that affectation/superstition. Sir Francis Chichester, who broke the single-handed sailing record in the sixties racing from Southampton to

Newport, revealed in his book about the passage that his hands were on the helm of his boat less than two hours in total. (Single-handed boats have a different sort of autopilot, calibrated by the wind, because they do not have generators to load up batteries with the power to handle an electrical autopilot.) It never upsets me to see a member of my crew—I often do it myself—flick off the autopilot for the sheer fun of handling the helm. That's one thing; entirely another not to have an autopilot when you want one.

Allan was impressed by my gravity and said he would do what he could, but he was not confident. "The instrument on *Sealestial* is twenty-three years old."

"If necessary," I said, "install a new one." Not easy to do, granted, in Lisbon, one day after All Saints' Day.

We traveled together by taxi to the little wharf alongside the huge dock where the big passenger boats come in. It does not dismay me to see a sailboat undressed, having seen so many of them in that condition. I am sure that one half hour before the young woman emerged on her way to Westminster Abbey to become Queen Elizabeth, anybody who had gone into her dressing room would have shrieked at the utter inconceivability that all those gloves, decorations, hairpins, girdles, stockings, shoes, jewels, tiaras could come together on schedule to make a beautiful princess, fit to be a queen. *Sealestial* was a mess, but there were a half-dozen men there who seemed to know what they were doing. Liz Wheeler, our peerless young chef, was off buying something. But Martin was there (Martin Joesbury—a wonderful name, belonging to someone who deserves a wonderful name): he was—you may want to concentrate on this, if interested in lines of authority—captain of the *Sealestial.* However, for this trip, Allan Jouning had been brought in by me. To serve as captain? Not quite: I was captain. But Allan was senior among the paid crew. Moreover, by agreement with the owner, if I should decree a course of action which Captain Jouning thought imperiled the vessel, he would have the right to overrule me. If, for instance, I were to say, "I think we can ignore the Selvagens Shoal light and head one hundred and forty degrees, never mind leaving it to port," Captain Jouning could say, "Er, Bill, I don't think we'd better risk that." And we would proceed to leave it to port. In three ocean passages together this kind of thing has never once happened, though from time to time I have left it to his initiative to suggest which combination of sails he thought would be best: his knowledge of *Sealestial* (and of its eccentric inventory of sails) exceeds my own. As a matter of fact, he's a better sailor than I am.

It took me two hours to stow what I was ready to stow in the cabin. Much left back at the hotel would need to stay there until we were ready to set off, including my computer and printer and the ton of papers, overdue correspondence. But all the clothes needed for the trip I proceeded to stow, most of the ocean-oriented medicine (scopolamine patches, Percodan, antihistamines, laxatives, the stuff—the trade name escapes me—that binds rather than flushes), Mercurochrome, saltwater soap and various exotica pressed into my hand by my wife and my internist, sextant, spare sextant, chronometer, Air Almanac, plotting sheets, dividers, parallel rules, HP-41C calculator, stopwatch, HO-249 tables, guidebooks, Columbiana, and—our ace in the hole—the prototype Thrane & Thrane Satcom unit which, if it worked, would permit me to communicate with any telex unit anywhere.

My cabin, the "master cabin" I would share with Van, has on the port side two beds, one above the other, slightly to one side, permitting the two beds to become one double bed, if desired, when the top one is lowered. A dressing table with drawers on either side. There are lockers above the upper bunk (mine), and below the bottom bunk (Van's), and a deep locker at the foot of the two bunks. Opposite them, forward, is a hanging locker. Between it and the aft mast hanging locker are still other lockers, and then a huge, comfortable armchair in front of which an aluminum bar reaches from the sole of the cabin to the ceiling, providing, I assume, structural support for the cockpit above, but also serving anyone in the cabin with something to grab hold of when the boat is heeling or pitching; and also serving anyone sitting in the armchair as a pillar against which to exert pressure with one or even both legs, to maintain sedentary stability when the boat is hard heeled to port. In other words, allowing you to keep your seat and keep from crashing to the deck if the weather should be rough. A very comfortable cabin, especially in contrast with the two other passenger cabins which are best described as utilitarian. They will be described in malicious detail in my companions' journals from which I shall be quoting.

At center aft of our cabin is a companionway leading to the after cockpit. A heavy glass vertical hatch closes when guarding against wind, rain, or ocean waves. A small port above the upper bunk, when left open, permits a draft of air to run through the cabin. There is also a small fan at the foot of the upper bunk. I had crossed two oceans in that cabin, and sailed happily about the Caribbean in it a half-dozen times. I could get about it confidently in the dark, as I would often be doing in the days and weeks ahead.

I sat down for a moment in the large comfortable armchair, the one solid bit of comfort on board. After a time, scribbling on a notepad a list of things to do, I reflected on a trip four years earlier, aboard a Broward, a 93-foot luxury motor yacht I found myself on.

To give just an idea of the kind of thing you can expect on such palazzos, the master stateroom—the status equivalent of the little room I now sat in—had His and Hers Jacuzzis. The interior of the boat was done by John Bannenburg, who also did the interior of Malcolm

The Broward 93

Forbes's (R.I.P.) new *Highlander*—another way of saying that you can't buy higher-priced advice on higher-priced interior decoration. Granted, that's not the same thing as saying that Bannenburgiana are for all people the optimal utilization of a ship's cubic potential. I last took a Jacuzzi (as it happens) an hour or so before writing these words—had a hot bath right here where I live—which proves that I am a practitioner, not unacquainted with or hostile to sybaritic way stations. It doesn't follow that I would devote one fiftieth of the area on a boat to that particular diversion. For instance, I'd rather have an electric organ—I had an upright piano aboard my schooner *Cyrano*. The point of course is that there are true *luxury* boats, and in the days ahead, in some circumstances, we would be experiencing the ineffaceable difference.

I would never undertake to cross the Atlantic Ocean on a Broward, though it can be done, with careful forethought. I thought back to one of my favorite passages from one of my favorite books. It is a captivating line in *The One Hundred Dollar Misunderstanding*, by Robert Gover, a novel that thirty years earlier was the season's rage. The author's clever formula was to alternate diary entries kept simultaneously during a tryst between a smug twenty-year-old Ivy League college senior and an eighteen-year-old black hooker with whom the Ivy Leaguer was spending a one-hundred-dollar weekend. The book's sheer joy lies in her hour-by-hour outwitting of the young pomposo, who on Sunday morning explodes in his diary: "Sometimes I wonder just how all this could happen to a bright, white, Protestant college senior like I." Beautiful!

Most sea people who grow up on sailboats are instinctively suspicious about power boating. The provenance of my trip had been a blend of curiosity and opportunism. I was curious to have the experience of life on board a powerboat, two years after sailing across the Pacific on *Sealestial*, occupying this little cabin. And the venture was opportunistic inasmuch as the ride wasn't costing me anything: the Broward had in any case to travel north, where its owner cruises during the summer months. The ingenious and thoughtful broker, a friend of long standing, thought to advertise the Broward's availability as a charter boat in my magazine, thereby accumulating credit points for a trade-off. Which is how come a sixty-one-year-old bright, white, Catholic college graduate like I found myself, that evening in mid-May, ushered into a master stateroom either one of whose two Jacuzzis would have consumed more space than my present cabin. But when I got up from my reverie, I was happy to be here—on the *Sealestial,* a lovely sailing ketch. I'd have another Jacuzzi when I got home. When I got home? Thirty days, 4400 miles.

I said good night to the hardworking crew and technicians and told the captain that if he needed me I would be in my room at the hotel, to which I repaired now, resolved to do an evening's paper work and to be prepared, after a night's rest, for the arrival of Dick, Van, Danny, Christopher, and Tony. I spent a long evening dictating answers to overdue correspondence. My anxiety to get my work done was fueled by a mounting sense of excitement, what Ishmael describes in *Moby-Dick,* when he knows that the time has come to go back to sea.

· CHAPTER TWO ·
The Crew

A strange experience when I woke at daybreak—what *was* the time? Beginning tomorrow I'd know the time of daybreak to the minute, else how know when to prepare to shoot the morning stars? My watch said 1:05 P.M. Ridiculous—I could see the shimmer of gray coming up over the sea, visible from the window of the Ritz. I looked at the digital band on my watch, set to New York time. It registered 7:05 P.M., the appropriate six hours earlier than the dial. Come on! I turned on the lamp and fished in my briefcase for the alarm clock. Not there: I had stowed it on the boat. *I did not know what time of day it was* and I don't think that had happened to me since I was oh, six, and began wearing watches.

I like to know what time it is to within seconds, partly the offshoot of my (however brief) training in the CIA, where punctuality is held to be a matter of life and death and sometimes is, but most pronouncedly since I took up celestial navigation twenty-five years ago. Not long after that we were ushered into the age of the VCR, and when you want to tape a program coming on at 8 P.M., you very much do not want your tape to begin at 7:58 or, especially, at 8:03.

I had access, of course, to the hotel telephone thirty inches away. The Reception Desk would give me the time right now. . . . Let me guess. Between 5 A.M. and 7 A.M. We were closing in, on November

3, on the shortest days of the year, and there was that gray light out there. But what would it prove?—my establishing that it was 6:42. Without a functioning watch, a few minutes later I wouldn't know what time it was yet again, not until I got a fresh battery for my BMW watch. So?

I went back to sleep, consoling myself that it wouldn't be possible to sleep past the hour of 9 A.M., because I had placed an order for breakfast at that time.

I had MCI'd (the electronic communication mode he and I—and many others—use) Dick, who is a fellow subscriber to the doctrine of punctuality, the day before. Pass around the word (I said), to Van and Danny, Christopher Little and Tony, that after they check in at the hotel they should have breakfast or not, as they chose, and then go to sleep, and meet me at 12:30 in the main dining room for a briefing, followed by lunch, followed by a trip to the boat for stowing their stuff. Accordingly I heard from no one when they arrived at the hotel. It was only just before I was preparing to mail the cassette to my assistant Frances Bronson at the office that, playing it back for a routine check, I discovered that it was nonfunctional. The long hours of work the previous evening had been in vain.

It's hard to relay to anyone who hasn't had the experience the agony of needing to do all over again work already done, the Sisyphean Curse. I'd rather write two new columns than rewrite one lost in my computer, and now the prospect of going back over ten hours of work and doing it all over again depressed me much more than the meteorological report I picked up at the bulletin board advertising the possibility— note "possibility"—of blustery southeasterly winds, southeast being the direction we would be heading tomorrow, about noon. So: between nine and ten I went shopping for a new battery for my watch, and for a cassette recorder that was not defective.

But top priority is the fax that arrived this morning from *People* magazine, which is doing a two-page spread on the need for national service, as elaborated in my book *Gratitude*, published a couple of weeks ago. They sent a reporter to see me on Monday and he had cranked out a Q&A based on my voice-recorded answers to his questions. Alas, it needed complete revision. There are people who can craft

Q&A's that make the A's sound like the person they are interviewing. They all work for *The New Yorker*. Well, important to get it right, so I started from scratch: using the same questions the reporter had used, and extemporizing my answers:

What was I proposing, actually? That Americans, beginning at age eighteen, be encouraged to devote a year of their lives to civic or philanthropic work: for instance, helping the elderly and the sick, teaching illiterates, doing environmental work—there are over three million slots where national service volunteers could profitably serve. Who did I suppose would primarily profit from such a system? Primarily those who served, rather than those who would be served—their profit would be substantial, but should nevertheless be thought of as derivative. It is the effect on the character of the volunteers I am mostly concerned with.

Some practical questions: Would they be paid? Yes, but only pocket money, about a hundred dollars per week, plus room and board where relevant. But there would also be incentives, and these would add up. Only graduates of National Service would qualify for federal college loans, much as in the G.I. Bill. Everyone needs enough money to live, but after that other considerations prevail, principal among them the judgment of their peers. I stressed that those one instinctively thinks of as likeliest to beat National Service—the affluent and best educated—wouldn't want to live with the ignominy of having declined to serve their country.

How to handle the point that we are living in times that put to sleep idealistic impulses? By denying it. There are eighty million Americans who donate more than five hours every week to philanthropic or civic service. But it isn't just idealism that needs to be appealed to. Young people need to be told (and retold, and told they've been told) that they profit every day politically, culturally, and materially from enormous endowments of which they are the beneficiaries; that Thomas Jefferson, William Shakespeare, and Thomas Edison are people to whom we owe a continuing debt, and one way to discharge this debt or try to is by making sacrifices. When the country is in genuine need, youth have volunteered to defend it. We need to focus on needs that aren't expressed by the threat of sending Americans to help foreigners, using tanks and rifles.

"How does healing the elderly or cleaning up a park teach the volunteer about his or her 'patrimony'—how does it teach them to appreciate the Constitution or the Bill of Rights?" the *People* editor had asked.

I answered: "It should be made plain beginning on Day One what the meaning of national service is: That it is exactly that, an act of *gratitude* for the benefits of living in our society, sating ourselves with what others have given us. Call this indoctrination if you wish, but distinguish it sharply from the kind of indoctrination associated with totalitarian societies. There they are taught to worship the state. Our volunteers would be taught to worship a society that keeps the state at bay. The effect of national service would in my judgment affect the citizen's disposition toward his society and toward his neighbors for the rest of his life." I closed by insisting that yes, spiritual aims were being advanced: "The work is of course secular, but much secular work generates spiritual animation. Most of the time Mother Teresa is engaging in manual labor—but her work is self-sanctifying. Those who have served in the military, or engaged in the work of Boy or Girl Scouts, are psychologically advantaged over those who have not had such cohering experiences."

At about the time the *People* interview appeared, Congress passed a Citizenship and National Service bill, generally known as the Nunn bill, which appropriated several hundred million dollars to establish a nonpartisan commission to explore the whole business of national service. Six months later, the President had not got around to naming the members of the commission. It was discouraging to me and others who had been thinking, in terms of activity generated primarily by the individual states coordinated by a government commission, that the feds should be taking the lead. The campaign for national service continues and opposition to it comes from left and right: the left sees lacking in the Nunn bill the compulsory element it tends to deem indispensable; the libertarian right disapproves because it is a statist enterprise, and a pox on all statist enterprises. A well-earned pox, on the whole, but it pays to remind ourselves that the Constitution is a state charter, the Bill of Rights generally an anti-statist element of it, and that the best defense against usurpatory government is an assertive citizenry.

. . .

The hunk of mail I brought with me to Lisbon has a letter from
Edward Pulling, age ninety-one, the founder of the Millbrook School,
which I and my three brothers attended. He was (he died in April 1991,
aged ninety-two) a remarkable human being, about whom I had written
in the *New York Times Magazine* on Millbrook's fiftieth anniversary.
A few years ago, delivering the commencement address at Millbrook,
I told the graduating class that when at age fourteen I arrived at the
school and first experienced Mr. Pulling, at six foot four the most
imposing physical (and moral) presence I had ever come across, I
simply was not able to understand how it was that when Mr. Pulling
entered the British Navy as a midshipman, the Kaiser, on hearing the
news, hadn't simply surrendered. I dedicated my book *Gratitude* to
him, who had selected *Non sibi sed cunctis* (Not solely for oneself, but
for all) as the motto of the school he founded. He thanks me with his
distinctive courtliness for the book, and passes along a copy of his
introductory remarks delivered at the inauguration of the new head-
master of Millbrook, the fifth since his own retirement. Knowing his
interest in the subject I now send him a copy of my upcoming exchange
with *People* magazine.

Professor James K. Galbraith, son of my old friend John Kenneth
Galbraith, writes from the University of Texas to urge me to attend
a conference "of especial merit" being organized at Austin under the
auspices of the Lyndon Baines Johnson Foundation and Library on the
general subject of "Government and the Arts." "Dear Jamie: I hope
you will pass along my regrets. I fight valiantly, and on the whole
successfully, to avoid participating in conferences, pleasurable though
it would be to see you." I arrived at this formal insight, on which I have
instinctively acted for a very long time, only during my last few years
in charge of *National Review,* and I am surprised there isn't a more
general allergy to the "conference." Perhaps I am lucky. At *National
Review* decisions are quickly arrived at because lines of authority are
clear. There are times when it is absolutely essential to confer, but I
incline to believe that when it is not necessary to confer, it is necessary
not to confer. So much easier to read the views of others nicely trimmed
for economy's sake, than to sit with a dozen people who in some cases

aren't given the time necessary to develop their thought, in other cases
don't have sufficient thought to justify the time they are given to
express it.

Stuart Little, father of Christopher, sends me a copy of his letter to
the acting president of Boston University (President John Silber is
running for governor). B.U. had paused to consider taking on what used
to be called the "Buckley–Little Catalogue." My idea, ten years ago,
was to do something to preserve titles that otherwise disappear. There
are 45,000 books printed every year in the United States and 85 to 90
percent of these are remaindered in six months or so. The phenomenon
is therefore frequent that John Jones looks for a book title to which he
is attracted only to find that it is out of print. He can perhaps find it
in a remainder store, or get it from an outfit that specializes in finding
out-of-print books. Or he may not find it. Or he may not trouble to look
for it, on being told it is out of print.

My idea was to encourage authors to buy as much of the remaindered
stock of their own books as they chose to do, and store these in the
cellar. We would list these books every year, for a modest fee, in a
catalogue. Libraries and bookstores would stock the catalogue. On
establishing that a desired book was out of print, the bookseller would
consult the catalogue, find the title, and order the book for his customer, keeping 40 percent of the price and remitting the balance to
the author, who would go to his cellar once every month and mail the
requisitioned volumes to the buyers.

We published the catalogue for three years and learned that the
enterprise would need either more working capital or else a parent
company that had regular traffic with libraries and bookstores, to ped-
dle the catalogue along with other inventory.

A buyer came along. Stuart and I kissed our project goodbye, happy
that it was securely in the hands of a large organization that could make
it prosper. One year later they were bankrupt. Boston University, after
much thought, decided it didn't want to risk the seventy-five thousand
dollars per year necessary to nurse the project along until the catalogue
became universally known and used. I am very saddened by what looks
to be the end of a splendid idea, and write to tell Stuart that although
we have no formal responsibilities (the buyers, in fact, still owe us

money), we should continue to keep our eyes open for someone willing to give the project life.

Pastor Richard John Neuhaus has been for several years an extraordinarily influential neoconservative and Christian (*The Naked Public Square* is one of his books, in which he struggles to understand the progressive dogmatism of the First Amendment secularists who, e.g., want to make war against public celebrations of Christmas). He writes, and encloses a copy of a letter sent out to personal friends, expanding on an earlier, more or less public communiqué, in which he gave the reasons why he had decided to leave the Lutheran church, to become a Catholic priest. I reply to him, "Did I forget to tell you how very beautiful I found your statement announcing your entry into the Catholic Church? It is rich and resonant and worthy of its author." It's funny, but governing protocols make any public celebration of another person's conversion to one's own faith somehow, uh, *infra dig.* You would think the home team would be permitted at least a small measure of the joy and enthusiasm we license and indeed encourage when a star pitcher leaves the New York Yankees to join the Boston Red Sox.

Sherwin Nuland is a brilliant member of the faculty of the Yale Medical School who at my urging a year or so back personally took charge of the tatterdemalion body of Fernando Valenti, the great harpsichordist and musician, just now dead. He writes, "I was deeply saddened to hear of Fernando's death, especially because he seemed to be doing so well at the time he went off for Majorca. He spoke to me a day or so before he left, and was in high spirits, even beginning to be somewhat optimistic about the possible completion of his Scarlatti book. And so another brilliant star flushes itself out, after spending a few decades dimming its own light in self-destructive behavior. I don't know which troubles me more, the havoc he wreaked on his own potentially stupendous career or the actual fact of his death." And the doctor concludes, "Envy is not ordinarily one of my sins, but I must confess to being jealous as hell watching you enjoying yourself so much on Sunday afternoon [when I performed with the Yale Symphony orchestra]. It was a wonderful thing for you to do, and Fernando would have been button-busting proud. Many thanks for sending me *Grati-*

tude. I have tried to live my life in such a way that I can at least partially repay the huge obligation I owe to this great country—I have brought up my children the same way and the concept of service is so bred into the older kids that they consider it a straightforward fact of their lives. I hope that *Gratitude* will begin a national tide of discussion that has been long needed." I acknowledge the letter, and thank him for what he did for Fernando Valenti.

Peter McWilliams is a bird of paradise who sought ten years ago to entice skeptics into trying out computer word processing. His how-to computer books have been triumphs of lucidity and fun. "I received your letter dated October 1 claiming that I was incorrigible," he writes. "Yes that's true but what specifically am I being accused of incorrigibility for (of? to?): Incorrigibly yours, Peter."

I reply: "How on earth would you expect me to remember which of your incorrigible acts especially caught my attention at that moment? I am going to sea and am laconic."

Jim McFadden, one of my oldest friends and colleagues at *National Review,* is incensed that *Life* magazine has listed the 100 Most Important Twentieth-Century Americans in its special issue and "disincluded Clare Boothe Luce (*Life* was CBL's idea!), but included the likes of Betty Friedan, even Billie Jean King." I share his indignation and recall an exasperated letter from Mrs. Luce when Mother Elizabeth Seton was canonized the first native-born American saint and *Time* carried on its cover a picture of a mutt, describing pet life in America.

I write to Jack Muggeridge, brother of Malcolm. "Forgive me for intruding, but Bob Tyrrell sent me a copy of your letter to him which gives me an update on Malcolm and Kitty. If you can think of anything in the world I can do to help them, I do wish you would let me know. I last spoke with Malcolm on his eighty-fifth birthday and he told me then that he would not be responding to any letters, having lost the powers of communication." Before Jack received my letter, his illustrious brother had died, news I received on arriving at Madeira, where I wrote an obituary and sent it out as a column.

. . .

Professor Charles Moskos, who is the most mobilized academic in favor of national service, and the architect of Senator Sam Nunn's national service bill, writes, *"Gratitude*'s core idea of two classes of citizens (which I was groping toward in my own book) will revive public philosophy from its present moribund state. Likewise, it will shake up both the libertarians and the paleo-liberals." It is a thesis of my book that there is nothing at all wrong or undemocratic in recognizing that there are two classes of people, first class and second class, provided that there is always and everywhere mobility and encouragement to move from the second to the first echelon, inhabited in my essay by those willing to give a year of their lives to national service. I thank him and express interest in an essay he has written questioning the idea of women fighting in battle in the armed services. "I have long urged the producer of *Firing Line* to try to drum up a debate on the subject to take place in West Point or Annapolis, where the issue, as you know, is very much alive at this point."

I was exhilarated on finding that between ten and twelve-thirty I had done the exchange for *People* and reproduced one half of the ten hours' lost dictation. This time around I did not need to slow down in order to read material I had already read the night before, so that I was able to dictate more or less continuously. The speed of it all left me in just the right mood to welcome my pals when I went down to the dining room.

It really is a fine moment in life to see assembled for a joint enterprise people you know, people you love to be with. I remember what I felt as a thirteen-year-old schoolboy in England. Every other Saturday two of my (six) sisters, at boarding school at Ascot nearby, were permitted to pick me up at my school at Old Windsor. The rendezvous were always for four o'clock. They would drive in, one sister eighteen months older than I, the other eighteen months younger, the chauffeur at the wheel and the French governess-chaperone in the back, and we would drive into Windsor, have a gluttonous tea, exchange news, gossip, talk of the high and low moments of our fortnight, and be back at school by six, sad to be separated, elated at having been together even for so brief a period. On the right Saturdays, I would walk down a half mile to the school gate at three-thirty and wait, and if the car was ten minutes late the pain was keen. It was hardly comparable, fifty years later, but when I saw them—Van, Dick, Danny, Christopher Little, Tony—I felt the surreal pleasure of it all, the whole messy, expensive, intricate, vexing business of getting a boat and a crew, the right boat and the right crew, plotting a course, justifying an idea, and preparing to set out with your friends for a protracted adventure. There was so very much to do. . . .

So what. Departures are almost always hectic, and maybe they ought to be. I recalled what my wife and I went through a couple of years back, before boarding the *Sea Cloud.* Unlike the *Sealestial,* the *Sea Cloud* justifies—to compensate for the boat's luxury—an ordeal in preparing to reach it. Before boarding a boat for a trip which by its comprehensive hedonism would rip out the eyes of a Calvinist, it helps to have struggled right up until you get there with workaday problems. You wouldn't want to start in on Scheherazade's one thousand and one nights having just finished a hundred nights of debauchery, interrupting only the rhythm at which you consume bonbons. The burden of a million things that need to be done before setting out on a vacation, especially if one million things go wrong, accentuates the pleasure felt when the boat finally weighs anchor, vacation-bound, or the plane, finally, is airborne.

The twenty-four hours before *Sea Cloud* were created to absolve the conscience. My wife, Pat, was nearing the end of an eternally long hip-replacement recuperation, as also the end (we liked to think) of the most hectic social-civic week of her career in New York City.

During the preceding twenty-four hours I presided at a two-hour television debate in Houston featuring the six Republican candidates for President together for the first time, and, the following morning, attended a breakfast given by the sponsors of the debate. This was followed by two one-hour *Firing Line* television tapings, musing, along with political specialists, on the performance and prospects of the candidates and on the political questions they had raised. A private jet would guarantee my arrival early in the afternoon in San Francisco, giving me plenty of time to rehearse for an evening's long-planned public social event at which I'd serve as master of ceremonies and which required me, among other things, to perform two pieces on the harpsichord. A second private plane would guarantee my arrival at the

Marjorie's SEA CLOUD

airport in Los Angeles before my rendezvous with Pat, "with over an hour to spare," my hosts had promised me. . . . We would meet at the Continental Airlines gate in Los Angeles in time to catch the plane at 11:50 P.M. for Papeete, a ten-hour flight, intending to spend, in Tahiti, a leisurely thirty-six hours before boarding *Sea Cloud.*

You guessed it. 1) En route to San Francisco, the winds required an unscheduled stop in Albuquerque, for refueling. Delays at the S.F. airport, another hour of waiting. 2) Got to S.F. only just in time to dash to the harpsichord, already onstage and, sick with nervousness, rush through my pieces. Cocktail reception, dinner, the affair . . . 3) I slaughtered Bach . . . Was rushed out to the airport, to learn 4) that we were fifty-fifth in line for takeoff (two of the runways were out). 5) It wasn't a jet, as promised, but a turbojet. However, a car *was* waiting when finally we landed at Los Angeles, which drove me at furious speed to Continental at the other side of the airport where I checked my bags. I was carrying one handpiece, a porter another two. Together we sprinted over one of those endless LAX airport passages from check-in counter to departure gate, arriving at the gate at 11:45—five minutes before departure time—to face a wife whose face was glacial with fear and loathing, emitting at virago speed her lacerating software lecture

on how Husband Cannot Manage His Life Properly Going Always in
Overdrive. . . . All I needed; except 6) the ensuing announcement of
an hour's flight delay. Followed by the announcement of a second
hour's delay. Followed by an announcement of the flight's cancellation
and news of the unhappy coincidence that, the defective fuel pump
and hydraulic gear having been fixed, this last—and conclusive—delay
was caused by the refusal of the cargo door to close. Any cargo door
that cannot close, we were left to reason, presumably can't open, which
meant that 7) our thirteen bags might as well have been in Tahiti. At
2:20 A.M. a scramble for Continental's emergency toothbrush kit, then
a bus to a motel. Three hours later a 6 A.M. a phone call: the plane is
fixed, will depart in exactly forty-five minutes, all but precluding even
somnambulistic toilet duties. But we were there in forty-five minutes
to hear 8) the announcement of an hour's delay. Followed by the
announcement of a second hour's delay. Followed by the announcement of the flight's latest cancellation. Back to the motel, we order
lunch, wife steps gratefully into bath, phone rings: plane fixed, immediate departure, quick, *hurry* up. We were there, and this time were
actually led to our seats and given a glass of champagne, Château
Triumpho . . . Followed by a second glass, followed by—a third,
sorrowful notice of 9) the flight's newest cancellation. We were led to
the Air France waiting room, having been advised, resignedly, by Continental to switch allegiance. Air France flight, 10) delayed. Two hours.

But then it did leave, our baggage was waiting for us in Papeete
(Continental finally made it), we got to bed, rose, had three hours to
survey and map Papeete, quick lunch, and on to:

The *Sea Cloud*.

Mostly, at lunch at the Ritz in Lisbon, we talked about boat details.
Yes, at the airport Danny had handed Allan Jouning all the spare parts
needed for the generator and the muffler. Danny would write the next
day in his journal:

> Arriving at the International Airport in Lisbon was less than easy. I
> strolled merrily toward Customs with my single duffel bag and two
> Comsat Communications Systems, boxed and looking like giant camera
> equipment containers, and a ship's muffler. Yes, a muffler for the newly

broken, hopefully about-to-be-fixed generator. I was plucked by the Customs officer to the right lane, while my friends walked through the left, "Nothing to Declare" lane, without so much as a blink.

"What you have in that?" he asked, pointing to the Comsat suitcase.

Oh, just two of the most sophisticated communications units known to man, lent to me by Comsat, to test while crossing the Atlantic; and in this box, a muffler.

"What's Comsat do?"

"Look, why don't you read the brochure I have here, because it would take me all day to explain." ENTER DICK CLURMAN with an official-looking document of some sort in hand and a tongue of fire. Dick looks at me and says to pack all that junk up, he will take care of everything. Okay by me.

Dick called the official over, told him how important we all were, said how vital it was to go immediately to the hotel to give our stuff to the captain, therefore we should have his blessing and be let go. It worked. Off we went. The four of us with our thirteen bags, most of which were accessories and parts for the trip, and miscellaneous items for WFB. Such as a spare computer, 100 pounds of mail from the office, and a few birthday presents from Pat and friends. You know, the usual stuff for a trip across the Atlantic.

Now Danny Merritt is not a smart alec, and I know he wouldn't have sassed the Portuguese Customs. Moreover, his face radiates the innocence of St. Sebastian, and I don't doubt that he'd have got through Customs all by himself in due course. But I don't doubt, either, that when he saw Dick Clurman, cigarette in hand, tooling in, his heart burst with gratitude, because Dick is the Man Born to Cut Gordian Knots. For one thing he is, as already noted, Solomonic by nature—if he'd thought there was duty to pay on a muffler needed as a spare part by an outgoing boat he'd have said so. He knew there was no such levy, and his knowledge of where the truth lay, expressed in English only just understood by officials whose English was insecure, had the effect of burning a hole in bureaucratic skepticism. (I have witnessed Clurman as acetylene torch going through bureaucracy before. It is a beautiful sight.)

So, I learned, the all-important ship's gear was safely in the hands of Captain Jouning. Tony Leggett expressed genteel indignation, as he dug into a huge papaya, at the owner's having given us a boat, eighteen months after we had contracted for it, in which the engine needed to be rebuilt and with generator mufflers in advanced decomposition. I told them that I had called the owner three nights before in New York, when told about the engine by Allan, and that he had said he could *not understand it,* that he had spent *two hundred and fifty thousand dollars* on *Sealestial* during the last twelve months and had been assured two weeks earlier that everything was in super shape.

In all my dealings with Dr. Papo up until that time I had never had serious problems with him, but it is true that he is presumptively opposed to innovative ideas. As for instance when, after I was told by an experienced friend that the Bay of Biscay at that time of the year often develops fearful easterly currents, making it hell to get started across the Atlantic, I resolved to take off from Lisbon instead of Marbella, which is east of Gibraltar. I had a telegram from Allan Jouning: "Dr. Papo telephoned last night. He does not like the idea of starting the trip in Lisbon. He wants to move the starting point to Puerto Banús (Marbella). I am not sure exactly why. Someone has been advising him not to go to Lisbon. He said it was dangerous, that there were 10-foot tides. I am not sure what is dangerous about 10-foot tides. In northwest Australia on *Freedom* we have 25-foot tides."

I have had 28-foot tides in Plymouth, Massachusetts, and 40-foot tides in New Brunswick.

"I do not mind where we start," Allan's telegram went on; "my only problem is that I have paid two thousand pounds for travel and accommodation for my family that I will not be able to refund if we start other than from Lisbon." Allan had planned to bring his family to Estoril, nearby, for a week of beach life while he supervised the preparation of *Sealestial.*

I said to the owner: Lisbon.

The hell with it all, Van said, dismissing all problems as merely distracting. Indeed, the hell with it. As things stood we would leave the following day as scheduled, provided the sea trials that afternoon were uneventful. Christopher Little wanted to know how Liz Wheeler was doing. I reported that I hadn't actually laid eyes on her but that from all reports she was in a fine mood. Christopher said he had tried out some of the recipes in her recently published book, *The Yachting*

Cookbook: Glorious Menus and Quick Dishes Afloat and at Home, and found them splendid. Danny asked why I had ordered yet another sextant, and I told him the ship's sextant was not in reliable shape, and I needed a standby for my own. Oh, I suddenly remembered, had they seen Liz's memo on Sea Bands? I had sent them copies, but not, evidently, in time to reach them before leaving.

"Sea what?"

I pulled the brochure out of my folder. "Here's what Liz's flier says. Listen hard—it's good copy: 'I was nineteen then. I was crossing the English Channel. I would be in Paris that night. Spain a week later. I felt my life was about to begin. I felt also I was about to be sick. In front of everyone. In front of the girl there at the railing, the girl with beautiful black long blowing hair. Everyone was chatting. Laughing. Being debonair. Being insouciant. The deck of our small Channel boat was overflowing with nonchalance. Only I seemed to notice something was wrong. That day I learned it isn't the epic storm at sea that makes us epically sick. Oh no, it's the subtle, oddly squirming uncertain movements of a deck that do it. Somewhere in the bottom of my stomach (or inner ear) a tiny voice of nausea was rising, hinting that things far worse were on their way. . . . That afternoon, years ago, Sea Bands were as yet uninvented, still years away; a small miracle that eventually would rescue people like me, stuck in veering cars, trapped in boats, confined to airplanes, locked in long elevator rides. Sea Bands work. They operate by asserting imperceptible acupressure on the Nei-Kuan point inside both wrists. No drugs. No drowsiness. No hocus-pocus. Made in England, today Sea Bands are used routinely by submariners, professional divers, hospitals, yachtsmen, pilots, high-steelworkers; and prescribed by physicians. Wish they'd been around long before now. So will you. Sea Bands. Price: $16.95 per set. We pay shipping. (To order call toll free 800 231-7341.)' "

"That took rather a long time to read," was Van's comment.

All right, all right, I said, Were they prepared to put on their scopolamine pads? Or were they interested in trying Sea Bands? Hardly feasible at this point, but they could order them, if they liked, and have them waiting for us in Madeira. Everybody said they would indeed put on the scopolamine pads that night before going to sleep—which, I knew from experience, most of them would forget to do.

These are gentlemen who acquire a confidence about not getting seasick and more often than not they don't get sick—unless the seas are unruly, and the skies turn that gray, emetic shade some of them soon emulate. It is harder for me to deliver the annual lecture on seasickness given that, for some reason, I don't myself get seasick, not since a particular Atlantic crossing in December 1938. Notwithstanding my apparent immunity, two years ago, preparing to go down in the French Navy's little sub *Nautile* to examine the corpse of the *Titanic*, I slipped on one of those scopolamine tabs, just in case. As it turned out, there is no motion whatever once you get a hundred feet below the surface of the water, and I sank utterly without stomach problems the two and one half miles to where the *Titanic* lies. There are other things to vex you when you enter that little submarine for nine and a half hours, to forage for *Titanic* memorabilia: the cold, the insufficient room to stretch out your legs, a steel bar that presses against the chest as you fix your eyes on the mini-port window, searching for *Titanic* gold. But no sea-sickness.

"Let's go," I said, and they jumped up, eager—first to go to their rooms to fetch their sea bags, then to the boat to stow their gear. We would reunite at seven that evening for our last dinner ashore. DANNY: "Do you want me to bring some champagne from the boat?" Absolutely, I said; a fine idea that would save us, at the rate at which the Ritz charges, a million dollars.

They were off in two taxis. I went back to my mail and to producing another column, an "evergreen," as they say in the trade—i.e., a think piece not likely to be too badly mauled by anything that happens between the time it is written and the time it is published. Important, since I was talking about a column to be run the following Wednesday, and this was Saturday, and in between was a national election.

We reconvened in my small suite wearing coats and ties, that being the rule for dinner downstairs, where we had reserved a table. Danny poured the champagne.

Dick offered a toast: "Van, your political comings and goings are actually responsible for our sailing tomorrow." Van was promptly toasted.

And indeed it was so. Because early in the spring Van had decided

The last meal with coats and ties

he would campaign for the Republican nomination for Governor of New York. At first I thought this a diversion, but I soon found that a) he was dead serious; b) he thought the impregnable, imperious Mario Cuomo highly vulnerable; and c) he fully expected that if he fought for the nomination in a primary, he'd win it, and of course win the backing of the Conservative Party, and probably win a Republican primary—and probably go on to win the election.

At that point I had scheduled our passage to begin on November 1. It occurred to me sometime in May that the voters of the State of New York would find it odd if the Republican gubernatorial candidate left off campaigning six days before the election in order to travel on a sailboat across the Atlantic. Obviously the point had also occurred to Van, but he is the type who does not like to inconvenience others; he waits for them to act. So . . . I said to him that, while I did not agree that he had a chance in the world of winning the election, I conceded that he had a good chance of getting the Republican–Conservative nomination; so, if agreeable, I would put off sailing on our trip until November 7. Agreed.

What then happened was that the New York courts disqualified
Van, on the grounds that he had been a resident of New York State
for only four years. The New York State constitution requires five years'
residence of a gubernatorial candidate. It is different when one is
running in New York for other offices. When I ran for mayor of New
York City, I had only to point to a dwelling place in New York the day
of election, and it didn't seem to matter that I have always been
domiciled in Connecticut. When Bobby Kennedy ran for the Senate
he quickly bought a big house in Long Island, and whee! he became
a New Yorker. My brother was elected to the Senate from New York
(to Bobby's old seat) under a similar chimera, except that he did not
bother to buy a big house in Long Island. His "residence" in New York
caused one columnist, after the surprise election victory, to comment
that Senator-elect James Buckley "lives modestly in New York City,
sharing a two-bedroom apartment with his mother, his sister, his wife,
and his five children." Van put up a valiant struggle to construe time
spent in Paris as ambassador as constructive residency in New York, but
when the highest court voted No, 5–0, his campaign came to a stop.
I then moved our trip forward from November 7 to November 4—it
was too late to go back to the original date of November 1.

Van was, as usual, enlivening, predicting that next Tuesday Cuomo
would do less well, even against undernourished candidates, than expected. (He was right.) Christopher Little asked me if I had cooked up
a diversionary theme for our idle hours on the ocean. On the first trip
we had written anti-Communist declarations, *National Lampoon*–
style, which we dispatched in emptied wine bottles, tossing them
overboard and painstakingly recording the texts of these messages in
the log, to enforce the No Repetition rule (no two messages were
permitted to be the same). On the third trip the idea, once a day, was
to come up with the question that would make appropriate the pre-
stipulated answer, as in: *"Dr. Livingstone I. Presume"*—that's the
answer. The question to which it is appropriate? *"What is your full
name, Dr. Presume?"* Tonight, Van had a maddening one. Answer:
"Winnie-The-Pooh and Alexander The Great." We pondered that—
for a moment Danny thought he had the appropriate question, but we
groaned at its inadequacy.

"Give up?" Van smiled.

"What two characters, one fictional and one historical, have the same middle name?"

We gave him the prize, unchallenged, and went down to dinner. But first a bizarre comment from worldly-wise Dick Clurman—absolutely vintage stuff. He looked out the window of my room at the full moon over Lisbon harbor and said, *"Gee, that's beautiful!* When will it be full moon in New York?"

Dear Dick. Those dinners, pre-flight, are high moments.

· CHAPTER THREE ·

Setting Out

We would meet at the boat at eleven, so Danny and I located a church
nearby where a Mass was scheduled for nine and set out by foot to go
there. The weather was nicely fall-like, and our city map guided us
through a green park, up a broad avenue without much traffic, and then
hard right: at the dead end was a chapel. Inside it looked like so many
European chapels, congested with decorative materials mostly made
during the seventeenth, eighteenth, or nineteenth century, a lot of
gilt, a lot of paintings, statuary, dim light, the faint odor of incense.
The elderly priest spoke in Portuguese, easy (relatively) for foreigners
with a little knowledge of Italian or Spanish to decipher in print, impossible to understand when spoken. ("If you want to learn to pronounce Portuguese, practise saying 'Tottenham Court Road' as a single
syllable . . ."—Sacheverell Sitwell). The congregation, as everywhere in
Europe, was 85 percent female and the same percentage over the age
of fifty-five, and the chapel half empty. It always heartened Malcolm
Muggeridge to note that it is spectacularly different in catacomb country: the churches in East Europe bulge, and why not? In countries
taught to revere historical idealism, who is a greater visionary than
Christ?

From Christopher Little's journal:

I approach the trip with more trepidation than the previous two. Whether this is a function of advancing years—it's hard to remember that it has been ten years since *Atlantic High*—or due to increased nervousness on [wife] Betsy's part, I cannot say. Whatever the case, I brought up the subject on the plane to Danny in the careful manner men tend to do when they discuss such things, i.e., "I'm not scared but Betsy sure is." Danny immediately said that [wife] Gloria felt the same way. We talked about it for a time, reminiscing about the previous adventures, and we all agreed that neither of us had ever been really spooked before. Although Danny admitted to one brief moment in the gale the night before we passed the Strait of Gibraltar on Atlantic High.

I think it correct to say that for reasons that attest either to dumb faith or to ignorance I have never felt these trepidations, on setting out. The statistics are very reassuring, though I was perplexed on attempting to get the same insurance policies I had gotten for the crew on our last passage. For one hundred dollars, I had got a million dollars' coverage for each of them against loss of life. Asking this time around for the same policy for Ocean4, I was told (without explanation for the inflated figure) that the same policy would now cost thirteen hundred dollars. That premium outdistanced my paternalism, and so I sent the information to individual members of the crew, leaving them free to take out the policy or not.

I did pray, that Sunday morning, for a safe passage, and for other concerns, and when Dan and I left to go back to the hotel I knew that both of us walked with lighter step.

We were all there at eleven, including Allan's little boy, two, and girl, five—Jessica was born while her father was sailing with us in the Pacific, north of the Marshall Islands. Her mother, Daphne, clutched the little children's hands, even though they are old salts—Daphne estimates that Jessica has sailed twenty-five thousand miles aboard *Freedom* during the last three years. The boat looked truly resplendent, one of those transmogrifications that happen to boats in the half day before they set

"I rather regretted the total absence of any ceremony
remarking our transoceanic departure."

out to race or on a long passage. We were busy for a few minutes stowing gear that had been kept in the hotel. Tony wrote:

> Dick picked me as his cabin mate, I found out when I did an overnight *Patito* cruise with Bill late in October. The reason? Christopher Little with his cameras had too much gear all the time, and Danny was a "pig."

I regret to pass on this animadversion, all the more so since the identical obscenity has been used by Dick to refer to my own habits aboard ship. I should make it clear that he was not referring, in either case, to physical cleanliness, but rather to a mature perspective having to do with tidiness. Dick cannot walk out of his cabin (or his living room) without storing away the loose paper clip. I find it much easier to wait until the paper clips accumulate and, say once a month, sort things out. Danny, who has always been precocious, follows my habits, and in doing so disturbs me not in the least *except on those inexcusable occasions when he neglects to replace my divider or my parallel rules which belong in one and only one slot in the navigator's drawer!*

I have to confess that I rather regretted the total absence of any ceremony remarking our transoceanic departure. No such trip should, in my judgment, set out, so to speak, unlaunched. In 1958, preparing to go off to Bermuda in October, we served beer and champagne and pretzels at the marina at Twenty-third Street in New York and my oldest brother brought as a departure gift an 8-foot palm tree. Just the thing for a 42-foot cutter setting out on a seven-hundred-mile passage. We lashed it good-humoredly to the backstay and there it rested, clinging to life like the rest of us, right through the hurricane four days later, coming to symbolize for us Mother Earth, the staff of life.

One pleasant way to set out from New York is to hire the *Petrel*. It is a retired 72-foot racing yawl and works out of the Battery Park at the tip of Manhattan as a lunch-dinner "head boat." You charter the *Petrel* with its crew of five and sail off in the general direction of Ambrose Light, with food and fare for up to thirty-four guests. You take your little sloop and harness it to a winch on the *Petrel*'s stern. You join your guests for a couple of convivial hours of this and that, including the chef's Death by Chocolate dessert; and then, at about 1 P.M., you and your crew bring up the trailing line and do a little

Geländesprung onto the *Patito,* haul up your own sails, and wave at the *Petrel'*s landlubbers, one party going off to sea, the other back to land; one party wistful, the other exuberant, and no one ever knowing for sure which is which. But in Lisbon I'd have had to go to the highways and the byways to dragoon total strangers to any feast celebrating the departure of the *Sealestial* for the New World.

We needed to pause an hour or so to take fresh water from a tender, after which I slipped the gear forward, the lines were loosed, and we set out.

It is a long run from the heart of Lisbon to the open ocean, ten or twelve miles down the historic river. The surroundings are interesting, romantic even, and the great mastodonic statue in memory of Prince Henry the Navigator impressive; but I would hesitate to agree with Admiral Morison when he writes of Lisbon (in 1942, *Admiral of the Ocean Sea*), that it is "still the most beautiful of the world's greater seaports." Professor Morison, when he wrote this, had just finished

". . . the great mastodonic statue in memory of Prince Henry the Navigator . . ."

reminding the reader that in the fifteenth century Lisbon was "the most stimulating place in all Europe for an ambitious young seaman like Columbus." "Portugal, the ancient Lusitania, was then the liveliest and most go-ahead country in Europe. She alone had been enlarging the bounds of the known world during this tag end of the Middle Ages. Portugal not only discovered and peopled the Azores, where no human beings had ever lived before; for almost half a century she had been sending vessels further and further south along the West African coast. . . . The Infante Dom Henrique was the initiator of this forward movement. Men before him had the spirit of discovery; he organized discovery. His headquarters were on Cape St. Vincent, the southwestern promontory of Portugal and of Europe . . ."—the same point we had sighted, our first sight of Europe as land, on the transatlantic passage in 1975.

But it is inevitably the case when setting out to sea, or at least this has been my experience, that for everyone on board, no doubt for a variety of reasons, the experience is a solvent of sorts. There is primarily a sense of fatalism (you cannot now go back), combined with the knowledge that, after all, you are setting out on a trip for which you

volunteered. And, here and there, a true feeling of release. Danny wrote:

> My stomach knots begin to loosen as we head out the harbor. I confess that I needed very much to go away for a while. The strain of a new job, traveling in and out of New York, trying to create a marketing strategy, spending more money a month than I earn—all created the need to get the hell going. Sailing is such a reward that these everyday stresses quickly dissipate. Sailing with my friends, such as Dick, Van, Tony, Chris, and Bill, immediately takes effect, and like a drug works its way in the system and begins the healing process. We're off to a great start.

Our course was southwest and the wind was northeast; what could be happier than a close reach the first night out?—that and the moon full? My nonracing watch system, carefully evolved over thirty years, calls for four-hour stints, halfway through which relief is effected of the crew who has been on four hours. So that, for instance, at midnight, A, who will have been on four hours, the last two with B, will be relieved by C; and at 0200, B will be relieved by D. For only three hours a day would Allan Jouning and Martin and first mate Denis be responsible for sailing the boat: between 7 P.M. and 10 P.M. Those would be

our three hedonistic hours. The first for dinner, the next two for entertainment—a movie, of which we had on board forty, including the entire PBS series on the Civil War.

"Dinner was served up down below," Tony wrote in his journal (lunch was always in the cockpit, except when the weather was very bad), "since it had gotten pretty nippy, and it was in keeping with what I'd heard about Liz. A delightful something like red snapper, partially baked but finally pan-broiled. Served with style and followed by a simple green salad with a superb dressing, and then crêpes Suzette."

Dick had written out on the computer and printed a list of our movies and it was resolved that instead of the dreary plebiscitary business of what-would-we-show-tonight, we would be bound by the choice of one of us, whoever had the draw that night, which precedence would proceed alphabetically after tonight's draw—which I won. I selected *Monsieur Hulot's Holiday,* which I hadn't seen since it was first released in the early fifties, and was glad to confirm my memory of it as the funniest movie ever made, the genius of which lies in the director's adamant resistance of any temptation to over-milk a humorous situation; so that the young, gaunt, clumsy French vacationer, setting out for a week on the beach, gets into every conceivable difficulty but you never see him slip twice in a row on any one banana peel, and no banana peel is elongated.

I had the first watch and would be relieved at 0100. I was glad to

"Dinner was in keeping with what I had heard about Liz [Wheeler]."

hear from Van, our meteorological officer, that every indication he could catch on our wayward shortwave radio was to the effect that the front lying south of us would move well west before turning north, and so leave us undisturbed, heading as we were deep into the Atlantic Ocean toward Madeira. I made the log entries, shot a couple of stars haphazardly, using the horizon lit up by the full moon, and reminded myself lazily that with five hundred-odd miles to go before a landfall, I really didn't need to know with any exactitude where the *Sealestial* was at 0100 on the morning of November 5, 1990.

· CHAPTER FOUR ·

The Storm

This chapter may prove the most useful I have ever written about the sea, and for that reason I approach it with primary attention to detail.

Here are the relevant entries, excerpted from the logbook, mostly written by me, for November 5, 6, and 7.

Nov 5 1700. Did 178 miles in Day 1. Weather fax is reason meter low. No star sights acct clouds.

Nov 6 0100 Barometer down to 1017

1000 Unlikely sun sight acct clouds. Will do a DR [position estimated by Dead Reckoning] *based on log.*

1500 Barometer 1016

1700 Barometer 1013, took extra reef. Course made good, 260 degrees, approx 8.5 knots.

2000 Barometer 1012! [Exclamation point in the original] *Conditions uncomfortable. Mainsail is reefed, mizzen is down. Low overhanging clouds. Barometer lower to 1007.*

2100 DR plotted: To Funchal, 205 degrees, 110 miles

2330 Barometer down to 1005.

Nov 7 As of 0100 1) we tacked at 2130 to 180 degrees; 105 miles from Funchal, which lies at 205 degrees; 2) at 2230, we were going 9.5 knots. Lost furling line on genoa for 30 minutes; 15 minutes later, broke again.

Furling line fixed but couldn't do better than 165 degrees. 3) No change in barometer, still at 1005.

1245 Isla Porto Santo at 33–05 N, 16–20 W—63 miles at 260 degrees; 140 miles from Funchal. [If the Estimated Position was accurate, we had drifted away from Funchal twenty-five miles in twelve hours.]

What this tells you barely (other material is omitted) is that a) we experienced in a day a dramatic drop in barometric pressure; b) we needed to change our course in order to cope with the wind direction; c) we needed to reduce sail; d) I became unsure of our position and considered an alternative destination (Porto Santo).

Before giving my own conclusions about the thirty-six hours under review, I draw on excerpts from the journals of my crew, in so many ways instructive. To begin with the longest consecutive narrative, which is Tony Leggett's:

I came on watch at 0700, joining Chris, and came up just in time to have my first taste of a rain squall and some pretty strong wind. We were forced off our 230 degree course, and really had to button up due to the rain. After the squall had passed over, someone made a fateful comment: "That's my kind of a storm—intense wind, rain shower, launders the boat nicely—then it's over after five minutes." We pretty much agreed with his assessment.

But it started getting very difficult to do things down below. People started to stir, trying to make a regular day of it, but the day just wouldn't cooperate. Since Liz was unable to do much for breakfast she wound up with some wonderful bread and served it in a basket with jam and peanut butter. I was huddled up in a corner of the cockpit, to leeward behind the dodger, spreading jam for people, but I seemed to be my own best customer—there wasn't much appetite. Mindful of my advice that you never know when your next meal is coming, I ate about as much as I could handle, and then scooted off to my bunk for the rest of the day. Life aboard ship just plain isn't fun when the only thing to do is either to be on deck in the spray or down below in the developing muck. Now we were pounding along on a port tack, lee cloths up [a lee cloth is the equivalent of a lee board, the latter made of wood, the former of canvas. It serves to keep a body from falling out of bed: i.e., it keeps the body from falling out to leeward] since the cabin is to port, and things starting to feel a little crowded with the hatch dogged down tightly against the frequent spray coming on deck. With the cabin so small, it was absolutely essential to keep the door open. And so I tried to do the only thing possible: sleep; but for most of the day, nothing doing. Crowded, ship's bow slamming up and down, the moist and sodden surrounding air finally stinking. Some waste water or whatever just isn't draining . . . lingering in the forward cabins, which smell like a holding tank or sewage plant . . . makes it that much easier to be seasick.

I just lay there the whole day trying to sleep and not doing so, trying to read, not being able to do that without getting sick; and so ended up doing nothing. The preparation for the evening meal was enticing and we had wonderful smells of garlic and ginger to counterbalance the strong, mephitic quality of the general atmosphere. Still, I knew it would be unwise for me to try to sit up and eat with the boys. I contemplated asking for a bowl in my bunk, or else one I could take with me up on watch, but thought that would be a little self-indulgent. In fact during the entire time I never actually felt miserable. I had just decided that spending all day in the bunk was the best of my available options. With the slamming that's now going on I started having misgivings about the rig. Around midnight there was a terrible bang and then the sound of madly luffing sails. I was out of bed immediately, ready to tear on deck in nothing but briefs. I heard Chris say, "It's just the jib furling gear." So I jumped back into my bunk. After a few minutes the flapping was calmed and we were back on course. But a half hour later the banging resumed. I was feeling guilty about not going up and volunteering, but figured I'd be having some heavy duty myself so remained in my bunk until called at 2100.

Shortly after I joined Chris, things started happening. It was still a wild moonlit night and we were bombing along with a half-furled genoa and double or triple [triple—WFB] reefed main at nine to ten knots. In the moonlight I could see that the mainsail was starting to separate from the mast as one after another the sail slides broke on the lashing holding the bolt rope to the slides. I was on the helm, and asked Chris to check with Allan—who said that nothing could be done in these conditions.

The beautiful stars, moon, and occasional scudding clouds gradually went dark though we could make out some darker clouds to windward. We were starting to get some real gusts now and went from our 180

course to 150 or even 120 to give the boat an easier time of it. As we
headed off onto a broad reach we watched the speeds go upward of ten
to eleven knots, then get back onto course when things went normal.

Suddenly everything went white, the rain was pelting, the wind speed
shot up, and we were bearing away on a sleigh ride. Martin came on deck.
I ran off with the wind. It was eerie as the visibility dropped to just a
boat length. The stern area was all lit up by the stern light, as if we were
in a snowstorm. Sometimes, as we rounded up, the lee side dug in, water
cascading into the cockpit. Martin was keeping an eye on the wind speed
and yelled out fifty-five knots! We were doing ten knots through the
water. I think that's about the strongest gust I've been in. But oddly
there was no sense of real fear. *Sealestial* seemed built to take it and then
some. The only nagging thought was the visibility being down to under
a boat length and the image of a big black bow of a merchant ship
suddenly appearing. Not really worth it, to dwell on that sort of thing.

At 0100 I roused Danny, and Chris headed back down to try to sleep.
Danny and I swapped off every half hour and noticed that the wind
seemed to be hauling a bit [moving clockwise] and we could get up to
190 and sometimes even 200, but it was still very heavy going, slamming
into waves, rocking wildly, the spray coming in solidly over the weather
rail. Luckily it wasn't too much of a problem for me since my trusty
six-year-old Live-7 foul-weather gear with the Sou'wester hat kept me dry
except for the clumps of water that would fly in, in which case I got hit
in the face and some of it inevitably made its way down the neck.

About 0400, with Danny on the helm, the jib started luffing more than
usual. I thought he was just too high, but when he assured me he was
on course I looked below the mainsail and up at the jib and saw that the
sail had ripped, from the leech line right to the forestay on a seam.
Rolling up the jib would have been the obvious and easy solution, but
of course it had all been lashed down during the previous watches'
problems with the furling line. I looked down into the saloon and saw
Martin looking up at me from the settee to leeward. I was about to
launch into a detailed explanation of the problem, but he waved his hand
resignedly and said, "I heard it all."

We got Martin, Denis, and Allan and tried to analyze the situation.
Ultimately, the lashing had to come off and the sail wound around the
forestay by hand. A pretty daunting task since if it got loose it would
probably unroll all the way. With Allan at the helm trying to keep us
dead downwind to reduce the speed and blanket the genoa, Danny,

Martin, and Denis tried to haul down the genoa while I eased out on the two jib sheets. After fifteen minutes of backbreaking work, they got it.

As we came back up to course we realized that by now we had lost about half the slides on the mainsail, so it was now well away from the mast. Only solution: take *it* down. Tighten the main sheet, bringing boom to center line, let go halyard, and smother mainsail before it got too far out of control. The furling job was a real hash job, but as good as could be expected given the conditions.

Before getting the main down, we put up the staysail so at least there was some canvas up, giving us control and a degree of vertical stability. It seemed made of terribly light material and I was afraid it would go soon. Even though it is such a small sail, there were six wraps on the winch and the sheet was absolutely bar-taut. Gives one an idea of the forces involved. With only the staysail we were making now six to seven knots, keeping up to 180 or so, still not what was desired.

Dick was supposed to come on at 0500, but Dan and I agreed that he'd be worse than useless under these conditions. We didn't wake him. He made an appearance about 0630, hung around down below in his boots, but didn't make any attempt to come on deck. He demanded to know why he hadn't been awakened earlier, so I replied that we'd sorta had our hands full keeping the boat going. He good-naturedly disappeared back to his bunk.

When I went to wake Bill at 0700, he asked if the wind had calmed a little, since the motion was so much easier. He seemed pretty surprised when I said it was because we had only the staysail up, that the wind was in fact stronger.

By midmorning, with the wind coming back to a normal range (like twenty-five to thirty), we needed to supplement the staysail with some engine power, and that helped us point up a little too, but our progress was still not in the right direction, Bill said. It was starting to be clear that we were at this point, with all the zigging and zagging and no sun sights, a little unsure of exactly where we were, and therefore unsure what was the best course to Madeira, but that was Bill's job, and he was working on it.

The sun was now and again visible. We tried to get some sights by bearing off, to lessen the motion for the sight taker and also keep the sextant from getting soaked by the constant spray. First Bill tried a couple of sights in the fleeting clouds and then Danny. Each time I had to prop Bill up by grabbing his belt and making sure I was planted firmly.

Danny's technique was to wrap himself around the leeward shrouds for
stability, but the problem then was that he was exposed to more spray
and had to wipe off the sextant a couple of times. Given that the waves
were so big and we were jumping around so much it is a wonder that
they got anything useful. . . . Well, the sights helped confidence a little.
We appeared to be about sixty miles away from Madeira, which lay on
a course of 260 degrees.

By evening, things were getting back to almost the routine. . . .

I withhold comment and give now excerpts from the log of Dan
Merritt:

My thoughts, a time or two, raced to my wife and kids, but only for
a split second, because I couldn't afford to screw up in these conditions.
They were getting worse and worse. "Tony, who goes on watch after

you?" Pause . . . "You don't want to know." "Oh shit." It's blowing
fifty-two now in gusts, wave action is erratic, keeping the *Sealestial* on
a rough course is tough, and I'm about to have Dick come up for the
next two hours? I'll get Bill to rejigger the watch. I really began to pray.
What will Bill tell my wife? "Gloria, Dick was at the wheel, struggling
with lighting a cigarette in fifty-knot winds when suddenly Dan was
catapulted into the sea. . . ."

I must shift grounds for a moment because now that the storm is over
I can put into perspective why I did pray so earnestly. I adore Dick
Clurman. I enjoy his company and the fact that he allows us to tease him
a bit, it's one of his endearing qualities. But . . .

We all have seen on TV wonderful westerns mostly starring John
Wayne with wagons trudging up winding mountain trails on the verge
of toppling over a precipice to a certain death below. Dick steers the
Sealestial like a wandering snake and he gives the ship a winding path
even when the seas are calm.

Well, I was nervous. Dick came up and he took the wheel and we took turns every ten to fifteen minutes and I continued to pray and it went well. I was very proud of Dick Clurman. He did it if not wonderfully, he did great. As a matter of fact, I think he steered as straight in those horrible conditions as in the days before and certain days to follow.

The storm was scary from another perspective—danger to the crew. We had to go forward twice to fix the broken roller-furling system. The dinghy broke loose under a mountain of a waves while Allan and the first mate and I were forward furling the genoa in by hand. Lines whipped about our heads and arms with force to break either. I was on my back being careful not to be struck by the flailing lines when the damned dinghy heaved from its cradle and began sliding my way. I froze. I actually—and for the first time—did not know what to do. I could not go outboard of the lifelines—I'd be swiftly washed away. I couldn't get up lest my head would be ripped off by the lines whipping in fifty-knot winds. I thought, as the dinghy slid toward me, I'd be pancaked; for some reason it only tapped me and bent a stanchion and got caught in the lifeline just long enough for me to crawl toward the stern and with the help of someone tie it down. Allan was hit by a line and showed the sign of it three days later. Denis was whacked, thank God lightly, on the side of the head and knocked to the deck like being floored in a football game. Bill went forward twice to tie down sails and he brought down what was left of the main. I hate those moments. It's when you are most vulnerable to nature. And nature has no mercy on any of us who are careless. [This does not sound like Danny, who is relentlessly cheerful and omnicompetent in all situations. The melodramatic tone is sincere, though superimposed several weeks later when he tended to his journal.]

We are all very good sailors, and fully aware of the inherent dangers of storms. It's storms that bring out the fear in me and it's storms that bring out the strengths too.

I could not eat the meal last served before the storm ended. I felt queasy and I was exhausted. I could not sleep. Between the pitching and the howling of the wind and the state of mind I went sleepless for about forty-eight hours. I venture to guess my shipmates got not much more.

We go to Christopher Little:

Morale, as they say, made like the barometer, dropping rapidly. While nobody became exactly testy, we were hardly a bunch of happy campers.

Danny and I had the 0100 watch, by which time we were bucking 10-foot seas and thirty-plus-knot winds gusting to forty. At high speed trying to sail as close to the wind as possible steering was increasingly difficult. I wear glasses, and the salt spray made it impossible to see. When I took them off the stinging of the salt water made it equally impossible.

I was at the helm when we heard a sharp, very loud report a few feet away that brought all hands clambering naked out of their wet bunks. What the fuck happened? I initially thought we had blown out the genoa as we had done on the Atlantic trip, but it was impossible to see through the driving rain and spray. Bill had the quick instinct to illuminate the spreader lights which revealed that the roller reefing line had let go and the entire genoa (it's a big sail) was flying free, uncontrolled, snapping dangerously in gale-force winds.

Danny took the wheel and a group of us went forward under trying conditions. Violently flapping genoa sheets—["ropes"] nearly an inch in diameter—are potentially lethal on the foredeck. So with one arm protecting the head, one arm hauling in the enormous sail—without the mechanical advantage of winch—holding on for dear life, we eventually managed to re-reef the genoa. I took a glancing blow on the top of my head, and Allan came aft with a nasty welt on his forearm.

Every sailor has tales of storms at sea. Many sailors have encountered worse than we were about to, but I had not.

A very short time after the initial sighting of the squall line the wind surged with incredible intensity. Sound is a very important component of a storm at sea. Everyone's heard the saw about the wind singing in the rigging. The wind started to scream and cosseted us. In our foul-weather-gear hoods it was impossible to hear one another's shouts. We took a sudden violent gust and *Sealestial* heeled over so far it wasn't just the gunwales in the water, the leeward side of the cockpit went under. We righted a bit and Tony, at the helm, struggled to turn her downwind. The rain and the roiling seawater became one and we were thundering along utterly blind. The wind hit Force 11 [fifty-six knots—one force on the Beaufort Scale short of a hurricane] and I have to say I was momentarily petrified. I didn't have any idea what would happen. For me at sea that was the first time that had happened.

If you think that sleeping in such conditions is a possibility, let me disabuse you. *Sealestial*'s angle of heel was such that the full weight of my body after negotiating entry into my upper bunk touched very little if any of my mattress; I was lying on the cabin wall. The occasional violent roll would send me across my bunk to the canvas lee cloth—in this case on the windward side—which would save me from being tossed to the deck below. The plunges of the hull into deep troughs create a sensation of weightlessness as close as any short of a trip into space. In spite of my position, and due to the constancy of gravity without wind, my leaking hatch still managed to drip cold seawater onto my already wet and abused body.

And Van Galbraith:

Nasty it was—winds for two days from twenty-five to thirty-five knots (during a squall they hit fifty-six knots) and most on the nose. That, plus the adverse seas—big, swollen waves, 15 to 20 feet, made to look even more awesome by the upward view from the low deck of a sailboat. Oppressing to the spirits. The latter were further dampened by the swill that accumulated in the main cabin—foul-weather gear, clothes, cassettes, food, papers, books, bottles all shifting from side to side and stirring themselves into a great revolting stew. The damage to the boat included: the slides ripped off the mainsail; the roller reefing gear for the genoa fouled; the genoa ripped; the automatic pilot broken; the freon gas leaking from a hole in the refrigeration system; the Sat Nav navigation system knocked senseless by two flying sorties out into the saloon as the boat rolled violently; lost water pressure; shorted lights and electronic gear; a broken toilet seat; and water, water everywhere—going into the main cabin and mixing with that stew and steady streams into food and clothes lockers and horizontal sheets of rain through leaky hatches.

And, finally, Dick Clurman:

Everyone agreed it was either the worst night or second-worst they'd ever spent at sea. WFB: "A bloody nightmare." DANNY: "Just pure nasty. I counted thirty-five hours." TONY: "I've never been in that strength wind trying to keep things safely in control: forty-five on the speedometer and we were doing ten knots to leeward." ALLAN: "Pretty bad."

Others' tales aside, let's get one damn thing straight right now. I went off watch at 2300. The wind was blowing thirty-five knots, the seas about 10 feet. The worst of the storm was abuilding. That night I was on the

watch cycle that afforded me my first opportunity for a full night's sleep in two days. I wasn't due on watch again until 0700 the next morning. I climbed into my upper berth in the closet-sized forward port cabin. The hatch was battened down tight. The door was closed. The leeboard was pulled up high. I was snug in a cocoon. I slept soundly through the whole apocalypse.

The careful reader will have noted a few contradictions. For Christopher Little, sleep was out of the question, but Dick Clurman slept (and so did I, between 0200 and 0700). Dick Clurman was not given the wheel in the early morning but took it later on when the seas were still unwieldy, and performed well.

I add a personal experience, traceable to the effort (stupid, as you will note below) to keep track of the boat's zigs and zags after we lost the genoa furling line, after we lost it again a while later, after turning downwind to manage first the furling line, later the mainsail. I was perched at the navigator's table attempting to keep a record sufficient to give us a dead reckoning (DR) idea where we were vis-à-vis Funchal, our destination.

My particular predicament was something I had never experienced. The back of the navigator's chair had been removed before the wind became unruly in order to clear a view of the movie early in the evening. I snapped off the movie halfway through, at about 9 P.M., when to continue it made no sense because of the mounting discomfort. But to replace the chair back was not something to do now, requiring intricate placement of two aluminum rods in remote holes obscured by cushion material, a high-definition enterprise impossible in our condition. Alongside the navigator's table is another of those aluminum rods that go from the sole to the ceiling against which you can support your body, maintaining you in place at the navigator's table. But that rod, removed in order to make the television/movie screen visible to those in the settee opposite, had been replaced but now crashed down. The attachment at the bottom end holding it to the floor was broken. Repairs were out of the question.

This left anyone sitting at the navigator's station literally without the means to stay in place when the boat heeled hard over to port. Four—f-o-u-r—times I was catapulted out from my station, flying 17 feet to leeward, my motion arrested only when my feet hit the settee opposite. It was worse merely than that I lost my place and my instruments went flying in every direction. The force of my body movement was, well, bruising, and each of the four times I crawled back to my station, I needed to establish that my body was whole.

But here is a diagnosis, generally useful to men and boys at sea.

To begin with, the ship was not soundly rigged. If the furling line to the genoa had held, much that you have read would not have happened. A line adequately strong would have held even if that much of the genoa then exposed to the wind had ripped apart. If the clew of the genoa goes, the clew is rotten. There is no point in maintaining a genoa-furling apparatus unless you can count on its working in the most severe conditions. It should never countenance a genoa overextended to the point where it becomes impossible to furl the genoa in completely.

That responsibility—defective rig—belongs to those who maintain boats when they set out to sea. We had a weak furling line. The mainsail was worn, and the mainsail slides were irresolute, old and tired.

But the tactical mistake was my responsibility, as captain in charge of the boat.

When the wind gusted up to over thirty knots in turbulent seas with the barometer down as sharply as it had gone, presaging worse yet to come, I should have given one simple instruction:

Gentlemen, we will heave to.

1. Pull in the genoa, entirely.
2. Pull down the mainsail.
3. Put up a staysail and lead it aback. That means, lead the clew not to leeward, as one would normally do, but to windward, as tight as it will go.
4. Raise the mizzen, and tie in a reef. Tighten it right to the center line.

Play with the wheel until the boat is heading practically into the wind. The headsail, lead aback, will nudge the bow of the boat just off the wind. The moment this happens, the wind will hit the mizzen, edging the bow back up toward the wind. At which point the headsail once again takes over.

The little routine is repeated, and the helmsman soon comes to know exactly where the rudder is ideally situated to bring about: *equilibrium.*

Yes, we'd have had equilibrium for the twenty critical hours. The boat would have slid slightly to leeward, and the forward speed would have been about two to three knots. In the resulting stability, one could have played a game of chess in the saloon below. The two men in the cockpit would have little to do. In some circumstances a little forward engine power, say 800–1000 rpm, would enhance stability.

The loss in distance-made-good toward the objective, Funchal, would have been less by far than what we lost by storming 90 degrees and sometimes 180 degrees off the wind, which was coming in, roughly speaking, from the direction of Madeira.

I have had several experiences of bad weather at sea, and recall one recently in which I made a decision of considerable practical consequence.

A sloop hove to. Note the (storm) jib led aback.

Twenty-four hours after bidding goodbye to the *Petrel* in New York Harbor in 1989, bound for Bermuda aboard my little *Patito* with Danny and Van and my friend Patrick Ciganer from San Francisco, we exchanged reflections on the data Van (as ever, our meteorological officer) had discreetly (he had not circulated it among our families and guests aboard the *Petrel*) collected after three days' phone calls to the National Hurricane Center in Miami. A tropical disturbance. Five hundred miles east of the Antilles, working its way westward, and projecting a northwesterly swing . . . perhaps achieving hurricane force, and projected to pass 5 degrees east of Bermuda. But, said the gentleman on the phone, you can't ever track tropical disturbance itineraries with exactitude, and what and where Hurricane Barry (as it would be designated a day later) would be doing about the time we would be approaching Bermuda was . . . unknown, and for the time being unknowable. But there was sufficient apprehension, in U.S. meteorological headquarters, to dispatch an airplane to probe the disturbance. We would need to be careful.

We don't have a single-sideband radio (the ship's equivalent of a long-distance telephone) aboard the *Patito*, and would therefore need to rely on shortwave and on inter-ship communications. Meanwhile we had set our course—147 degrees—and were headed, close-hauled on a port tack, toward Bermuda. The watch system was activated and the sun gave way to a black night, followed by a refractory dawn.

Oh my, don't we all know what it's like. The skies get grayer and grayer, the wind more and more huffy, the boat increases its heel, like a mountain climber facing an incline increasingly steep. Twenty-four hours after waving goodbye to the *Petrel* I had, in the course of one three-hour period, a) taken a single reef on the main; b) reduced the genoa by one-half its area; and c) taken a second reef on the main. The layman should know that these are steps designed to reduce the area of canvas exposed to the wind. Carrying the striptease to the end, you are left with what they call "bare poles"—i.e., no sail whatever, the resistance to the wind reduced to the mast(s) and the freeboard—i.e., that much of the boat that is above the waterline and a target of the wind.

Alas, the energumen that roams the seas seeking the destruction of well-being began to score. Patrick would not eat lunch. Van nibbled. Danny bravely cooked a three-course meal, which he then—transcended. Van had been hard at work on the Sony shortwave. But coastal America was uninterested in the huge front that was now giving us thirty-knot easterlies, rain, and a waspish sea. It was so for ten hours and at about 3 P.M. Van made contact with ("spoke," as they say in orthodox ocean lingo) a vessel only dimly visible on the horizon. A Dutch sailor fluent in English told us that the front we had penetrated was forecast to follow us down to latitude 36 degrees. That translated to one hundred and forty miles southeast of where we were, suggesting more of the same for, oh, thirty hours. And then, our Dutch friend added, it wasn't yet known whether the tropical disturbance, which was now moving in our general direction at about twenty knots, would dissipate or accumulate to full hurricane force.

What-to-do time.

Just Say No reached my mind as plainspokenly as if Nancy Reagan had been sitting there in the cockpit, dispensing basic lessons in rudimentary morality. The memory flashed back to the Annapolis–Newport Race of 1967. We had beat bravely down the Chesapeake. Pulling out of the bay, the winds increased. The #2 genoa blew. Up went our #3; in an hour it was gone. I didn't have my second #3, made of tougher material, on board. I hoisted the storm jib and the storm trysail and we bobbed along comfortably—but the boats behind us, more appropriately rigged, began to slide by. After a few hours such boats as we could spot seemed to have been arrested by the furious wind. I decided to quit the race and return to the Chesapeake and in one hour reversed the distance it had taken us a grueling six hours to climb. We felt better, the following morning at Norfolk, when we learned that thirty-four boats—a whopping 24 percent of the fleet of 125—had said No. It is much harder to say No when racing than when cruising. Cruises are undertaken with greater emphasis on the marginal delights of the passage than on the delights of successful competition. We were racing against nobody. Still, to say No is psychologically vexing (should we have persevered, never mind that no point of honor hung on our reaching the top of Mt. Everest?), and spiritually taxing—at sea one expects mortification of the flesh; were we shrinking from our Lenten duty?

I reflected briefly on these questions, and decided to Say No to the temptation to go ahead. So . . . we came about, and headed for Atlantic City.

There was no Atlantic City handy to us, one hundred miles northeast of Madeira. When there is no sanctuary at sea, you do the best to make your own, by heaving to.

It haunted me for the balance of the trip that I didn't have the judgment there and then to give the right commands. I have hove to three times in my sailing life, every time with total success. I don't doubt that both Allan and Martin, if they had thought themselves in charge, would have given the right orders. Instead we acted like amateur racers, trying to make time with an inadequately rigged boat. I am still embarrassed by my lack of forethought. The idea that rough weather at sea is good sport is nicely handled by Professor Morison. "No mariner in a small sailing vessel welcomes rough water, which renders navigation more difficult and dangerous. He accepts foul weather or heavy sea, but never likes it, and is not afraid to say so. Columbus explains that he welcomes the high sea merely because it enhances his reputation among the men. And when he has smooth water, he ejaculates 'Thanks be to God.' It is the nautical bluffers who pretend to glory in stormy weather and rough water, and affect to find smooth-water sailing dull." There were no nautical bluffers aboard the *Sealestial*.

· Chapter Five ·
We Arrive in Funchal

By the afternoon of Wednesday, the barometer had risen to 1010, an upward jolt, in a couple of hours, of 5 millibars and it was time to concentrate on finding our position. It is humiliating to make further confessions of ineptitude on top of one so major as the item with which I concluded the last chapter but, as I have confessed in another book on the sea, I almost always make—and almost always at the beginning of a trip rather than at its end—foolish navigational errors. (From Clurman's journal: "I am said to move at a fast pace in most things. But Bill makes me look like a sluggard. No matter what, he is always in a hurry. Mellifluously so, but nonetheless in a hurry. To eat, to set sail, to see the movie, to move on to the next passage. On land he is just as hyper.") If those errors I made and discovered to have made during Day 3 and Day 4 had been made by a midshipman, he'd have been sent to the horse cavalry for life.

I was vaguely dissatisfied with those few sights successfully brought in during the occasional shafts of sunlight we were graced with in the ugly weather. Celestial navigation is interesting in the way in which it communicates its dissatisfactions. Most obviously, of course, bad sights will cause you to fail to produce the island at the time and place you ordained that it should be. Actually, that hasn't ever happened to me. But well before landfall time, celestial will reproach you in one of two

ways. The kindest way is by giving you a preposterous "intercept"—
that word means the difference between your Assumed Position and
your actual Line of Position—an intercept of, oh, 3,042 miles. Since
the seasoned navigator always gives an Assumed Position smack on the
nearest coordinate to where he thinks the boat actually is, measured by
dead reckoning, you can be suspicious of any intercept of over thirty
or forty miles. When you get one that is outrageously wrong, you have
done something outrageously incorrect, e.g., you have given a position
in the Eastern Hemisphere when you are actually in the Western
Hemisphere.

But the more subtle ways in which celestial navigation can bedevil
you is with genteel little anomalies. If by independent measurement
you find that your taffrail log (which measures speed over the water)
is running very accurately, but there is a difference of twenty-five miles
between the distance your taffrail log says you traveled and the distance
your celestial sightings say you traveled, you wonder if there was an odd
current that accounted for that twenty-five miles. Or? . . .

I hadn't done celestial navigation for a year or so, and I discipline
myself, usually on Day 2 or 3, to put away my calculator or my computer and work out the whole thing by hand, as you would do in the
gymnasia of trigonometry. It takes a while to remember all the things
that on the calculator get done automatically: but they come back. We
are talking about an hour's work, maybe two. And what did I find out?

That at the misdemeanor level I had in fact made *no* mistake.
Something else was wrong—on another level. You then begin ticking
off, one by one, the generic elements of celestial navigation. If it isn't
the calculation, it *has to be* that the sextant sight was off, or that the
wrong time of day was put down. I had taken enough sights in a lifetime
to know that my problem could not just have been a matter of a series
of bad sights. And so I pondered. . . .

And indeed, there it was. I was using an Index Error of zero: which
is what the Index Error of my old Plath sextant was when last I used
it. Inquisitively, I leveled the index mirror on the horizon and found
it was now: *Minus eight.* That means that I had been exaggerating the
size of all sights by eight minutes ever since casting off. Eight minutes
of arc translates to eight nautical miles of earthly distance. It doesn't
really much matter if you are eight miles away, in mid-ocean, from

where you think you are. It gets to matter a great deal as you approach land, particularly if you are avoiding the hazard of a shoal.

The end of my problem? Oh no. On Day 3, the Index Error corrected, there was still . . . something wrong. It is uncanny how, almost always, you can depend on an accident-of-nature's calling your error to your attention. Dick was trying, with that zeal he brings to the operation of all radios, to bring in WWV, which is the station in Colorado that beams you the time of day, day in day out, every hour of the day. The signal comes in at 5,000, 10,000, and 15,000 MHz. That means that on one of those frequencies, wherever you are, you are supposed be able to get the absolutely correct time. The trouble is: You *aren't* able to hear the signal everywhere in the world, and we weren't able to pick it up (nor could we for a week or more), in the eastern Atlantic.

Now Dick was not looking for the correct time because he wanted the correct time—to get the correct time, all you had to do was ask Captain Bill, who would cheerfully give it to you after looking at his snazzy, aforementioned BMW digital watch. Dick was trying to find the time in order to coordinate with a Voice of America news broadcast he was trying to bring in. Having failed to get the time from WWV, he switched to a frequency that brought in London. At the end of every hour, BBC habitually pauses a few seconds, and then a clipped English accent comes in saying solemnly, *"This is London,"* followed by a couple of bars of martial music. And then the hour, Greenwich Mean Time. Instinctively I flashed a look at my watch and *found it one minute slow.*

Impossible! But for the first time at sea I had on board a crown jewel chronometer. It is hideously ugly to look at and hideously expensive, this Japanese quartz chronometer the size of a small portable radio, made by Seiko, which I bought from a gentleman who handles only chronometers, is a learned student of horology, and a stylish correspondent. He enticed me—after years of resistance fortified by my unhappy experience with my first Hamilton chronometer, bought in Gibraltar in 1955, which never quite worked—into buying this Japanese model. I keep it on my desk in Stamford and once or twice a month I look at it and make adjustments on my BMW watch, as required. And then every now and then I pull up the aerial on my little Radio Shack crystal weather and time receiver and push down the WWV button to check

Clurman and WFB, checking it out. Note that the steering is at this point being done by foot.

the chronometer: which has not lost or gained one second in the three years I have been observing it. (By the way, *never* trust the time signals you get from the telephone company. They can be as much as three seconds off.) I tore down the companionway and stared at my chronometer: *It too was one minute behind.*

According to BBC.

I waited impatiently one hour for the next BBC news hour: again, by its signal, I am a full minute behind. I think back: When last did I tinker with the minute hands of the chronometer? Simple: the day I packed for this trip, when I turned my chronometer from local time to Greenwich time. Could I have moved the minute hand one unit less than I should have done? Answer: Yes. Obviously I had done exactly that, there being no other explanation for it.

Painstakingly, I reset it. A lot of fuss about a minute? If your time is off by one minute, your position at sea is off by fifteen miles. Depending on the situation, that fifteen miles would be added to the eight miles by which the Index Error was wrong, in which case I'd have been twenty-three miles away from where I thought we were, or else—fifteen minus eight—seven miles. I drew a breath of satisfaction, confident that there would be no more errors of this nature. Moreover, when I got to the Canaries I would get in the mail an updated copy of What-Star, my navigational pride and joy, as we'll see.

The storm had knocked out our Satellite Navigation unit. This made me feel more at home on the *Sealestial*. It didn't work going across the Atlantic in 1980, didn't work going across the Pacific in 1985; and now after two days at sea, once again it wasn't working. If necessary we would home in on Funchal using the Radio Direction Finder. Which by the way . . . I asked Martin, Where is it kept? The answer: Nowhere. There isn't one on board.

The navigator's inventory of tools was diminishing. I wrote in my last book that as luck would have it I had yet to make an ocean landfall other than by sextant. Loran didn't extend to Bermuda in my racing days, does not operate in Europe or in the Pacific or in the Caribbean east of the Bahamas. So. My job, post the convulsions of the storm, was to establish where *Sealestial* was. I spent the evening of Day 4 grappling with the stars, working them out not through WhatStar, but on my calculator. I was satisfied that we were within ten or fifteen miles of where I thought us to be, and gave course directions to the helm and, at midnight, asked to be awakened in time to get the morning star sights. Shortly after 5 A.M. we spotted the twenty-seven-mile light on the northwest point of Madeira. Out of habit, I took the helm. And still had it when, just before noon, we turned into the harbor, halfway down the eastern coast of Paltea, and tied down on a busy dock, berthing alongside a fishing boat, there being no clear area on the dock that we could claim for our own.

We had done the first leg, 525 miles, through some very unpleasant stuff. Shore assignments had been made. Danny would attend to the laundry (62 kilos); Tony would find us a small Volkswagen-type bus, with or without driver; Van would find out where on the island sails get repaired; Dick would line us up a hotel. Liz and Allan had one thousand things to attend to. And I gave first priority, after the sails, to finding someone to fix the autopilot, sick as it was, a definitive casualty of the storm.

Another casualty of the storm was our itinerary. Because of the storm we were a day and a half late in arriving at Funchal, and here we would

Funchal. Sanctuary.

need to remain for at least two and a half days to make essential repairs, a full day longer than planned.

It was Van who had first blurted out the alternative as, with several hours still to go before reaching port, we were ticking off the boat work and related problems that still needed doing: Why not, he said chirpily, just skip Cape Verde? I was momentarily impatient with Van, which is not my way. To "skip" Cape Verde en route to Barbados was on the order of saying, Why not skip Hawaii en route to Japan? Cape Verde is a convenient and interesting way station on the trade-wind route to the New World. I then brooded on his suggestion for a full five minutes. The pieces came quickly together: He was absolutely right. There was no sensible alternative, not if we were going to keep to our schedule at the far end of the journey, in Barbados. And on the reasonable punctuality of our reaching there, several of my companions' tight schedules hung.

Yes, then. We would proceed as planned on to the Canaries, and leave from there for the Caribbean: a huge leap, 3,100 miles, but one Columbus had, after all, managed. This meant massive administrative rearrangements. A kind gentleman in Cape Verde, who works for the United Nations Development Fund—whose president is William Draper, who would be coming on board in the Canaries—had gone to the most extraordinary pains to line up, in islands that are sparse, undernourished, underpopulated, and underprovisioned, everything we would need on landing there after a 1,069-mile sail in anticipation of a 2,172-mile sail. Getting to Cape Verde by commercial plane is done all the time, but not every day, and to get there involves connections in places like London, Lisbon, and Angola. We would need to make fresh reservations for three people joining the *Sealestial* and for three leaving the *Sealestial.* We would need somehow to abort the huge shipment of foodstuffs ordered by Liz from Lisbon for delivery in the Cape Verde Islands at the time we were scheduled to arrive there. All of that was my job and, of course, became Frances Bronson's job at my office in New York; and because Frances took it all on, it would be done expeditiously.

I had been in Funchal once before, with my wife on a Royal Viking tour ship aboard which I was the lecturer. Madeira had been the stop between Casablanca and Fort Lauderdale, a very long way. I remembered Madeira, from the half day we spent here, as thoroughly Mediterranean: warm, fragrant, pretty and green. Fifteen years later it struck this traveler as something other than a mid-Atlantic historical and pastoral oasis—though, true, I came down with a one-day grippe and have come to recognize that biological distempers season one's judgments whether of places, food, or manuscripts.

But the impression of Madeira taken by my companions (as would be the case down the line in the Canaries) wasn't buoyant either. Tony wrote about our Hotel (Casino Park): "Breakfast in the dining room confirmed everything about the place I'd been thinking. Simon & Garfunkel arranged by Muzak at too high volume, and hordes of fat, contented heavy tippers." Van wrote, "Madeira itself is interesting but not a spot where I would vacation. First of all it is crawling with tourist groups from Germany, England and Scandinavia. Most of them are tour walkers and guided-tour takers, not the athletic types. Breakfast at the Casino Park Hotel, where the guests faithfully ate on their package deals, was institutionally depressing. The older attractive architecture is disappearing—only a small part of Funchal has Old World charm. There is an island atmosphere—isolated, cramped, homoge-

Atlantic Islands

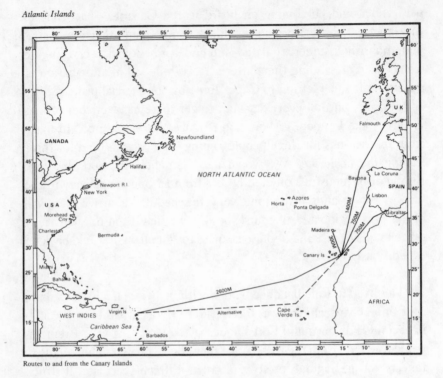

Routes to and from the Canary Islands

neous, inbred. This is not to say that Madeira is without beauty. . . ."

Danny? "Dick found us a hotel that resembles the HoJos back home, except this one is expensive. I find a casino. Oh my God! I need the sleep, but a casino only 100 yards away?"

I have seen that spell work before on Danny. When, two years earlier we had turned our back on the storm and headed for Atlantic City, he slipped away from *Patito* in midafternoon. The rest of us cleaned up, relaxed, and waited for him; but finally decided, along about 7 P.M., that young Danny was fatally in the coils of Mr. Trump, mortgaging his next year's salary. I wrote out a note telling him where we would be for dinner. As we were leaving *Patito* he showed up, a shy but triumphant smile on his face, Hannibal coming down from the Alps. He opened his right hand wordlessly and counted out eighteen one-hundred-dollar bills, handing to me to keep, against later temptation, fifteen of them, leaving him with only three to disport further—and to pay the cost of our dinner, which he triumphantly did. After which we visited Caesars Palace Casino.

I had two quarters, and was resolved not to go beyond them to my wallet. Within two minutes, they had multiplied to thirty-eight quarters, which I distributed among the senior crew. Danny had perched at a blackjack table. One half hour later, the senior crew were down to the two quarters—just enough to buy *The New York Times* and retreat to our little *querencia*. *Patito* was snugly dry, after six hours of sun; and we played Red Dog and I won twenty-three dollars. Danny showed up (I learned) at 5 A.M. It was difficult to revive him when at 8 A.M. I announced it was time to resume sailing. But we succeeded, and he opened his eyes, and managed a broad smile, reaching into his pocket to exhibit forty-eight one-hundred-dollar bills.

But tonight (for the time being) he would resist the casino at Funchal.

CHRISTOPHER LITTLE: "If you ever have the opportunity to visit the charming town of Funchal, Madeira, Portugal, 450 miles off the coast of Morocco, make absolutely certain that you do not stay at the Casino Park Hotel. Clurman, our pal and resident man-about-the world, was given as his *petite commission* the task of finding us a 'charming hotel, not too expensive, not too fleabag.' Well, the truth is he failed. The Casino Park, by no means flea-ridden, is a colossal chrome and glass and marble behemoth with about as much Old World charm as Donald Trump. When we checked in they slipped onto our bills without so much as a how-do-you-do a handful of extra chits for the dinner-and-show special, admission to the casino, plus one free cognac etc., etc. Extra price: 300 escudos ($50). Happily, WFB threw a fit and ceremoniously tore up the chits at the front desk, to the consternation of the staff, who are more accustomed to a more pliable breed of tourist." (Melodrama rides again. Tearing up chits is not my mode. I gave back the chits and told the man at the desk—but yes, sternly—that we would select our own amenities and pay for them.)

And anyway, it wasn't *all* that bad. The day I lay sick in the hotel was the day Our Gang toured the island. Tony writes: "We moved up into some spectacular forests, which looked like northern California, and then at the top into an area that looked like the Rockies, with steep

pine-covered slopes going down into ravines, and broad open pasture-
lands with sheep grazing and then terrific moonscapes of steep, almost
perpendicular cliffs and peaks. Pico de Apeiro has on top of it a cement
structure which brought the elevation up to 1,870 meters. Then back
down across the high plains and switchback into the eucalyptus forest,
a brief stop at a wicker place which was overrun with overweight Brits,
where I picked up a series of sewing trays for Liz and a big straw hat
for me. It could be a lifesaver for the run to Barbados."

To pause and reflect on the above entries: Christopher Little is the
son of a Scandinavian mother, the granddaughter of a sometime foreign minister, as it happens. Van Galbraith grew up in Toledo, faithfully attends the reunions of his public high school. If there is a human
being alive who thinks of him as snobbish that man will believe the
world is flat. Danny grew up in the lower middle class in Stamford and
would not hurt the feelings of a streetwalker. Tony is to the manor born
and has manners appropriate to his station: I would not believe it if he
spoke harshly or disparagingly to a subway token vendor. Dick Clurman
wages class warfare against such as Mrs. Helmsley, not against her
customers.

And yet . . . Here they are, writing in their personal journals express-
ing entirely extemporaneous reactions to a certain kind of hotel and to
certain kinds of tourists.

Is there a problem here? One worth pausing over? We had all come
off the ultimate cloister: a small sailboat with a prime cook and a couple
of hands to look after us during the few hours when we were not
ourselves engaged in labors sometimes demanding. The sudden change
in focus is entirely relevant to the question being explored: from the
tiny *Sealestial,* 71 feet long, to the behemoth Casino Park Hotel; from
the utilitarian arrangements of a seagoing boat to the modern rococo
of a flossy inn. And—most important, really—a half-dozen old friends,
ranging in age from thirty-five to sixty-five, preselected with some
reference to congruent backgrounds and interests and dispositions,
away for a day or two from the singular, sequestered exclusivity of an
oceangoing boat. There we shared an experience the intensity of which
immanentizes a certain quality of life aboard the vessel, the kind of life
in which people are called up at three in the morning to stand watch,

Tony writes of "spectacular forests . . . steep pine-covered slopes . . . broad, open pasture lands . . . terrific moonscapes of steep, almost perpendicular, cliffs and peaks."

custodians for four hours of the general welfare; from that to the huge caravanserai with one, two, three hundred, eating breakfast together, touring the island together, swamping the shops—it is the contrast that brings on what might in different circumstances be mistaken for flat-out snobbery. Such a contrast brings them to write about "overweight Brits," "fat, heavy-tipping Germans and Scandinavians"—as though there were an organic objection to their being in Madeira in the first place, or for that matter, special repulsion over their failure to look after their waistlines, or to their uneffacing manners. Yet nothing in the varying credenda of Our Gang is offended—quite the contrary—by the idea of The Vacation for working people, vacations made possible by the fruits of surplus. The very idea that in A.D. 1990 millions of people routinely traveled to places their fathers, let alone their grandfathers, could not dream of hoping to visit is a progressive idea by no means unrelated to the pleasures and excitements we ourselves were seeking out, crossing the Atlantic not because we were fleeing religious persecution or seeking political sanctuary. Ours was an entirely nonutilitarian trip, like that of the tourists who were flooding Madeira. And if it is true that most tourists are happier in such places as the Casino Park

Hotel than in hostels more apollonian in design and deportment, what does that tell us that Professor John Kenneth Galbraith didn't preach to an enthusiastic following of redistributionists when he railed against the new designs of the Ford Motor Company back when the company came up with the Edsel, a venture that ended by costing Ford a fortune and catalyzing *The Affluent Society,* which made Mr. Galbraith affluent? What else have we learned than that socialists and individualists alike often rail against popular culture or popular enthusiasms?

It is best summed up by saying that people who have the advantages of private, or relatively private, lives, and of enjoyments of their own design, seldom go gladly to massively patronized festivities, the most prominent exceptions being political rallies, I suppose, and opening nights at the theater. I guess one might add that it is true that youngish men who begin counting—and working off—calorie intake on the tenth anniversary of their graduation from Harvard are at least instinctively put off by those with avoirdupois, though in my experience they are not uniformly or obstinately affronted by it, for instance when the phenomenon occurs among chairmen of the board or fathers-in-law.

And there were of course other highlights than those Tony described, bounties of nature.

Danny won at the casino. . . . We visited for lunch Reid's Hotel, where we should have stayed—lovely, Old English, calm. Tony called home and wrote in his journal about his wife, Claire: "Her agent is very enthusiastic about the book [a primer on career alternatives] and . . . she's pregnant! Me a father? Wait a second, isn't this just a little too fast now? I mean, how long have we been trying? Less than a month. I thought it took a year or so. I guess we've got some adjusting to do. [The five other parents among his companions could have advised him.] *And when can we start telling people?*" When? About a week later, it transpired. Just before the crew change in the Canaries.

But then I don't think anyone would disagree with what Danny wrote at the end of our short stay at Madeira: "Two days here was plenty. I could not wait to be back on the *Sealestial,* in open water, with good food again, and some good sailing ahead."

Back at sea

CHAPTER SIX

Knocking About

I understand the distaste for true blackness at sea. It doesn't often happen, not the real McCoy, but it did happen as we pulled out of Funchal. No stars, no moonlight, no ambient lights from neighboring islands or from ships. Tony Leggett shares that feeling. "Very rapidly the lights of Funchal narrowed into just a small patch on the stern, making the darkness ahead all that much eerier. One had the sensation of floating a few feet off the surface of the water, but without any sense of direction. Just a void ahead, especially since the light shining up from the cabin below cut out night vision. Not a pleasant sensation at all. For some reason I found myself yearning—to head right back to Madeira."

I had no such yearning, but I did yearn, heading south from Madeira toward the Canary Islands, to avoid shipwreck. Yes, the guidebooks are quite schoolmasterish about the Selvagen Islands and the wrecks they have collected over the years. The Pilot Chart is reassuring: such current as is indicated in the area comes down from the northeast. I designated a point ("A") on a major coordinate and gave a course to A, 30 degrees North Latitude and 17 degrees West Longitude, a comfortable sixty miles west of the westernmost of the Selvagen Islands. The lazy wind was northeasterly, as well-behaved trade winds tend to be. Upon reaching Point A, we could decide on alternative courses. Either head for Lanzarote, the easternmost large Canary, or else head for Palma, the westernmost of the islands. We could of course have our pick of any of the four or five principal islands in between, but having accumulated just a touch of leisure time (the fruit of the decision to skip Cape Verde), my objective was to enjoy a relaxed cruise in the Canaries, as it would be seven days before we gave up our Leg One crew and picked up their substitutes for Leg Two. Seven days of pleasant sailing and sightseeing. Actually, more like five and a half, since we would need a full day and a little more to provision the boat for the long, long haul to the Caribbean.

The distances were nicely modest. Point A lay 138 miles to the south, on a course of 190 degrees, which meant that we'd be going by it sometime around noon tomorrow, a nice hour for confirming a boat's position.

That done—it was just after 11 A.M. that we passed Point A—we weighed now the alternatives. The wind having shifted from northeast to east, a course to Lanzarote would have meant a close haul, for which we were in no particular mood. By contrast, going to Palma was a blissfully short eighty-nine miles on a broad reach. The guidebook, moreover, came up with an interesting anomaly that would serve us when heading to the big city for provisioning. If you stick fastidiously close to the eastern shore of Tenerife heading north (northeast, actually) you find, lo and behold, a contrary shift of wind that runs you right up the shoreline, just like that! This would mean that we would not need to beat against a northeasterly as we meandered our way east toward our destination, the metropolitan city of Las Palmas in Grand Canary. Moreover, we would be visiting two ports in Gomera and one of these was where Columbus shoved off on that fateful day in September to discover, among other things, our homeland. It seemed a pleasant itinerary, but as a matter of fact turned out not to be, though the initial stretches were just fine.

That second afternoon out of Funchal was pleasant, the easterly wind transporting us at seven or eight knots right toward our destination, the island of Palma (not to be confused with Las Palmas, the city just cited, which was 120 miles east, on Grand Canary).

As sunset approached, the wind subsided. I took some measurements. At cruising speed of 2,000 rpm we would reach our destination, Santa Cruz de la Palma, at 0700. At 1500 rpm it would take us another two hours. The argument for the slower speed is obvious: there isn't much point in arriving at a harbor so soon after daylight. And anyway, the noise from the engine at 1500 rpm is about one third what it is at 2,000 rpm.

I recalled the trip on the big luxury Broward. That first day we sat there at lunch, in that three-million-dollar-plus boat. The stabilizers took good care of us and there was little heel. What struck me most forcibly?

Well, the noise, actually. Now that is not entirely just, because the sailor is always making comparisons, and of course when you sail without power you hear no noise, except those sounds you associate with the elements. On the Broward we heard a great deal of engine noise. But then the captain was moving the Broward at full cruising speed. He was doing about 2,000 rpm, which is also the cruising rpm of *Sealestial,* but the Broward was using both of his Twin Cat 3412 diesels, with their three-to-one reduction transmission. That and also the generators: Twin Cat 55 kw 3304 diesels.

I traveled up to the top deck, where the captain mostly operated from. (It gave him, he had told me, fore and aft views of everything from markers to little fishing boats.) I asked him how much fuel he was consuming?

About sixty-five gallons per hour.

I gasped, but the noise of the engines drowned out my disbelief. But later calculations confirmed what the captain said: it takes about five gallons of fuel to drive the B93 one mile.

How much fuel did he carry?

Six thousand gallons. . . . I withdrew to make calculations, and then asked how was it possible to advertise this B93 as a boat capable of crossing the Atlantic?

The answer is that it is perfectly capable of crossing the Atlantic but that when you do this you operate the ship differently. You use only a single engine—"for maybe a week." Then you turn on the other engine, shutting off the first. What does that cost you in speed? Oh, about one and one-half knots. How much less fuel is consumed? Well, said the captain, we use about sixty-five gallons with both motors and generators on, about thirty-five gallons with just the one engine.

I did not pursue the question why the extra one and one-half knots (thirty-six miles per day) was worth burning five hundred gallons of extra fuel. I asked instead whether it was quieter with just the single engine going? No, he said—as a matter of fact, it is a little *noisier.* More vibration. I didn't say anything until the following day, but after asking my sister Priscilla three times as we began lunch to repeat what she had said, I got—FLASH!—my inspiration. Without saying a word, I rose from my chair and walked—mysteriously, obviously on a Mission Bound—up to the top deck, leaned over to the captain, and asked him: Would he be good enough to reduce the revs while we ate lunch? He looked at me with some surprise, but his acquiescent instincts won out, and he replied, "Certainly!"—and we reduced to idling speed, which propels the B93 along at seven and one-half knots, a loss of five knots.

Ah, but the difference below! I remember that we treated ourselves, around the dining room table, to lasciviously whispered conversation, dragged out our post-prandial coffee, and it was a full hour before I went back to tell the captain that he could resume blasting when ready. On *Sealestial,* if you drop just about one knot, from 7.7 to 6.7, you reduce your fuel consumption by 40 percent, and diminish the noise by about the same measure.

We had a lazy dinner, a movie, and maintained the usual watch system.

"Sitting up together, huddled against a mild chill between three and five in the morning encourages intimacies," Christopher Little wrote. "Last night Dick told me the extraordinary story of his brother Bob's life and death. After a long first marriage, Dick's brother came home one afternoon to find that his wife had jumped out of their apartment window. Six weeks after he had remarried, Bob Clurman hired a car and driver, giving him instructions to go to Atlantic Beach on Long Island, upon reaching which he dismissed the driver telling him that he was on an assignment for his employer, the *New York Times.* He then neatly folded his clothing and swam two miles out into the Atlantic. A fishing boat spotted him, and though exhausted, he fought off their attempts to save him. They overpowered him and dragged him on board. He agreed with his new wife and Dick to commit himself to a closely watched stay in a New York psychiatric hospital: from which he promptly escaped, to go home to his high-rise apartment and, as his late wife had done, jump out the window.

"I don't think I've ever heard a more tragic suicide story, all the more so because of the love and awful sense of loss in Dick, so sadly authentic as he told the story. In turn, almost out of a sense of communal intimacy, I suppose, I told him the tragic tale of my own brother-in-law's suicide during his freshman year in college."

Such exchanges happen at sea in lonely circumstances, though a great deal depends on the mood of those on watch and on the emotional initiative of the sailor, as also, of course, on his confidence that his companion welcomes the intimacy. Nothing aborts a confidence more quickly than any suggestion that it is not welcome. That doesn't tend to happen among sensitive people, though all of us know sensitive people who would sooner dive overboard than talk about themselves, never mind the receptivity of their companion.

Working below on the star sights I overheard Tony, earlier in the evening, wonder out loud why I was going to such extraordinary lengths to see to it that at Palmas we'd have a working autopilot—Who really needs one? was his infuriating postulate. I was tempted to pop up the companionway and bark out two orders, one to him, the second to Danny, an order that would require simultaneous effort by both of them—with only one motive in mind, to hear him object that how could they carry out my commission since one of them was needed on the helm? But no, I didn't, though I made a mental note at some point in the next twenty days to impale dear Tony on his professed indifference to the principal labor-saving aid to navigation ever discovered. I wanted the autopilot, promised now by Allan to be waiting for us five days down the line, and I wanted the update on my WhatStar, which would do for me as navigator what autopilots do for helmsmen.

We came into the little harbor at just about the time calculated, once again needing to berth alongside another vessel because the harbor is so tight. We had this and that to fuss with, after which we set out on an auto trip of the island, heading up toward the 8,000-foot-high observatory which the guidebooks acclaim as a vital organ of meteoro-

Approaching the observatory

logical and astronomical science. We would stop for lunch somewhere en route, returning to the boat in the afternoon and setting sail for Columbus's Gomera, a mere fifty miles, reaching there about midnight.

Dick Clurman obviously went to such extravagant pains to indite his slanders, I have no chivalric alternative than to reproduce his journal entry on the subject of me as driver of one of the two cars. Earlier, having written that I am "hyper" while at sea, he had declined to specify that I tend to be hyper at sea only when he is at the helm. . . . But now he goes on:

Dick Clurman, practicing libel

On land WFB is just as hyper, only at times it can be more hazardous. Consider the scene on Isla de la Palma, our first stop in the Canary Islands:

He enjoys taking the wheel of a car on mountainous roads almost as much as he does taking the helm of a boat in rough seas. At sea he excels. The same cannot be said of him on land. I know of only one person who drives a car with more absent-minded indifference than he—me. But at least I dislike driving. He relishes it.

We embark from the pier in two rented Volvos to explore the astronomy observatory atop the highest peak (8,000 feet) on the mountainous island. Engineering ingenuity has laced this Spanish outpost with necklaces of serpentine, two-lane blacktops rising and plunging, edged all the way by dizzying cliffs. The two-hour, steep climb brakes his Le Mans driving proclivities. So the ride up, with Bill at the wheel, is relatively tame.

The steep ride down is another matter. Bill is winding and weaving at never less than fifty—up to sixty—miles an hour. I am in the passenger seat on the right, my seatbelt fastened (as, foolishly, I never do when driving with anyone else). Bill slows down not one whit as he pulls his

Tony and Van

La Caldera

crew-necked cashmere sweater over his head. "Grab the wheel," Danny shouts to me from the back seat. Good thinking, because Bill's sweater is snagged, covering his face and eyes. "Pull on my sleeve," Bill says calmly, as I hastily reach with my right hand to oblige. My left hand is clutched to the wheel. Bill's foot is still on the accelerator. The sweater maneuver completed, he resumes his conversation in midsentence where he left off, never deigning to mention his murderous and suicidal auto-gymnastic undressing.

In the same headlong descent, this time at a freewheeling 60 mph, Bill casually reaches over with his right hand and extracts from its plastic wrapping his daily upper pill (as if he needed it). Down his gullet it goes, assuring that his adrenaline will flow as fast as the gas fueling the hurtling car.

People who make vulgar comments about my ineptitude as a driver (my wife principal among them) are, I have concluded after consulting psychiatric specialists on the subject, finding ways to express their jealous resentment of my fifty-year record of never having had an accident, which of course does not count the two occasions when mad drivers banged into me. But let it go. What do I care? I, Master of the Universe?

When we descended from the observatory we were very hungry, and it was fine to be able to use the native language, as, in Spanish territory, we were now rescued from Portuguese. Dick was very anxious to find a *good* restaurant, which shouldn't be easy to do in this remote little island on the forlorn side of its only city. We came to a crossroad in a tiny village and I spotted a rusty yellow sign indicating that under that sign was—a restaurant. I accosted an elderly gentleman using a cane and walking down the block we were approaching. *"¿Es este re-staurante"*—I pointed to the yellow sign—*"de primera categoría?"* He looked over his rimless glasses to my question about whether this *restaurante* was first-class, and replied, *"Pues es donde como yo."* (Well, it's where *I* eat.) He resumed his walk, we piled out of the car and had, I swear it, one of the best meals I have ever had anywhere. This was a subject we needed to treat with some care because Liz was with us and the pains she takes to give us scrumptious food at sea, ornately prepared, was in sharp contrast to the little country restaurant

At the peak: Tony Leggett, Dick Clurman, WFB, Dan Merritt,
Van Galbraith, Christopher Little

where, written on a hanging blackboard, were three words: *"Pescado.*
Cerdo. Conejo." We could have fish (they had five tuna fish, no more),
pork, or rabbit. Moreover, the food was served quickly, together with
a local rosé wine, great slabs of freshly baked bread and a mound of
butter. With the main course were fried potatoes and hour-old ripe
tomatoes. It always surprises me what a direct effect truly good food
has on the morale, which is why Liz's contribution to the voyage has
been so critical.

None of us found the island particularly interesting, its observatory
to one side, and it is not a gathering place for tourists. Five hours later
we were ready to sail away, venturing out for fifty miles on a memorable
sail: the wind's velocity—about fifteen knots—could not have wavered
by more than a half knot during the seven-hour passage. The seas were
docile, the stars and the diminishing moon fresh and hospitable as if
egging us along toward the little island unknown and unremarkable
save for its historical connection with Christopher Columbus, whose
little house we would see (or, rather, the little house where he is said
to have stayed); seeing, also, the little church where he prayed on the
day he set out, its original nave still there; and see, too, what is left of

the extraordinarily small edifice—it is square, but built more as a turret than as a true fort—from which the widow of the viceroy ruled the island in the fifteenth century. Here, to quote the guidebook of Donald M. Street, Jr., "was the fortress of Doña Beatriz de Perona, who entertained Columbus during his trip through the Canaries on his first voyage of New World discovery. The second time he came through she welcomed him with fiesta and fireworks; but the third time, she had lost interest in him and had apparently taken a new lover. Doña Beatriz," Mr. Street concludes his vignette, "was big on revenge. When one of her lovers was too loud-mouthed about his conquest, she invited him to her castle for a banquet, then after dinner had him seized and hanged until dead from the castle walls." I asked Dick, after the passage was read out loud to us by Van, what did he suppose Doña Beatriz would have prescribed for a bad—"driver!" he interposed quickly, leaving the word "helmsman" stuck limply in my open mouth. Frustration, frustration.

· CHAPTER SEVEN ·

Traces of Columbus

Getting into Valle Gran Rey was a singular and exciting ordeal that reminded me of the strength of illusions at sea. The harbor lay on the left, its entrance not more than fifty feet wide. In the darkness I needed to maneuver exactly, i.e., wait until a tiny flashing red light was at exactly the bearing I wanted it to be at, then turn to an exact azimuth and slowly, slowly, move in the indicated direction, straining to see the outlines of the harbor's mouth.

I executed my maneuver a few degrees prematurely. Allan was all the way forward, and the crew strung out so that anything he observed he could communicate back to me via the pony-expressed voices that wired us together. I was pursuing my azimuth, eager to spot the entrance to the harbor when the word came back, the high pitch of Allan's voice, so seldom high, faithfully replicated by the strung-out transcribers: *"Go right forty degrees!"* I did exactly as instructed but then with my own eyes I found myself heading for a hundred-foot-high cliff that was not, I'd have sworn, more than thirty or forty feet ahead of me. Was it possible that Allan, so much closer to it, standing as he was at the bow of the boat, hadn't seen it? Inconceivable: but I followed my own instincts in the matter and turned sharply to the right, executing a 360-degree turn to give us time to take in the perspective, to verify it all, to see just exactly where that cliff was, and where the jetty signaling the opening to the harbor lay.

It worked. Suddenly we could see. It was there, fifty or sixty feet away. Where it should have been. We crept up on it and docked by a quay. This turned out to be futile. Great swells kept coming in, and the spring lines would certainly not take the strain; at this rate two of us would need to be up all night tending to the docking arrangements. Tony volunteered the suggestion that, what the hell, there were enough of us awake and active, why not go on twenty miles to the next harbor? But Martin came up with a better suggestion, and I turned the helm over to him to execute it. It called for two crew to take a line attached to the stern of *Sealestial* and purr up on the dinghy to the perpendicular dock and tie it to a fixture there. We turned *Sealestial* around, threw out an anchor, and soon found ourselves sitting peacefully in the middle of the harbor. "At first I thought our warp was going to be banging against everyone's hull," Tony fretted, "but in fact it led out beautifully straight to our stern. There was no reason for us to be sheepish at all. Sleep was very sound."

Chatting with Allan, after all was quiet, I described to him an instrument even the great *Freedom* doesn't have, but which the *Patito* proudly has. With all the satellites now up, I said, such problems as we had faced tonight disappear.

"When the appropriate charts are done," Allan commented. Indeed.

The new "NavGraphic" had been the special excitement on the trip to Bermuda aboard the *Patito*, when we landed instead at Atlantic City. The Trimble GPS NavGraphic is the ocean equivalent of the postman who knows how to find 22-A Maiden Lane, undistracted by 22 Maiden Lane which is a half-dozen beguiling yards off to the right.

My very first experience with it, sailing into New York from Stamford, was engrossing. I designed the installation so that in inclement weather I could situate the monitor to that navigational miracle on the cockpit, under the dodger. That way we could all actually *see Patito* sail, second by second, westward from Stamford, past Execution Rock, up into the East River, past La Guardia Airport and Rikers Island and Hell Gate to Gracie Mansion, and then south down the length of Manhattan. On the screen, a tiny facsimile of a sailing boat, sliding along an illuminated chart, identical to your sailing chart, expanding

Finally, snug in Valle Gran Rey; which wasn't worth it.

or diminishing in scale accordingly as you push ZOOM IN or ZOOM OUT, keeping always in front of you the course to your destination and the distance to it, the Estimated Time of Arrival, the Course Made Good—all of those plums to which Loran has accustomed us; but now all there on a live TV screen in front of you, so that when you get to the Brooklyn Bridge *Patito* is shown under the Brooklyn Bridge— uncanny. Assuming the availability of detailed charts, and a disk that covered that part of the world—and all of this will be with us in a matter of a year or so—we'd have glided into Valle Gran Rey as confidently as we slid down the East River. Granted, it is a luxury item. The Trimble unit retails for about ten thousand dollars. But it is delivering up to you, at no supplementary cost, the fruit of about twelve billion dollars of Department of Defense technology. The Department of Defense's GPS satellites are to the NavGraphic as the alphabet is to a typewriter.

It wouldn't have been a bad idea to have slept through to noon the next day, which is when we set out for San Sebastián. In my journal I nominated Valle Gran Rey as "the ugliest town in the sea world."

I wish I could do justice to its ugliness. Every building standing up is utilitarian and unfocused. The beach with its rolling surf would be splendid for swimming except that the rocks make swimming impossible. A little further up from the beach is a fetid lagoon which swimmers at Valle Gran Rey presumably need to settle for. There was no reason to stop over here except that it was a convenient distance from our starting point the evening before, and the entrance to the harbor was nicely challenging, the kind of thing that adds to one's experience. I remember trying to sail into Cancún one night in 1966 aboard *Cyrano*. The boardwalk was entirely lit up making it inconceivable that we could distinguish the tiny red light marking the entrance to the canal we needed to find. I paraded the schooner up and down the brilliantly illuminated lights, the two ship's binoculars heavily used, but the mission was on the order of distinguishing the relevant light bulb in Times Square. On that occasion I finally called the Coast Guard and, in Spanish, was told that the thing to do was to start at the south end and begin to count hotels, which *were* distinguishable. "The light you are looking for is between the sixth and the seventh hotels." Boat lore. Sea lore. Valle Gran Rey gave us that, sea lore. The supply is inexhaustible.

We headed up around the island to San Sebastián on its eastern coast. That was where Christopher Columbus set sail. To see that little harbor, in the shape of a half-moon, is moving, quietly—hugely— exciting. It was there that they lay, the *Niña*, the *Pinta*, and the *Santa María*. This last was the flagship, and Columbus never particularly liked it—a bulky, routine cargo vessel with three masts, a square rig, and a crew of forty. Robert Fuson quotes an authority who tells us that the ship displaced 202 tons, almost three times what *Sealestial* displaces, was 77.4 feet long (6 feet longer than *Sealestial*) with a beam of 26 feet (10 feet more than our own) and a draft of 6.9 feet (ours is 8). The *Pinta* was a little smaller all the way around, did several crossings including an exploration of the Amazon River, and went down in a hurricane in the Caribbean in 1500 (explorers are still searching for the remains). The *Niña* was about the same size, but carried four masts. She was Columbus's favorite, and he took her across on his second and third (out of four) voyages.

I read out loud, to the amusement of my watchmate Danny, the decree that explains how Ferdinand and Isabella came up with these vessels. The town of Palos had offended their majesties in some connection or other and earned a black mark, in the tender of those days redeemable by the service of two caravels, as their sailing boats were called, for a period of one year: to be claimed at their majesties' convenience. Why not have the Palos people come up with the ships for Columbus? Why not indeed. The letter addressed to the local governor:

> Know ye that whereas for certain things done and committed by you to our disservice you were condemned and obligated by our Council to provide us for a twelvemonth with two equipped caravels at your own proper charge and expense. . . . And whereas we have now commanded Cristóbal Colón to go with three *carabelas de armada* as our Captain of the same, toward certain regions of the Ocean Sea, to perform certain things for our service, and we desire that he take with him the said two caravels with which you are thus required to serve us; therefore we command that within ten days of receiving this our letter . . . you have [,] all ready and prepared [,] two equipped caravels, as you are required by virtue of the said sentence, to depart with the said Cristóbal Colón whither we have commanded him to go. . . .
>
> Given in our City of Granada on the 30th day of April, year of Our Lord Jesus Christ 1492. I THE KING. I THE QUEEN.

I had waded a bit in Columbiana during the preceding days and would continue to do so for a couple of weeks, eschewing only ritual iconoclasms. Excepting rare, authenticated historical revisionism (Vatican II cost me my St. Christopher, whose name and patronage I had invoked when my son was baptized), such stuff (Columbus was a "cruel mercenary," a "genocidal prototype," a "lazy leader," an "inept naviga-

tor") is washed away with the tides of history that come along with
blessed frequency to cope with such festering effluences. I don't have,
about Columbus, the intense personal curiosity that has animated so
many scholars, and I accept as established that Professor Morison was
wrong about where exactly he made his landfall, but it is primarily on
Samuel Eliot Morison that I'll be relying as I reflect, as we did so often
on the trip, what little our voyage from the Canaries to the Caribbean
had in common with his. I have never doubted that my companions
would have preferred thirty-six days even in the Casino Park Hotel to
thirty-six awesome days on the *Santa María.* But there in Columbus's
passage lies a tale that will always continue to exhilarate. I do not doubt
that five hundred years hence a small sailboat will home in on San
Sebastián, as we were now doing, just to lay eyes on where the great
event began which, whatever historians finally decide about the personal character, eccentricities, ambitions, habits good and not so good
of Christopher Columbus, changed the shape of the world as no other
exploration, not even that giant step forward for mankind in 1969, has
done.

We wandered about San Sebastián for traces of Columbus. There
are three. The remains of the fort of Doña Beatriz, now being recon-
structed, the house where he lived during his stay in Gomera, and the
little church where he worshipped. The fort I have described. The
house is now a little art gallery, with four or five rooms. It is, was, of
modest size, as one would have expected, and of course there is no way
of knowing whether so much as a splinter of it was around when
Columbus slept on the island.

The church is a different matter because although it was sacked in
the eighteenth century supposedly by the Portuguese in one of those
endless encounters that stain the epoch of exploration and empire,
experts avow that the central section, the nave, is pretty much as it was
in 1492, a dozen years after the first of the Canaries had been colonized
(the Guanches fought the Spaniards off here and there over a considerable period of time). One would hardly have expected to find, in so
remote a part of colonial Spain, a grand church, any more than one
would a grand fort. But the relic is symbolically important in grasping
the character of Columbus. Professor Morison himself went to that
chapel to pray before undertaking his own voyage in 1939 retracing

Columbus's passage. I paused there too to pray for a safe and happy passage, and contemplated what Morison wrote, in his scholarly anxiety to distinguish between the genuine faith of Christopher Columbus and the ritualistic faith of so many of his contemporaries. Morison would write about Columbus the Discoverer and about his singular gifts without committing psychobiography.

Casting his mind back to re-create the flurry of exploratory activity that was triggered by Columbus's discovery, Morison wrote: "As the caravels sail on tropic seas to new and ever more wonderful islands, and to high mountain-crested coasts of terra firma where the long surges of the trade winds eternally break and roar, I cannot forget the eternal faith that sent this man forth, to the benefit of all future ages. And so, writing in a day of tribulation both for Europe and for America"— Morison wrote these words just after Pearl Harbor—"I venture to close my prologue by the prayer with which Columbus began his work: *Jesus cum Maria/Sit nobis in via.*"

Jesus and Mary/Be with us on our way.

· CHAPTER EIGHT ·
Las Palmas

The point now was to wend our way first to Santa Cruz, the big city in Tenerife where the updated WhatStar would be waiting and where we expected to pick up the new autopilot. But a phone call by Allan brought the advice that the autopilot would arrive not at Santa Cruz but at the other big city in the Canaries, Las Palmas, on Grand Canary. So much the better, because most of the international flights go there, and there we would be picking up the new crew.

It's a short run from Gomera to the southern tip of Tenerife but on a route due east. The wind is fickle, manipulated by the high mountain in Tenerife, and as we pulled out of San Sebastián, paying lavish attention to the last sight of land Columbus saw, I called to put up the spinnaker. Before it was up the wind had died and we were under power. Ten minutes later we were close-hauled, and ten minutes after that we tucked in a double reef. I was most eager to experience the miraculous southerly wind current at Tenerife, whose hospitality would spare us a long day's tacking, permitting us to sail directly up to Santa Cruz.

You guessed it. The southerly did not/does not exist. I gave it every opportunity, going in practically to the beach and working bit by bit offshore hoping for the lift. No such luck. Tack tack tack, against a stiffening breeze. Toward late afternoon I decided we'd stop short of

Santa Cruz, at the town of Candelaría, whose harbor we located with some difficulty, arriving tired from a hard day's work on the wind.

Reflect on our ability to take that option, of pulling into a convenient harbor. It is a great luxury of cruising at sea in a region profuse with shelters. New England is perhaps foremost among all cruising areas on earth. (How many harbors are there between New York City and Eastport, Maine? One thousand? Ten thousand?) Aboard a boat there are only the geological limitations—you can't travel as the crow flies, given the physical obstacles, ranging from shoals to peninsulas, but there are no better ways to meander. Ten years ago my wife and I "cruised" to Curaçao. But we were aboard the *Queen Elizabeth 2*, not to be compared with a sailboat which, with modest limitations having to do with the depth of your keel, permits "gunkholing," as they call it: a kind of sea-spelunking. When you go there on a luxury liner, you don't get to see in Curaçao what you ought to see in Curaçao. You get only the whiff of the place, and a chance to buy a beautiful set of 7 × 50 binoculars with inbuilt compass for two hundred bucks. Pat and I finally saw "Roques" (Islas Los Roques), but on a sailboat, as it should be seen—not as we had seen it fifteen years ago, flown there by friends from Caracas on a nice little jet, met by a powerboat that zoomed us off to a 50-foot Chris-Craft for two nights and a day of sunbathing and snorkeling, the mother ship never once moving its anchor; yes, a floating hotel or, better, motel, cozy but sedentary, no way to explore.

On the other hand, let's face it, we had had a rocky afternoon on the *Sealestial*. If it had been the big squat Broward 93-foot motor yacht, we'd have been much more comfortable. For reading a book, just for instance—an interesting point here. Aboard a sailboat, even fully crewed, there is more often than not something that prevents you from total repose. You are perhaps heeled over, and suddenly you are dumped from your seat or bunk. Or else someone comes smilingly to dislodge you—the grapefruit juice is in the locker just under where you are sitting. Or there is a squall and you need to get out of the way to permit the ports to close, after which you suffocate. By contrast, at sea in a modern powerboat—provided the fore-and-aft pitching is not too distracting—you are free to immerse yourself totally in your reading, your writing, your card playing, or your desk work. That may be among the reasons why the Broward has such varied electronic gear as a telex machine and—

Yes, a Satcom. I have often envied the boat that permits you to pick up a telephone wherever you are at sea and simply dial away, just as in the television ads, as though every day were Mother's Day and every editor you write for were a mother. (Though, in fact, I don't like editors very much when they can ring in: better, at sea, when exploring, only you can ring out.) It transpires that the wonderful Satcom, indeed a miracle, comes with certain economic depressants. Like ten dollars per minute's use. The only time aboard the Broward we ever used it was to make a single call of instrumental purpose, to relay to the wife of one of my friends our estimated time of arrival at Charleston, by all odds the most laconic call this friend ever made to a wife of forty years' standing. This time, when he announced that he had just one thing to say, he did have (or allowed himself) just one thing to say and did— cost: twelve dollars. The Satcom, by the way, if you feed it thirty-five dollars a day, will give you a daily news bulletin that stretches seven paper-feet long, reaching right to the extremity of the day's news, like how many Contras can dance on one Boland Amendment.

If peripatetics is your bag, you need to keep reminding yourself that when you travel, what you see, as well as what you experience, depends greatly on the mode of conveyance. This is obvious when you fly across the Atlantic instead of going across on a liner, or when you take a raft down a canyon instead of driving a car alongside. The same word—a "cruise"—is assigned to cover a passage aboard any type of boat. But there has got to be room to accommodate those who want to explore islands from aboard a boat over whose movements they have control, which is hardly the case with the QE2. Though, come to think of it, there is the modern fantasy, another version of control, and the musician Peter Duchin told me it happened to him when he married, and was invited by Aristotle Onassis on board his colossus, at anchor off Casablanca. After dinner Duchin was given his wedding present: He could command the movements of the yacht for the next twelve days. You can do a lot in twelve days, starting at Casablanca, on a ship that travels at twenty-four knots, and so Peter buzzed about for two happy weeks, finally debouching with his wife at Alexandria, why not?

It is of course a blessed part of the experience of traveling, this independence of movement. With a car or a bicycle or walking shoes you can move when you wish to, but only in accessible directions. A boat will move in any direction, save straight up. (One doesn't want a boat to go straight down, though sometimes of course this happens.)

What needs to beat within you is the desire to see, and if you wish, explore, islands at your own speed, traveling to any spot in the area that will accept the draft of your vessel. And you will know the distinctive pleasure that comes when the anchor is down and you look out over the cockpit and find, as we did on the offshore islands in Venezuela, that you are alone, or in the company of only one or two other boats, and that as far as your eye can see there is no habitation, only the shrubs and the palm trees and the white-powder beaches girdled by the pale turquoise waters; but you are not frightened or lonely because you are protected from the elements, and you have at hand everything you absolutely need (food, shelter) and practically everything you might want (good company, and a variety of planned distractions).

After dinner, tied up alongside the quay at Candelería, we viewed all three hours of *A Bridge Too Far*, the World War II movie about the bloody engagement in Holland where the British general sets his sights too high (. . . a bridge too far), wonderfully well made and wonderful raw material for Professor Paul Fussell in his ongoing historical campaign to establish that, in wars, nobody ever gets things right. (Except in the Persian Gulf.) Afterward we stretched our limbs, making it up into the town a few blocks to a little beer parlor.

As sometimes happens, we were buoyed by one of those people who occasionally give the earth a happy face. He is a middle-aged bartender who arranged a table outdoors (he thought we would like the view of the harbor), insisted that the beers he first served weren't really cold enough, bringing a second set, and opened up (no charge, señores) two tins of crackers and a can of nuts for us to nibble on. The talk was relaxed, maybe even inert. I established that a taxi to take me north to Santa Cruz the following morning to pick up my WhatStar would take two hours round trip, decided the hell with it, I would contrive the means to get it forwarded to us up ahead in Las Palmas, and we were all in bed by midnight and off to an early start for the big bustling capital at Las Palmas, where there was much to do.

. . .

We would set out for America either from there or from Puerto Rico, at the southern tip of the island. It looked for a while as though the wind were northerly enough to permit us to round the northern tip of Grand Canary without tacking. But it wasn't, and we had a one-leg tack before rounding about and sailing comfortably into the big municipal port which, along with Santa Cruz, shares the heavy burden of European tourist traffic. Beginning in the early spring there is a planeload of tourists coming down here every hour, and, during Easter time, every half hour. The Canaries are the Caribbean of Europe, is the simplest way to put it.

And Las Palmas is for sailing boats the major way station to the Caribbean. Whether they are coming in from the Mediterranean or from Scandinavian or British waters, they will stop at Las Palmas for provisioning before making the long run to Antigua or Grenada, the most common stops. We learned soon after getting there that a race regatta would set out a few days after our own departure. The race to Antigua—run on informal grounds, I gathered—made a convivial occasion for fifty boats to make their way west, bound for the commercial trade from December to May. Mostly these were boats designed for the charter business, but among them also were a dozen or more smaller boats, some of them manned single-handed—a part of the gypsy community of the sea. They would make abundant use of their radios en route, reporting on weather and other phenomena.

Because of the regatta there was no space for us in the huge city wharf, not on the first night; but the next morning, while taking fuel at the dock, I struck up a friendship with the gentleman at the marina who seemed to be running everything this side of Houston Control. He would, he said, acknowledging my requests, get us fuel, carpenters, autopilot specialists, empty 50-gallon drums, and hotel space for the incoming crew. Before he was through filling *Sealestial*'s fuel tanks we had become blood brothers. I took the opportunity volubly and dolefully to regret, in Spanish, *Sealestial*'s physical alienation from his enterprise, stranded as we were at anchor 100 yards away because of the lack of dock space. He winked in the direction of the space right by the marina from which a large sailboat was departing and suggested

Regatta-time at Las Palmas

that if we were to occupy that space *inmediatamente* there wasn't much he would be able to do about it if and when the gentleman who had reserved it hove in; and anyway, such people are often late; and anyway, somebody would surely pull out of a space somewhere else along the large quay, leaving room for him when he came, and *¿Ud. me entiende?*—did I get the idea? Instantly: three and one half minutes later we had backed *Sealestial* into the space we would occupy for two busy days.

It is worth touching on the autopilot only because logistical frustrations associated with preparing to go to sea have something to do, I think, with the character of the experience. Without them there would be less of that distinctive sense of relief of which I spoke in Lisbon, when one pulls out, finally dependent only on one's own resources. The unit from London had, of course, *not* arrived. It was "somewhere in Madrid." Allan, no doubt influenced by the way in which his boss William Simon attacks a problem, suggested two possibilities: that he himself fly to Madrid, locate the damn thing, and bring it in; or that a mechanic from London be engaged to bring one down from London and install it. Desperate though I was for the unit, I found these alternatives pretty pricey, and decided to lean on the chance that the unit would indeed arrive on Monday. This was Friday.

We made one desperate, final try to get our old one fixed. This required the seduction of two overburdened technicians who came on board at noon and were treated like surgeons arriving at the bedside of a dying king. Their "impression" was that what was defective in the old unit was two diodes.

Could we get those two diodes in Las Palmas?

They would see; they would call us on the radio at two.

At three I gave up monitoring the radio, finally succeeded in locating their boss, who reported that the critical diodes were not available.

I'll have them brought from the United States, I said, by son Christopher! And so I went to a hotel with long-distance telephone booths, called Frances Bronson, who after a call or two to New York provisioners took my troubles to my friend of last resort, Heinz Hary of Norwalk, Connecticut, who runs a television laboratory. He spent three hours on the phone, located the two diodes in Fort Smith, Arkansas, as I remember, got them to New York, to Christopher, arriving at *Sealestial* just two days later. They didn't work. I did manage, courtesy of Cook

Travel, to get my updated WhatStar transported from Santa Cruz, and
Allan got busy on two vital matters on which we had conferred: extra
fuel, and the cockpit table extension.

You see, when you go over a large tract of water on a sailboat you
want to have enough fuel to keep you in motion when there is no wind.
I asked Tony to make the calculations based on our getting four 200-
liter barrels at Las Palmas, strapping them on board as reserves. (We
had done exactly this ten years ago, traveling the 1,900 miles from
Bermuda to the Azores.) Assume, I said, a fifteen-day passage. Tony
worked it out:

> • The total capacity of the ship's fuel tank is 1,600 liters. With the
> four extra barrels we would have 2,400 liters.
> • The generator needs to run six hours every day to sustain the
> batteries and everything the batteries in turn sustain. That is an irreduci-
> ble constant. The generator burns 3 liters per hour, 18 liters per day, or
> 270—call it 300—liters for the trip.
> • The motor, running at 1,500 rpm, consumes 10 liters per hour;
> giving us 8.75 days of engine time on the fifteen-day passage.
> • The motor, running at 2,000 rpm, consumes 12.5 liters per hour;
> giving us seven days of engine time.

In sum, with four extra barrels of fuel we could count on using the
engine as much as 50 percent of the time, provided we watched the
speed at which we ran it. I would keep a log every day noting exactly
how much fuel we had used during that day.

The social life around us was hectic and vinous. Dick Clurman noted
one expression of it in his journal, as he might have noted an encounter
with Indians in 1762 at a nearby wigwam. "A cocktail party on a
neighboring boat, two down from us, began at 7 P.M. and went far into
the night. At 3 A.M. it grew into a wild, drunken melee stretching to
the quay. It seems that someone vengefully had plunged a knife into
someone else's rubber dinghy. A screaming argument rent the night,
conducted in a crossfire of French, English, Spanish, and Swedish.
Only two words, throughout, were perfectly articulated, recurring in
every exchange no matter in what language. 'Fucking' and 'asshole.'

Four of these, just in case

They are America's contribution to a lingua franca. The first is often used, but not inevitably, as modifier of the second. After a boathook was broken over one combatant's head, the Policía arrived. They tried unsuccessfully to conduct a dockside inquiry, then—I suspect for symbolic purposes primarily—they carted off one alleged malefactor without ever having succeeded in establishing just who did what to whom. By the time the sun came up, all seemed to have been forgotten. The crew on board the scene of the crime are cheerfully going about polishing up their beautiful vessel for the big annual race across the Atlantic to Antigua."

It's interesting how, as one grows older, one somehow contrives to avoid that kind of thing—wild parties—even as one becomes progressively resigned to their going on, which is okay provided they don't go on on one's own turf. Sailing into Las Palmas yesterday, after the ten-hour sail from Candelaría, Dick commented on the general scene aboard *Sealestial:*

The cozy refuge—the *Sealestial's* saloon—with its electronic navigational devices, TV screen, video player, tape and stereo decks, has additions when we are on board. Our working quarters in the small saloon could pass for a *Saturday Night Live* set mocking the cockpit of a spacecraft gone haywire. A spaghetti roll of wires and extension cords oozes out from a multiple outlet attached to the single 110-volt plug. The strands reach the two or three laptop word processors in use and are otherwise engaged in charging computer batteries in two "toasters," which is what WFB calls his multiple-battery chargers. He is now unsheathing his second portable printer, with its attachments, on the dining room table, where he's printing out the last two of his columns before the scheduled hiatus. Someone is fiddling with the switch, trying to discover whether it belongs to the generator or to the inverter. Nobody is even sure which is which, or which is on, which off—or is the current coming in from the engine's alternator? There are questions. Who has a flashlight handy? (I always do.) [Also: a cigarette lighter, pliers, a set of screwdrivers, tape, screws and bolts of different sizes, lubricating oil, a battery tester, spare batteries, a rag, and a Swiss Army knife.] Where are the AAA batteries? Would you please pass the music box? (WFB—he means his portable cassette player). Please turn off the fluorescent lights. (Bill again.) Where are the hurricane candles? Anyone seen my blue ditty bag? (me).

Okay—then a scattering of topics touched on at dinner.

ME [Clurman]: "Why did Tom Selleck shave his mustache?" (It was missing when he presided at *National Review's* Thirty-fifth Anniversary last month.) BILL: "For a new movie role. Did you know that Abraham Lincoln grew his beard between the time he was elected and the time he arrived in Washington? November to March. Please pass the red wine." DANNY: "Whose turn is it to pick the movie?" VAN: "I don't think I stayed awake through one movie on the Pacific trip." DANNY: "Allan's mustache is beginning to make him look like a Mexican bandit." TONY: "I like to think I could play Jeremy Irons." BILL: "By the way, this (he points to the surrounding situation) was exactly the scene in which Van was videotaped ten years ago saying he would never work for the government." ME: "Yeah. He said only an 'asshole' would. It was a premature public use of that now popular word. I still can't say it." VAN: "Asshole was still in the closet then." [From Admiral Morison, quoting a contemporary of Columbus on language aboard his fleet: "And (Columbus) . . . was so great an enemy to cursing and swearing, that I

swear I never heard him utter any other oath than 'by San Fernando!'
and when he was most angry with anyone, his reprimand was to say, 'May
God take you!' for doing or saying that."] ME: "What the hell kind of
music is that—can we turn it down?" [Dick *listens* to music only in
Carnegie Hall.] CHRISTOPHER LITTLE: "Is there any more red wine?"
BILL: "That camera reminds me that Jack Heinz lent me a tricky wide-
luxe Russian camera about ten years ago. A year later I looked for it to
give it back, damned if I could find it. It showed up after Jack died. It
was under a pile of magazines in a bathtub." DANNY: "We should have
a telex in two hours telling us whether Frances got our message." TONY:
"Is there anything sweet—I just feel a need for it—a little chocolate?"
CHRISTOPHER LITTLE: "Bill, can I have the battery tester? Under the
National Review behind you?" Bill gropes for it: "No. That's the volt-
meter."

. . . Bill reported to Christo when he arrived to join us: "The only
things that worked on the boat all the time this leg of the trip were the
movies."

Not quite. I have a crucial amendment. The people worked even
better.

Having got the name of a pleasant seaside hotel about ten miles
south, one third of the way to Puerto Rico, Dan and I drove out and
made reservations there for the incoming crew. They would need the
morning of the following day to de-jet. Their instructions were to
expect someone from *Sealestial* to materialize at lunchtime, who would
drive them and their gear to the boat, wherever it was.

That, I had decided—after Van reported a conversation with one of
the gypsy sailors walking about barefooted—would be Puerto Rico, a
half day's sail to the southern tip of the island, several thousand miles
from the Puerto Rico with which Americans are familiar.

Everybody knows about the value of local knowledge, but it is also
true that some of us (I am exceptionally guilty) don't take the trouble
to ferret it out. A year ago, in Curaçao on *Sealestial* on Christmas Eve,
I had such an experience, one of those little, incidental exchanges that
change itineraries. It was a native sailor, a Dutchman, who approached
me on the street. He had read, he said buoyantly, one or two of my
sailing books. He asked where were we spending the night. I nodded
to where we were docked, along the main waterway into Curaçao.

". . . But why don't you go to Spanish Water?"

Spanish Water was just ten miles southeast, and if you aren't looking studiously for the entrance to it, you are not likely to find it. (In that respect it is like English Harbor in Antigua—perfect for protection from stray pirates.) You snake your way in and after the first turn there is a beach, this one quite full of people and of cast-off bikini tops. A half mile up is a pretty little yacht club with mountains of green on either side, like New England in the summer. Where we anchored we had perfect protection, and the lights of the Dutch-cleansed yacht club buildings shone out at a respectful distance, and the beach, now deserted, was within reach. The moon elected that night to stay with us through the evening, and ahead of our anchor, rising thirty feet as if to comply with a decorator's plan, was a little navigating light, an eight-second red flasher (every eight seconds a one-second light). Christmas Eve on the *Sealestial*, with decorations by Patricia Buckley, with more lights in the saloon below than in all of Curaçao. . . . All of that, courtesy of a passing stranger.

Puerto Rico sounded pleasant, and pleasantly removed from the hectic life at Las Palmas. . . . Might as well go there for the final launch,

On the Zodiac, out of the harbor for a quick swim

The final run for Dick, Danny . . .

since nothing could be done on a Sunday about the autopilot, which would, or would not, come in from Madrid on Monday. If it came, we would assemble it en route.

We set out early. Dan and I, alone in my cabin, read the Mass before lunch, giving again thanks, among other things, for having survived the storm. This day's sail would be the final passage of Ocean4, Leg One. An uneventful but pleasant run down to the southern tip of Grand Canary and around to the relatively new little tourist port, itself only a half-dozen miles from Mogán, a second and even more picturesque tourist spot. At Puerto Rico we rented a car which would be kept busy the next day. "God, how expensive," Danny wrote. "The rental is the same as a round trip to London. That sounds expensive, because it is. A one-day rental is 150 U.S. dollars. I could fly to London and back for $138 U.S. according to a flier I just picked up." Allan would need the car to motor back to Las Palmas to check on the autopilot, and Dan would need it to go to the hotel at noon to rendezvous with the new crew. They would yield their hotel rooms, in which they slept after coming in from the plane in the morning, that night to Dan and

. . . and Christopher Little. Note grief.

Christopher Little and Dick Clurman; who in turn would yield their ship's bunks to Christopher Buckley, Bill Draper, and Douglas Bernon. We would all dine together—nine people—on the *Sealestial*. After dinner the lame ducks would drive to the hotel in two taxis and the following day we would set out for Barbados.

· CHAPTER NINE ·
The Crew Changes

I have written elsewhere about the importance of knowing well anyone you ask to join you on an ocean passage of any length and now I was violating my solemn counsel in the matter. As is obvious, a commitment to such passages is serious for both parties. The sailor who undertakes to give over an entire month out of his year—or even, in this case, two weeks—has much he needs to weigh. He might be using up vacation time a spouse feels, understandably, is owed to her. There is inevitably that element of apprehension, more keenly felt, as a rule, by those who do not come aboard and are left at home than by those who make the journey. Or, it may be that the period will coincide with a crisis in his professional life.

Still, the commitment having been made, it is not lightly set aside, a point I have always stressed because my own commitment is to put together a crew that, for all that there is variety among them, effects harmony; or, if a little less than that, never effects disharmony. I have once or twice in the past decided against reinviting to sail with me persons who committed offenses that would be deemed trivial on shore or in the office, simply because the social membrane at sea is delicate, the more so because behavior sometimes needs to be strenuous, emphatic, authoritative, even raucous. In issuing, from the helm, a call to tighten the main halyard instantly, it may prove necessary to shout in order to be heard through wind and rain: all the more necessary that it should never cross the mind of the person being shouted at to doubt that the intentions of the shouter are instrumental, not censorious.

This passage needs an ode to Reggie Stoops, who shared all my ocean passages with me.

My son, Christopher, had called me from Newport on a Wednesday morning in September 1988 to give me the news of Reggie's death. Christo's second sentence—perhaps his training as a journalist prompted it—was, "It happened at eleven twenty-two." My eyes turned to the gaudy new chronometer, already described, sitting on my desk, guaranteed not to lose more than seven tenths of one second in one year. The exact time was 11:45. Ten days earlier I had told Reggie over the telephone that our navigational worries at sea over the question of the exact time of day were finally ended, that the next time we set out to cross Long Island Sound—or Narragansett Bay—or the Atlantic Ocean—we would never again have to worry about exactly what time it was in Greenwich, England. He said (from his hospital bed) that he longed to see the new clock. Our studied fantasy about the months and years we would continue to sail together after his freak illness was finally diagnosed had never flagged in our thirty brief telephone conversations during the preceding two months. I commented that no doubt he would insist—Reggie was an M.I.T. graduate, and *that way* about contraptions—on taking my chronometer apart and ridding it of that seven tenths of one second annual problematic. I went on to ask him what his weight was that day and he said one hundred and thirty-seven pounds (down from two hundred), which permitted me to observe that we would have no further excuse for singling out slender Danny Merritt to go up to the masthead when we had trouble up there; and he had laughed his gentle laugh and said with that little hoarseness I was becoming used to, "I guess you're right. On the other hand"—his voice registered now a trace of curiosity—"they're giving me something to make me fatter, so don't count on it." I didn't count on it, because of course I knew; he by then knew it, and he knew that I knew it, and so it goes.

I had known it three months before, on that day in June when he was remarried and I had served Reggie as best man (I had been that also for his first wedding, and this time around warned him that I

limited myself to two such services per friend). A very few others knew
it then also, who managed more successfully than I to internalize that
knowledge. But when Christo gave me the news I had expected to hear
at any moment I thought less of what had happened at 11:22 than
about all the years I had known him. Was it one hundred nights or was
it one thousand and one nights that we shared in fine and awful
circumstances the cockpit of a boat and I had experienced the quiet
delights of his understated company? He could, mind you, drive grown
men to tears with the deliberateness of his reactions. Rehearsing an
emergency drill, the second night of our Pacific crossing in 1985, Dick
Clurman asked him where the life jackets were stored. He reacted as
if he had been challenged to give a brief definition of the Fourth
Dimension. The pause, the slight clearing of the throat, the innocent
look of a man accosted by an angular question, a question followed by
the exhilarating frankness of his innocent reply ("I'm not quite sure at
this point"). In the book that sprang from that passage I quoted from
Christopher's journal. He had written, a few days before we landed in
New Guinea, "You find out on a trip like this who you can *absolutely*
depend on. And really, the answer is—Pup [WFB] and I agreed—that
the person who is absolutely dependable in every situation is Reggie."

We didn't mean—I added in that book—that any other crew member had ever abandoned courtesy; merely that Reg was a critical mass
of composure and intelligence and good nature. He never complained.
A year later, at a reunion party of the crew, he presented us all with
T-shirts on which the entire paragraph I have written was reproduced
in *Drink Coca-Cola*–sized type.

When finally I visited him other than on the telephone—face-to-
face, two days before he died—we embraced, after his very best friend,
coming into the hospital room ahead of me, my son, Christopher, had
kissed him on the forehead. Reggie was able to pronounce my name,
and he had managed a smile. I looked at his fine face and thought back
that time to another moment of great strain. It was mid-March in
1957. The little dinghy in which we had set out to retrieve a duck blind
a mile in front of my house on Long Island Sound had capsized, and
we realized, all of a sudden, that our lives hung on our ability to swim,
in our heavy winter clothing, in freezing water, to a promontory a half
mile away. For a full minute we could not judge whether we were

making headway against the northerly wind, but we did. Gradually, painfully, we made our way. Fifty yards from land he looked at me and said, "Go ahead. I can't make it." I could not help him with my frozen hands, so I sang raucously to him and I prayed with unfeigned imperiousness, ordering him to continue to beat his arms, however limply, against the waves. In five more minutes we were there, crawling on our stomachs to shelter.

Three days after Christo's call, serving as a eulogist at Reggie's funeral (my son's eulogy was a lyrical masterpiece), I told that story, and went on, "What brought this to mind was the infinite dignity on his frozen face that afternoon, thirty-two years ago, which I saw again on Monday night, on his pallid, skeletal face: struggling to live almost as a matter of good manners, but resigned to die; determined only that he would never complain, never let go that fierce dignity which he carried in good times and bad times, drunk or sober, exhausted or animated, in sickness and in health.

"I had a bouncy friend who once managed a witticism. 'When I get to St. Peter,' he said, 'I'm going to ask him to take me to the man who invented the dry martini. Because I just want to say, Thanks.'

Reginald Stoops, 1925–1988

"I am a Christian who, believing as I do that our Redeemer lives, knows that one day I'll be once again in Reggie's company, on that endless journey in the peace he now enjoys. When that time comes for me, as for others here, I shan't forget to say, as in my prayers I have said so often during the last days, Thanks. Thanks for the long play that came before that fatal bullet struck him down. Thanks, everlastingly, for the memory, everlasting."

So, the problem of a replacement was compounded by the special void. I had then an interesting experience, though the ending was instructive and disappointing. I had known slightly, not well—we had had a half-dozen engagements, primarily professional in character—a fellow journalist. During one of these he told me how much he loved the sea, and I would learn from Christo, who was his friend, that he was a highly competent sailor who had taken his own boat to Bermuda a year or so back. When Reggie was not able to make the little summer cruise I had planned in 1988 I spontaneously picked up the phone and asked the journalist if he would like to come. He could take three days of the cruise, he said, and would happily be there.

We had a fine time. Danny was along, and Van, and they both liked him. My new friend was wonderfully candid in all conversational matters, he loved to be at the wheel; he got seasick and was overembarrassed about this, but he was in every way a fine sea companion. When Reggie died I invited him with some confidence to join us on this trip. But, I warned in my letter of invitation, although there will be no hard feelings if you decline for whatever reason, if you accept you must put this down on your calendar as a quite solemn commitment.

My friend, like other members of the crew, had a problem getting away from his work for an entire month and so had signed on only for the second leg. Two weeks before I left for Lisbon I had a message from him given over the telephone to Frances Bronson: for professional reasons (he was working on a book) he didn't "think" he could go after all. I reached him by phone that evening and managed a sternness of manner that does not come naturally to me. He pleaded guilty to every contractual and moral sin in the Western catalogue but insisted that the then-threatening war in the Gulf, should it break out, as he thought likely that it would, would absolutely require his presence in Washington during the last two weeks of November, when we were to sail together. It was left as follows, that he would have one final long night of the soul, struggling with his conscience, and the following day would give me a Yes, or No: but needless to say, if during the interval I should come up with someone to take his place, that would solve everyone's problems. I murmured something to the effect that one doesn't, two or three weeks before the event, come up with the right person to cross the Atlantic Ocean with, and he conceded that this was a problem. There comes a time when there is nothing, really, left unsaid, and so we ended the conversation on the understanding that the next day he would give me his final decision.

Early in the morning I was on the phone with Christo, giving him this quite disruptive news.

Pause. "You want to listen to something for a minute?" Yes, I said. "I have a very special friend. He's about my age [Christopher is thirty-eight]. He has a wonderful sense of humor and had an awful tragedy—his wife was killed by a bus a few weeks after they were married, ten years ago. Before then he did a lot of single-handed sailing in the Bahamas. After her death he went back to school and got his second Ph.D.—he's a clinical psychologist, practicing in Newport. He is re-marrying next Saturday and Lucy and I are going to Newport for the wedding. Would you consider him as crew?"

I said yes. "But of course he won't be able to go, I mean two weeks after he gets married."

"He is marrying Bernadette Brennan, the editor in chief of *Cruising World.*"

I smiled. That could make a difference, granted; such people *know* about sea voyages.

One hour later Christopher had issued the invitation to Douglas Bernon, Douglas had solicited the permission of his bride-to-be, she had granted it, he had got back to Christo, and Christo had got back to me. I asked Christo as a further favor to call the tortured journalist and tell him what had happened, that he was off the hook. He did so. "Should I call your dad?" the journalist had asked. "No. Just drop him a note, why not?" (He didn't. Nor a note nor a call a month later, to ask how the trip had gone.)

·   ·   ·

So . . . I would soon be meeting, for the first time, Douglas Bernon, Ph.D., Ph.D. And—tremendous news—Allan had arrived back from Las Palmas, the farking Decca autopilot *actually in hand*! ("What I can't promise is, Bill, can we install it? It must have three hundred wires running in and out.")

As we lugged the parcels that would, we hoped, unite into a functioning autopilot, the little sloop alongside prepared to set out, on the same route we would be taking, except that the skipper was bound for Antigua. We had had coffee together that afternoon, and I learned from him that in years gone by he had been skipper of a maxi, which is what they call sailboats over 72 feet in length. We ruminated about the pleasures of large vs. smaller boats. We had, it transpired, jointly discovered the pleasure of—smaller boats.

I remember many years ago when word went out that John Nicholas Brown was going to sell his fabulous *Bolero.* This 72-foot splendor had, at the time, the record for the fastest sail to Bermuda on the golden run from Newport, the Kentucky Derby of the ocean-sailing set. JNB was the reigning aristocrat of Newport. His stately home, so wonderfully different from those mausoleums that both fascinate and repel, looks on the Ida Lewis Yacht Club over an expanse of lawn of a dozen acres. So much a part of the Yacht Club was he that, a few years after he died, the Yacht Club bought his Newport property from his estate, and it is there, finally, that the New York Yacht Club has waterfront property. It was there that Christo and I gave the reception after Reggie's funeral. With a moderate-size telescope you can see over to Hammersmith Farm, where Jackie Bouvier Kennedy Onassis grew up.

When he sold *Bolero,* the big question among the proletariat boat owners was, What would John Nicholas Brown buy now, in place of *Bolero*? There was some talk that he would go to power boating, at his advancing age: maybe a 200-footer—something he could be comfortable in when cruising the Aegean or the Caribbean. Others swore he would never desert the sail. Surely he would revive the J-Boat, and come into the harbor at Newport next spring with a 150-footer, with a modest crew of nineteen?

What he did was buy a Block Island 40, which is 40 feet long. In those days it sold for about $35,000. It was all fiberglass, and the designers seemed to be selling them at the rate of about one every week.

Douglas Bernon, Ph.D., Ph.D.

It made absolutely no difference to John Nicholas Brown, who continued to race with the New York Yacht Club happily, in Class D, where once he had triumphed over Class A.

But the switch from mastodon to puppy was difficult for younger boat owners to understand. My first boat was 17 feet long, and I loved *Sweet Isolation,* as I named her when she came as a gift from my father, when I was thirteen. My next boat was a 42-foot steel cutter, which I raced eagerly, and unsuccessfully. *The Panic,* as we called her, was not a fast boat, and was disadvantageously rated. She was destroyed in a hurricane, after which I got *Suzy Wong,* another 40-foot boat, a Sparkman & Stephens yawl "laid" in Hong Kong and commissioned by four G.I.'s serving in Japan who wished a circumnavigation to come between them and a settled life of marriage & kids. They picked up *Suzy* in Hong Kong and a year and a half later arrived, broke, in Miami, and sold it to me.

But I was beginning to think big, and ten years later acquired my beloved *Cyrano,* a 60-foot schooner with an 18-foot bowsprit, a boat that gave the owner of a 40-footer the impression that he had inherited all of West Texas. I mean, it would sleep twelve people, including a crew of four. It would sail like a dream (provided you had at least twelve knots of breeze). You couldn't tell whether the motor or generator was on or off, so quiet and shielded was her engine compartment. I sailed her everywhere, including across the Atlantic, and sold her only after the wretched accountant thrust the raw figures into my face, and I recognized that a 60-foot wooden boat with a crew of four was another version of owning the Burton Diamond—I read somewhere that every time Elizabeth Taylor went out wearing that diamond it cost her fifteen thousand dollars, what with insurance, capital investment, and interest.

But doing without a sailboat was of course out of the question, as everyone will agree who shares the lunatic attachments of the sailor. But after *Cyrano*, what might one own, while maintaining self-respect?

I bought at the beginning of Mr. Reagan's decade of greed a 36-foot sloop designed in California by one of those firms that are always going bankrupt. So halfhearted was my involvement in the enterprise that I did not bother even to look at the boat, assigning power of attorney to Christo and Danny. I approached it for the first time in the dead of night, at Essex, Connecticut, after a long lecture in Hartford. It looked as though it might have served as a large dinghy for *Cyrano*.

But lo! Every year my attachment to *Patito* grows. It is a boat about which I once wrote that four people fit perfectly in it, and five are three too many. So, psychologically you swallow that limitation once, even as, I suppose, people who can't eat salt, or butter, decide to do without salt, or butter, and never give it another thought. My wife, after one ride in it, gave it up joyfully, and I did not retaliate by giving *her* up.

But I have traveled to Bermuda in it (two years before the aborted trip that led to Atlantic City). And to New Brunswick. And to Cape Breton, where the Bras d'Or Lakes camp down. And a half-dozen times to Maine. The keenest pleasure I get from *Patito* is my, and its, specialty: the short, quick overnight cruise. Set out at 7 P.M., arrive ninety minutes later at a little lagoon across Long Island Sound, consume a voluptuously good dinner with fine music on the cassette player . . . a midnight swim, a quick read, wake at seven for another swim, sail an hour and a half back to Yacht Haven East, and at your desk by ten, feeling like a million dollars, which is about what you have left over, having done without *Cyrano* for ten years.

To *inhabit* a small boat, as my seagoing friend and his wife did, is another matter. He told me he had got used to it. I told him I'd never attempt it. How long would it take him to make the passage? He estimated three weeks. . . . Now, as he pulled out, I stood at attention, and saluted him.

And we would be leaving in a matter of hours. Van pronounced in his journal: "So what do we think of the Canaries? Let's first be charitable: a) They are a marvelous place to sail. You get not only the northeast winds but all sorts of local winds blowing into and off the islands, whose high mountains create their own local weather. And they stretch east and west for 250 miles, rising stately from the sea. The climate is good in the winter and not, I am told, too hot in the summer. There are plenty of yacht marinas, the most attractive of which, of those we saw, was at Mogán on Grand Canary. b) The high mountains and barren land exude a Wild West beauty which however fades on

Content, aboard 36-foot PATITO

close inspection. In fact we were told Telly Savalas did a western up in the hills behind Mogán. c) Although the Canaries cater to the mass-packaged tourists, there are also five-star, indulgent hotels in scenic locations, if you like that sort of thing for a vacation. d) Spain is a very civilized place, with all kinds of people, and the Canaries are as Spanish as the mainland."

A little dry that, and hardly in harmony with the raptures of the guidebooks, but such was the impression of all of us, though we hardly gave the interior a chance.

Tony, who had signed on for the entire trip, wrote about the impending departure of our companions. "A certain nostalgia began to set in. Christopher Little in particular, I felt, was starting to get a little wistful. The sailing over the past few days had not been really interesting or exhilarating and the scenery after we left Las Palmas was not worth writing home about. However, the spirit which had started to build— the routine of meals and watches, Van's jokes, WFB's anecdotes, Dick's constant gossip—had created something no one wanted to let go. Dick and Dan both regretted out loud their imminent departure and the way Dan kept throwing himself into the next project or errand

Tony Leggett greets Christo; Bill Draper looks on

suggested to me that he was trying to block out the fact that he wouldn't be around in another day. For myself, I was looking at the past few days as just a shakedown in preparation for the real thing, the crossing."

Danny was restive and self-critical. "These last few days I have noticed my spirit out of sync. I have finished Christopher's book [*Wet Work*, the manuscript] and Bill's book [*Tucker's Last Stand*, the galleys]. I've lazed around a lot and lost myself in reflections, just like the first day out. I feel bad about going home, so does Chris. I'd rather be a part of the whole and not a part of the part, if that makes any sense. I wish I had had a chance to tell Bill how much I really am going to miss being with him on the big leg."

Liz, of course, gave us a great feast, the nine of us crowded about the table. Conversation was spry and the good humor undiluted. But such things don't always entirely work. "All of which brings me to the Last Supper," Christopher Little concluded his journal. "It's a mistake, I think, to invest too much emotion in a single holiday get-together. So many people experience a meltdown after Christmas dinner. So I think it was along these lines that my expectations were overinflated.

The crew for Leg 1 shares dinner before departing.

Of course we had fun; we always have fun. But there was something missing. Maybe it's the difference between starting and ending: after all, three of the group had just arrived. Maybe there was even some trepidation about the crossing. That wouldn't be surprising. What seemed to be missing was an emotional component. Too much yo-ho-ho, maybe not enough true intimacy. So I left disappointed in our final evening, and disappointed not to be continuing on board. I'll miss my pals."

My own feelings were dominated by the happiness of my reunion, at least physical—for many years we were never truly separated—with my only child. When I first proposed the trip to him he had been reluctant to make a commitment to sail with me, advancing reasons for his reluctance which I thought sincere, even if illusory. I was happy at the prospect of seeing him, and spending a fortnight with him. He was born in September 1952, preceded by a tubal pregnancy that elimi-nated one of his mother's Fallopian tubes, and followed by another which eliminated the second, leaving him an only child (a *fils unique,* they say in French; in his case I prefer a *unique fils*). In July (this had been a very full year) Pat and I had been married forty years, and at our little celebration, conducted annually but especially important to us on our fortieth, our five or six guests were herded into the little music room and on our giant TV screen we were shown an *hour-long* documentary conceived and written by Christo and executed with the help of his wife, Lucy. It was a grand tour de force. It had the expected features—wedding pictures and the lot—but the frame was: Christopher T. Buckley, sounding exactly like Mike Wallace, and asking such questions as Mike Wallace would ask in a *60 Minutes* exploration, the theme of this one being, "What do you make of Bill and Pat's being married for so long?" It was both hilarious and ingenious—among its players, Mike Wallace, Liz Smith, Aileen Mehle ("Suzy"), Dick Clurman, Keith and Laurie Mano (Ronald Reagan said he would do his cameo, but Christo ran out of time and couldn't manage the round trip to Los Angeles). It was capped with love and tenderness, and made for a few moments of great bliss—nothing can manage this quite like humor laced with sentiment, which is a great gift of Christo's. So . . . I'd have him aboard, the same year in which he made his debut as a television producer.

And, yes, I had my autopilot.

Christo

BOOK

Two

CHAPTER TEN

Leg Two, the First Day

We managed to get away under sail, as Columbus had done, but then we lost it, lost our fairweatherly fair weather and quickly scored our first advantage over him (*"I have been becalmed all this day and night, until three o'clock in the morning"* Columbus wrote in his journal about Day 1) by simply turning on the engine. The calm stayed on through the evening, through the next day, through the following day. The noise of the engine, though I kept the rpm down to 1500 to save fuel, was deafening because the port cockpit hatch cover had to be kept open. In that hatch, level with the engine, were Martin and first mate Denis, and what they were endeavoring to do was to install the brand-new Decca autopilot, an Augean challenge involving, as noted, dozens upon dozens of wires that needed to be inserted into tiny little metal slots where the old autopilot's wires had lain for so many years. And of course the unit had been modernized, so that nothing was exactly as it had been in the preceding model.

They worked four hours that evening, beginning in the late afternoon, going through supper and the movie (the first episode in the Civil War series), and then resumed at eight the following morning, coming up from their sweatbox every now and again for a breath of air and at my insistence at noon the next day for a swim. (Bill Draper wrote, "We stopped midday for a swim, absolutely spectacular. A great feeling of freedom, until I thought about how important it was to stay very close to the boat.")

Indeed. On the *Sea Cloud* I had been told by a friend of the principal a story that still freezes the blood. He had been called a few months before to help a friend in critical psychological shock. Four men had been sailing to New York from Cape May. Opposite Atlantic City, ten miles out, one of two brothers pitched overboard while tending a sail in rough weather. He was thrown a line and grabbed it. The other three then tried for a heartbreaking hour to lift him back on board: but, finally, in the swirling sea, they lost the fight. If they had had a fixed boarding ladder they could have managed easily. If they had had a sling and a tackle, rigged to the main halyard, they'd have managed. A grisly story, the implications of which I hastily shook off, on climbing back aboard *Sealestial* using the companionway, which is harnessed whenever anyone goes swimming. On *Patito*, I have a stern boarding ladder that hinges up to the transom. It is readily usable by a swimmer.

On the matter of man-overboard, I had given Tony, who is in charge of safety, the note Reggie had written me two years before—the new procedures recommended by the Coast Guard. They are instructive, and shrewd. The protocols:

1) Toss over a life cushion or two (time allowed: two seconds). 2) Assign a member of the crew to keep his eyes on the man overboard (time: one second). Then 3) come about, leaving the headsail harnessed exactly where it was, so that now it is aback (time: five seconds). 4) Sail on a broad reach for the few seconds required to position yourself to one side of the "victim" (as the C.G. refers to him). 5) Then sail downwind past the victim. Then 6) upwind, bringing down the sails as you coast up toward him. At this point you need either a sling, attached to your main halyard, to bring him up, or else a floating line to your fixed stern boarding ladder.

Another thing (said Reggie in his memo), you should test your E.P.I.R.B. (Emergency Position-Indicating Radio Beacon). The way to do this, he had explained, is to wait until the end of the hour. Between the hour and five minutes past the hour, Coast Guard monitors ignore all distress signals, on the understood assumption that they are listening to sets being tested.

"Where do you check to see if the signal is going out all right?" I remember asking Reg.

"On Channel 15."

But I discovered, the first time I went through Reggie's drill, that my radio didn't have a Channel 15. A call to the Coast Guard established that radios that don't bring in Channel 15 are allowed to verify their test signals on Channel 16.

When we finished swimming I could spot the light in the eye of the autopilot brotherhood; and toward six Martin yelled up to me at the helm to flick on the autopilot switch. I did so and the wheel began to spin at a furious rate counterclockwise. "Turn it off!" one of them shouted from the port inferno. I did. An hour later: "Try it now." I did—and: It worked.

Worked like a dream, after we had synchronized the controls below. I reflected for the one millionth time how useless I (and many of my friends) would be if I were the Yankee in King Arthur's court, asked

The new watch schedule

to demonstrate some of the advantages of having experienced the twentieth century, whence the time warp had brought me, to display the magic that lay ten centuries ahead. There is no doubt that pooling the concentrated learning of Van Galbraith, banker, diplomat, lawyer; Bill Draper, Silicon Valley entrepreneur, former head of the Export-Import Bank, head of the U.N. Development Fund; Douglas Bernon, doctor of clinical psychology; Tony Leggett, banker, lifetime sailor; Christopher Buckley, poet, editor, novelist, dramatist; and WFB, the Renaissance Man—we wouldn't have got that autopilot working notwithstanding that the schematics were there and are supposed to be legible to *l'homme moyen sensuel.* Martin and Denis deserved the champagne.

Which is a perfect moment to pick up a little entry in the log of the sea snob Tony Leggett who—you will remember?—was overheard a few days ago disdaining the entire project that so absorbed me. He wrote in his journal for that evening: *"The watches at night were blissful, because both watch members could lie back on the settee and relax, while the self-steerer did all the work."* Can you stand it? What

Bill Draper

I should have done was to forbid Tony to use the autopilot. Fun idea. I have always advocated two rates of electricity in areas where there is nuclear power. The higher rate, generated by coal or oil, for everyone who opposed the local nuclear power plant, the lower for those who did not. But, actually, it is better to see Tony eat crow in his journal, though I doubt he remembers making the earlier remark.

We are all intimately acquainted with one another except for Douglas Bernon, the Ph.D., Ph.D., who integrates himself in the fastest way known to man, by laughing almost continuously and causing others to do so. He had begun his journal before arriving at the Canaries and it led with: "It was not so many years back that the greater kick [than accepting my invitation to sail] would have been to entertain left-minded friends, regale them, really, with how la-de-da clever I was to *turn down* Bill Buckley—I mean really, of all people!—and his plush trip across the Atlantic. But I appear to be getting smarter. I don't know the man. . . . I am along, was invited, really, because of my friendship with son, not father, and I look forward to sharing the voyage with him, but I am also curious to come to know Bill, which on a transatlantic hop seems likely."

One gathers that poor Doug felt nervous about the company he was keeping. "I am the lone newcomer to the scene; everyone knows everyone else, either through business, blood, school, or some combination. I am the only Democrat, the only liberal, the only Jew. I wondered with amusement and concern how we would integrate over the next three weeks." I was in turn amused, on reading the passage, for several reasons, among them that I'd never have known he was Jewish (or cared, except that as an Onward-Christian-Soldier I pray for the conversion of everyone to my True Faith). And then too this trip turned out, on the political front, to be a curious and amusing exception. I never talk politics unless required to do so, and usually for that I require a huge fee. Probably I don't talk politics for the same reason that, oh, proctologists don't talk about lower intestines. But on this trip Van and Bill Draper became a continuous act, compared in two of the journals to aging couples who cannot stop quarreling, even though they continue to love each other. The casus belli triggering battles between them were anything that had to do with the administration of George Bush, who is a close friend of Bill Draper, and indeed a friend of several of us—I've known him since 1970, and we continue to belong to the same twenty-seven-member camp in the Bohemian Grove. Van is also a member of that camp, as was Christo (he resigned), who spent eighteen months at Bush's side writing his speeches in 1981–1982. *But,* you see, George Bush is a nonmovement conservative, and Van and I of course are of the movement, *pre partum, in partu,* and *post partum,* but Van is a more energetic proselytizer, so that whenever a question touching a public issue arose, and there would be a lot of news made during the two weeks that lay ahead of us, Van would slight the Administration's handling of the question, Draper would rise to the defense, Christo would look at Doug and smile, and the rest of us would go about our business.

"I am the new kid on the block for this trip," Douglas wrote, "yet everyone has embraced my presence with enthusiasm and good humor, with the inevitable jokes about the need for a clinical psychologist on board." But he was a little dazzled by blasé conversational familiarities. "Champagne, cheeses, olives, and Cuban cigars, compliments of Fidel Castro himself, who had dined with Bill Draper recently and bestowed upon him polished mahogany boxes of these gems. Laughter. The world's most ardent convert to communism, the provider of fine smoke for Buckley et al. Van suggested someone should field-test them in the event that Fidel had learned something from our own CIA"—Remember? In 1961, under the auspices of Operation Mongoose, a CIA figure passed a poisonous cigar along, designed for Fidel to smoke—"but improved upon over our CIA technique. The fantasy of a grand trip up in smoke as plastique-laced tobacco hurls us above the spreaders!

"I am not used to being at a table where there is such familiarity with the powers that be and have been," Douglas wrote. "Heady and amusing. And Draper, for whom I have developed an immediate liking, is a funny fellow who moves among the prime ministers of the world, doling out coin for development. He informed us that he must be back by December 11 to have breakfast with Bush. His buddies sympathized calmly with his time crunch, and WFB said he would do his best to accommodate. Bill D. knows George as 'George' and WFB talks of 'Ronnie.' "

There is no disguising the spontaneities that issue from very old friendships, not easy to match with others of a different generation.

With such men and women, indeed boys and girls, the friendship can be keener, and even more intense, but it is not the same. With Van and Bill Draper, my friendship stretched back to the day we were tapped to join a senior society at Yale, in May of 1949. We were subsequently ushers at each other's weddings. Although Draper, living as he did in California before becoming a monstrous international big cheese in Washington and New York beginning with the Reagan Administration, was less frequently with us, he was often there, and we shared experiences. Van and I have never been out of touch, even when he lived in Europe.

One night Douglas and I talked about the subject on watch, and I told him I had attempted to get at the nature of it in the context of the experience of our own college class at Yale. I had been asked, six months earlier, to deliver the after-dinner talk to our Fortieth Reunion, and later I gave Douglas a copy. It sought to convey the impact of myriad experiences that flow to one undergraduate class. I began by reminding my classmates how very old we had become. . . .

Some of us who wondered if we would ever be this old, now wonder whether we were ever young.

Most of us are older today than Franklin Delano Roosevelt was when he died, five months before we arrived in New Haven.

Were we ever young?

Three weeks before matriculating at Yale I was in a little hotel bar in Edgartown with my upcoming college roommate and two of my sisters after a day's sailing. I ordered a beer and was surprised when the waitress asked to see my driver's license. I was not quite twenty-one years old, and so was told to settle for a Coke or a 7Up. I remember the great well of resentment. Should I tell her that six months earlier I had been in charge of a detachment of one thousand men at Fort Sam Houston, Texas? I thought the indignity monstrous . . . but had the sense to keep my mouth shut. There wasn't a barmaid in Edgartown you could impress by reciting your war record. And anyway, it was all very good training for reaching Yale as a freshman.

There were eighteen hundred of us—double the normal enrollment—because one of Yale's contributions to the war effort had been to make a comprehensive promise to matriculate, once the war was over, every single student it had accepted, during the war, from the graduating secondary school classes. Never mind how many we would be: somehow Yale would find food, quarters, and teachers for us. It is a good thing the war did not go on to Peloponnesian length, given that even as it was, several hundred freshmen were forced to occupy old Quonset huts built during the war for service use, and the rest of us to double up. The shortage of teachers in certain fields was so acute that in my freshman year I found myself being taught economics by a freshman in the Law School, and the following year I, along with two other undergraduates, was teaching Spanish.

There was an indistinct class structure, I remember: the war veterans and the nonveterans. Formally, the administration pursued egalitarian policies in dealing with us, with only the incidental perquisites (veterans got the Old Campus, not the Quonset huts). In fact, a little winking of the eye was done at mannerisms and practices Yale would not, I think, have indulged a class made up of seventeen-year-olds. Frank Harman (R.I.P.), a notorious physical slouch who had spent three sedentary years in the army learning how to speak Japanese, was told matter-of-factly at the compulsory physical exam we were all subjected to at the Payne Whitney Gymnasium that he should proceed, like the student ahead of him, to leap over a vaulting board. He turned to the athletic examiner and said simply, "You must be joking"—and walked quietly around the obstacle, on to the next station, deciding, one after another, whether he would submit to it or treat it as he treated the ash on his cigarettes. He got away with it.

How do you handle freshmen back from Omaha Beach? I remember the tryouts for the Freshman Debating Team. One of the applicants we'll call Arthur Axelrod. He delivered a fiery oration. When time came for the septuagenarian historian debate coach to deliver his critiques he said quietly to Arthur, "Mr. Axelrod. You really don't need to speak quite so . . . loudly." He got back from Axelrod, "I'm sorry about that, sir. I got into that habit having to shout to my men over the roar of tanks." Roaring Art Axelrod (as we ever after referred to him), a college freshman, had been a captain in the artillery, and was living now with his *second* wife.

Arthur was not easily governed. I won't forget his encounter with Dean DeVane at the beginning of our sophomore year. Arthur returned to New Haven one week after the semester had begun, and one of the few regulations about which Yale was inflexible, you will remember, was the insistence that all students should be present on the first and the last day of classes. He was accordingly summoned to the office of that calm, courteous, scholarly Southerner, who asked why Mr. Axelrod had been late.

"Well, sir," said Roaring Art, "I spent the summer studying the Middle Ages, and I became so engrossed in the subject I completely forgot about the Gregorian calendar change."

The response of Dean DeVane became legendary. "Ah, Mr. Axelrod. In that event, you would have arrived in New Haven one week early." Roaring Art went into hiding for a while after that one.

My roommate, Richie O'Neill (R.I.P.), was not easily trifled with. He came early to a decision that he needed to do something to tame the fastidious dean of the Engineering School who, an inflexible disciplinarian, required attendance at all classes, that being the rule for all engineering majors unless, at midterms—which were several months away—they achieved the Honor Roll. When Richie slept in one Monday he found on Tuesday a summons to the office of Dean Loomis Havemeyer. Richie was six feet two, had fought in the Marines in Okinawa, was all Irish, and had the smile of Clark Gable; every time Richie smiled I was prompted to count the silver.

"Why did you miss your class yesterday, Mr. O'Neill?"

"Diarrhea, sir," Richie smiled.

He was thereafter immune to summons from that office.

I reflect on the extent to which lines were drawn between veterans of the war and apple-cheeked freshmen, straight out of high school or private schools. [Van was not a veteran. Bill Draper had served as a paratrooper.] At first the difference was marked primarily by dress: veterans were almost studiedly wedded to khaki pants. But after a month or so the non-veterans, following the lead of their grizzled seniors, adopted similar dress; and, really, it was not all that easy to stare into the face of an eighteen-year-old and a twenty-year-old and discern in the latter the distinctive scars of service in the military.

For one thing, there was no clear way, before the days of the super-directors of Hollywood, who learned exactly how to atrophy the young mien in order to document service time done in Vietnam, no way to distinguish between the features of such as another of my roommates, who had taken part in the invasion of Iwo Jima, his closest friend dying at his side on the beach from machine-gun bullets, and such as me, who spent twenty-four months in the infantry, stateside, miserably uncomfortable months, but the bullets we needed to dodge as we crawled on our bellies under barbed wire were carefully aimed several feet above our rumps.

If I measured it accurately, the veteran population in the class of 1950 wasn't an altogether wizening influence on normal campus activity. Perhaps we were noticeably in something of a hurry to get on, get some learning, get married, get started in life. Money wasn't much of a worry; the G.I. Bill was paying our way, or substantially paying our way. There was carousing, if nothing on the scale of *Animal House.* Those of us who drank had learned two or three years earlier how to do so and when to stop doing so. Much of the time.

Eighteen hundred bright, individualistic men cultivated a lot of unusual pursuits. Fernando Valenti was practicing to become the world's leading harpsichordist. Claes Oldenburg I guess was dreaming of great ironwork constructions, worrying only whether museums would be large enough to house them. Jimmy Symington was wondering whether he would ever learn enough to become a Republican. I rounded up a few friends and jointly we bought an airplane and learned to fly, and did a little crash landing, for instance one afternoon on the lawn of the Ethel Walker School, from which I was hauled out, along with my brother-in-law-to-be Brent Bozell, by three hundred girls in high hilarity at the ignominious end of the two fly-happy Yale freshmen. Friendships were instantly struck up, sometimes under the oddest impulses. I sat for the first lecture in Physics 10 alongside another freshman, a young man of grave countenance. We were two of perhaps one hundred students, and at the end of the lecture, which had been given by a retired naval captain, we turned to each other—strangers—and the extrasensory circuit was instantly completed: We burst out into convulsive, almost hysterical laughter. We had a bond. Neither of us had understood a single word uttered by the instructor. We ended fast friends and co-patrons of a private tutor who barely escorted us through the survivors' gate of Physics 10.

I think most of us, probably even including Arthur Axelrod, were struck by something we had not, for some reason, anticipated: the awesome, breath-catching brilliance of some of our teachers. The basic course in philosophy, a survey course that began with Thales and ended with Whitehead, was taught by Robert Calhoun (R.I.P.), a member of the faculty of the Divinity School. Remember? A tall, ruddy-faced man with crew-cut hair who wore a hearing aid. He spoke the kind of sentences John Stuart Mill wrote. Never a misplaced accent, qualifier, verb: sentence after sentence of preternatural beauty, formed as if in a magical compositor's shop, by golden artisans. Never pretentious, just plain beautiful. His learning so overwhelmed him that sometimes—and he was a man without affectation of any kind—sometimes as he traced a philosopher's thought schematically on the blackboard he would find himself lapsing into Greek, or perhaps Hebrew. When this happened there would be a quiet tittering in the classroom, but Professor Calhoun was deaf and didn't hear; so, after a while, we would just struggle to understand. Yet Mr. Calhoun, at Yale, was just another professor in a department of philosophy star-studded with learning and brains.

Lewis Curtis, professor of European history, had a lecture course, and each of his lectures—they ran exactly forty-eight minutes—was a forensic tour de force. His description of the Battle of Jutland could have had a long run Off-Broadway. Pyrotechnics were deemed, at Yale in 1946, a little *infra dig*, so it wasn't thunder and lightning and morning lights that Lewis Curtis gave his class: rather, wit and polish. We could not believe it, and I still wonder at it, that anyone could deliver, three times a week on schedule, discrete lectures sculpted so lovingly; they came out like Renaissance statues, buoyant yet lapidary. How do they do it? I think the wonder of scholarly profundity hit us as freshmen here, even if we were destined to wonder about the uses to which learning is so often put.

Another thing that struck us was something I came to think of as a genetic attribute of Yale, and this was a distinctive sense of gentility. We were addressed as adults. And, for the most part, treated as adults: by men sharply to be distinguished from those noisy martinets we had experienced at boot camps. We had, however briefly, a vision of an entirely different order of social arrangements, a community of scholars. We would eventually learn, through experience and through reading, that no petty human vice is neglected in the academy, that fratricide does not stop at academic moats. But as students we were substantially shielded from such frictions because students are after all transient, and we were not competing with the faculty for anything. Perhaps our experience was in that sense denatured, but it is an ineffaceable part of the memory of four years at Yale: the very idea of institutional courtesy. We have never been quite the same after those four years. Perhaps not better in every way, but certainly we were now men who knew something about the scales of human achievement.

I think, in these mellow circumstances, of the great centrifugal forces

4   THE YALE DAILY NEWS, FRIDAY, JAN

| "The Oldest
College Daily" | 𝔜𝔞𝔩𝔢 ⚜ 𝔑𝔢𝔴𝔰 | Founded
January 28, 1878 |

WILLIAM FRANK BUCKLEY, JR. Chairman

THOMAS HENRY GUINZBURG, Managing Editor   JOHN DeWITT MACOMBER, Business Manager
FREDERICK FRANCIS STANNARD, JR., Sports Editor   AL PAUL LEFTON, JR., Asst. Business Manager
WILLIAM JOHN CARR CARLIN, Vice Chairman   ALLAN McLANE, Advertising Manager
ROBERT WERNER DUEMLING, Asst. Managing Editor   EDWARD EAMES DONALDSON, Circulation Manager
STANLEY BURTON FEUER, Asst. Sports Editor   NORMAN KAVANAUGH, Editorial Secretary
            ARTHUR WILSON MILAM, Production Coordinator and Feature Editor
WILLIAM HENRY OTTLEY, Technical Supervisor   ALFRED KEMP STALLINGS, Purchasing Manager

SENIOR EDITORS

Clifford V. Brokaw, III   Daniel C. deMenocal   Andrew C. Hartzell, Jr.   Richard H. Lawrence
Newcomb Cleveland   George W. Gorham   Thomas M. Hopkinson   George Lee
            Sheridan N. Lord   Thomas N. Tuttle   Angus C. Wright

"Bright College Years" (Foreground: WFB, with bone in his mouth.)

in modern life. I sat late one night last week in the garage-study of my
home in Stamford, putting these words together. My wife and I have
lived there for almost forty years. Even so, I reflected last Monday, I have
only twice laid eyes on the neighbor north of my property, and have yet
to meet my neighbor to the south, who has occupied *his* house for fifteen

years. By temperament I am content with the doctrine that good fences make good neighbors; but good fences shouldn't evolve into barbed-wire barricades, though much of this is happening: the atomistic pull of high-tech living, in a high-tech age.

It was here at Yale, forty years ago, that a professor introduced me to a book by Anton Rossi, with its striking introduction that spoke of two Frenchmen, strangers at a sidewalk café, each one reading his newspaper and sipping his coffee in the late afternoon. Suddenly one raises his voice to the other.

"Say, do you like Jews?"

"No," the other man replied.

"Well, do you like Catholics?"

"No."

"Do you like Americans?"

"No."

"Do you like Frenchmen?"

"No."

"Well, who *do* you like?"

The naysayer raised his head slightly from his newspaper. "I like my friends," he said, going back to his paper.

So do I. And most of my friends I met forty-odd years ago, met them within a radius of two hundred yards of where I am now standing. It occurs to me that forty years is a very long time. Less than forty years went by between the day Lincoln was shot and the day Victoria died. Just forty years before we graduated was the year the Chinese abolished slavery, the year Edward VII died, as also William James and Mark Twain. Friendships that last forty years are something. Monuments, I call them. There are few better grounds for celebration. So let's toast to the class of 1950, and to the college that brought us together.

Douglas sensed the depth of the bonds that brought together three of us, but he came to know that our friendships were never exclusive.

The levities assuaged our concern for the missing wind. Where in the hell was the trade wind? Allan told me that coming across from Cape Verde several years ago he had gone *eight days* under power. Eight days' fuel is exactly as much as we have for the entire trip. . . .

The ship's logbook has the entry, "ENGINE TURNED OFF!!" It was 10 A.M. on Thanksgiving Day. I felt the trip had now really begun.

In my journal I noted chirpily that Liz gave us for lunch "wonderful ham-and-cheese sandwiches on dark brown toasted bread—what a difference between good and awful sandwiches."

On top of the repristination of the autopilot, this was a day in which our Comsat, about which enthralling subject more down the line, was working, and at cocktail hour I emerged triumphantly with: *News from Dick Clurman!* He had volunteered, as soon as he reached New York, to do a digest of the day's news for his departed comrades, and here was the first one, as only Clurman would have put it together:

Date: Tue Nov 20, 1990 12:40 pm EST
From: Richard M. Clurman / MCI ID: 338-8411
TO: National Review / MCI ID: 120-0058
Subject: Daily News for Sealestial, 2
Handling: Doc
Message-Id: 92901120174029/0003388411NB4EM
Filename: News 2.04
To: The Sealestial at Sea—November 20, 1990—0900 EST
From: Horace Greeley
SHIPBORED NEWS
    Word limitations prevent this reporter from giving all details of homeward passage by air. Most exciting event: After three beers, Danny slept six hours.
    LEDE ITEM: 245 cities in U.S. where Liz Smith's column appears, rocked by following items this morning's column:
    "CHA CHA: Did Pat Buckley and Lady Grace Dudley kiss and make up after their recent contretemps, which occurred when Her Ladyship attacked Pat's son, the writer Christopher, in public, denouncing something he'd written?
    "I wouldn't say they kissed. But after Grace apologized, the story made the rounds that Pat turned on her heel and refused to accept the 'I'm sorry.' Pat didn't turn on her heel. She did say, 'Let's forget it, Grace.'
    "Golly, let's all forget it."

Department of Clarification: 1) Christo had written the front-page *New York Times* book review the Sunday before of the unflattering life of Bill Paley, recently deceased head of CBS. 2) The review retailed with great wit the findings of the author, which were mostly at the expense of the late Mr. Paley; 3) Lady Grace was oh-so-fond of Bill Paley. 4) The day after the review appeared, Lady Grace, spotting friend Pat Buckley walking in at a cocktail party was heard by some to say, "I think your son is ca-ca," thereby committing one of the two torts not tolerated by Mrs. Buckley, the other being any animadversion whatsoever at the expense of her husband, so that 5) she allegedly let Lady Grace have it, within the hearing of all and sundry.

Addendum from your editor. I (RMC) have called her Ladyship Grace to tell her she should have stuck to her guns. Anyone who knows Christopher knows damn well that he's ca-ca. She was grateful for the information.

LOCAL: Governor-elect Weicker, moving quickly to deal with Connecticut's fiscal crisis, appoints William J. Cibes of New London, Democrat, who favors a state income tax, as his chief budget adviser. There are rumors that the state division of the National Guard has circled Buckley's home in Stamford.

DEPARTMENT OF CLARIFICATION: There is a Weicker-Buckley feud, details later.

INTERNATIONAL: Gorby in private dinner with Bush at Van's old digs in Paris. Serious difference between the two. Gorby irresolute about assuring support for military solution to Gulf crisis, urges negotiation and more UNing. Mitterrand and others similarly folding. Only Brit's Iron Lady hanging in, in the face of today's Tory party votes, which she had expected to win in close call. NYTimes–CBS poll shows alarming declining support for military action. Noted biographer John B. Judis [he had written a critical biography of me a few years before] in same paper argues Bush's international support heading the way of Woodrow Wilson's. Perry Worsthorne same paper Op-Ed says Brits really don't want to become part of Europe, says if Maggie were not around barking, some other dog would have to because anti-Europe union sentiment invisibly popular in UK.

• Saddam Hussein sending 250,000 troops to Kuwait, doubling his force there. Says if U.N. passes resolution on military action he will not send home all the hostages as he promised beginning Christmas Day.

• Cold War officially ended as 34 nations sign pact in Paris (Albania abstaining). Question: Whither defunct Warsaw Pact?

NATIONAL: Bill Bennett to head RNC [Republican National Committee], with ailing Atwater to be nominal chairman. Casting said to be engineered by Sununu. Bennett blasts affirmative action, supports Helms' campaign as hitting the right popular button.

• Thurgood Marshall and Sandra Day O'Connor join in dissent on SC decision upholding prior restraint on CNN broadcasting of Justice's monitored tapes between Noriega and his lawyer. Gov't not CNN screwing up in prosecuting case.

QUOTE OF THE DAY: from Teddy Turner, Jr., on sailing race against Soviet boat to get support for around-the-world regatta: "It's easy. You just kick a little foreign butt and whammo, people are hooked."

MARKET: up ten for various conflicting reasons, as usual.

SHOW BIZ: Ron Reagan, prex's son, working with Fox TV to host late-night talk show for a fall 1991 (!) start. He ought to be able to line up guests by then.

NOTE: Space limitations severe in these transmissions. Queries from you unfortunates, on specific questions, will be received and promptly answered. I'm dry, content, and wish I were there—now that I'm not. ENDIT.

There was a whole lot of inside language in that communication, but then that's what tailor-made news packages should contain, like letters from home. And then it is always interesting to muse on ten-week-old [it was ten weeks ago, at this writing, that my trip ended] news-and-punditry.

—Gorbachev did vote in the U.N. for military action against Kuwait, so did Mitterrand;

—The poll showed near-universal backing for military action after the U.N. vote;

—Bush's international support went exactly opposite the direction of Woodrow Wilson's;

—Under Prime Minister Major, Great Britain moved closer to the E.C.;

—Saddam Hussein did release the hostages notwithstanding the U.N. vote;

—The thirty-four-nation end-the-cold-war pact has not resulted in the evacuation of Soviet troops from Eastern Europe;

—Bill Bennett quickly resigned as head of the GOP;

—A U.S.–Soviet yacht race has not materialized.

We toasted Dick's health and went down for Thanksgiving dinner. Tony took note: "It included chicken, diced spinach, creamed onions, potatoes, cranberry sauce, and stuffing—the best, Bill Draper says, he ever tasted. Dessert was the pumpkin pie I had begged for and a mince pie as well. We gave her a round of applause." A lot of toasts for one day.

After viewing the next episode of the Civil War I stood watch and abandoned any idea, in the blackness, of trying to sneak a post-sunset sight. There was no stretch of useful horizon anywhere. It was indeed very dark, though not so much so as when eight days ago we left Funchal, but very dark, and I wondered how Columbus had dared to sail thus brazenly in uncharted waters. It isn't as though he and his immediate successors quickly and cleanly established that there was nothing to bump into between the Canaries and the Caribbean. Far from it. "Consult any terrestrial globe a century or more old," Admiral Morison wrote, "and you will find the Atlantic fairly peppered with imaginary islands, rocks, and 'reported breakers.' Brazil Rock, last of these phantoms, was not removed from admiralty charts until 1873. If every island were real that some mariner has thought he sighted during the last four centuries, they would be as close together as the Florida Keys."

But now with a new wind behind us we were steaming along at eight and a half knots, about the speed Columbus traveled at the fastest moments aboard his *Santa María,* which was a little slower than the sprinty *Pinta* on which Columbus returned. I knocked off the autopilot and steered the *Sealestial* for a few hours, in desultory conversation with Bill Draper, who is engrossed by the whole engrossing thing. I told him about the strange night aboard my friend Peter Flanigan's *Astraea.* I was in command, sailing toward Charleston from the Bahamas. We were a couple of hundred miles on our course (due north) when I got vaguely apprehensive, as one sometimes gets at sea. Something was telling us that there was confusion in the elements, and odd things were likely to happen. Not hurricane-odd—there was nothing on the barometer, or on the radio, that indicated any such danger. The weather report was of fifteen-to-twenty-knot winds from the southeast. But in fact the winds were coming and going, the sun was coming and going, the clouds ditto, as also squall patterns, off in the distance.

What does one do, asked Bill Draper, when one is "vaguely apprehensive"? "One battens down the hatches," I said. I remember the

opening paragraph in an issue of *National Review* back in the heyday
of the Warren Court. *"Oyez oyez oyez.* The Supreme Court is back
in session. Batten down the hatches." Hatches nowadays do not need
battening down; they slide in and out, for the most part, and don't need
battens. In any event, I continued the story, I came back on watch at
2300, and instantly undertook an extra reef on the mainsail. The genoa
had already been furled. We were on a broad reach with southeast
winds. And these were coming in gusts which a half hour later were
reaching forty-five knots, with shafts of driving rain in successive bursts
that lasted fifteen or twenty minutes.

I spotted a light at about eleven o'clock on our course, more exactly,
two tiny blurs of light visible with binoculars. Tony, though off duty,
came up to the cockpit (sleep below was impossible that night, as we
rolled and tossed). Tony suggested in his mild way that the ship was
bearing down on us and that he thought it would be appropriate to
come about. I recited my philosophy in such matters: I approach
oncoming ships until quite close, and only then make course changes,
definitive in nature. We watched in the blinding rain and howling wind
the ship, making out both its running lights. It didn't change on its
bearing to us, which told us we were on a collision course. (At this point
in my story Bill Draper was quite regularly scanning the horizon.)

What spooked us was that the ship seemed to come no closer. I doubt
it was traveling at four knots, let alone sixteen. Finally I came about,
primarily to ease the mounting psychological pressure in the cockpit, in
the anarchic circumstances of eccentric and screeching winds. An hour
later Tony was on watch with me and, suddenly, *there* was that same
vessel again, this time coming at us from astern. Again we watched for
fifteen, twenty minutes, wondering why it did not overtake us. Again, I
came about: with the purpose primarily in mind of losing the mysterious
ship. We had a little bit the feeling of a rudderless pursuer stalking us,
this time from behind, awaiting the auspicious moment to pounce. A
logical next step would have been to power on the radio and ask, "What
in the hell are you nice people dogging us for?" Tony allowed himself to
speculate that the Spookship was out here awaiting a drug drop. If so,
would it commit aggression against a 38-foot sailboat, out here in the
wild seas, that had spotted it?

So what happened? Bill Draper's voice was tense.

Nothing. The stuff of post-midnight fantasies in stormy weather. Although, I said, there was no explanation for the odd behavior of the S.S. *Spook*.

Bill told me he had kept his eyes open, and there was nothing surrounding us, nothing except blackness and the steady sound of a steady wind pushing us toward the New World.

I thought back on the most glamorous encounter at sea I had ever experienced. We were on *Sea Cloud,* and the information breezed in, routine stuff, blasé . . . It just happened, we were informed, that, headed in our general direction, bound west, was the *Eagle*. It is the three-masted bark manned by Coast Guard cadets, a vessel our own captain (Cassidy) had once commanded. We would effect, we were told—if all went well—a union at sea! A thousand miles from the nearest point of land! Very well.

At dinnertime the disappointing news was passed around that the *Eagle* was hopelessly off our own course, and would pass by sixty miles south of us. But then, just after eleven, we were told the *Eagle* would materialize in fifteen minutes.

Everyone did as one would expect: we lined up along the port deck.

The EAGLE

The moon was nearly full, but was playing tag with the clouds so that we had its illumination only momentarily. Came the magical moment when we spotted the dull yellow blur, two or three miles ahead.

It was a full half hour before the *Eagle* was opposite us, only a hundred yards or so abeam. All its sails were hoisted. So it must have been in these waters, here in mid-Atlantic, two hundred years ago when approaching ships were spotted and one wondered, in those bloody days, whether the ship was manned by pirates; or by a nation at war; or by privateers with letters of marque and reprisal.

But there was never, ever, a more fraternal by-pass than that night's, two sailing ships, one with its sails full, the second headed into the wind under noiseless power. The cadets' cameras popped in the night, opposite our own doing the same thing, a ghostly simulacrum of cannon flashes exploding at each other at sea. An unplanned moment, breathlessly beautiful in the off-again-on-again moonlight, the indulgent northeast trades blowing balm over the elated participants.

CHAPTER ELEVEN

In re Columbus

So we sail along, coping with problems as they arise, some major (the mainsail begins to tear), some minor (the shackle attached to the preventer snaps open). Most of the knowledge we dispose of, certainly in my case, is prescriptive. For instance, you know the world is round because you know the world is round. If you had to set out to prove it to yourself, you could rise to the top of any seaside skyscraper and with (or even without) the aid of binoculars you could train your eyes on that object on the horizon out there which is a black dot right now, at 11:05—but a gestating dot, as you will soon see. Because it is now (11:15) much bigger, in fact you think you can discern the shape of a bow. And by 11:30 you see the full outline of a ship steaming in toward you. The only way to account for this is the roundness of the earth. It has infuriated a legion of scholars that the myth persists that Columbus thought the world flat. Morison dealt with that canard:

> Of all the vulgar errors connected with Columbus, the most persistent and the most absurd is that he had to convince people the world was round. Every educated man in his day believed the world to be a sphere, every European university so taught geography, and seamen, though they might doubt the practical possibility of sailing "down under" or holding on when you got there, knew perfectly well from seeing ships "hull-

down" and "raising" mountains as they approached, that the surface of
the globe was curved. Aristotle was reported to have written that you
could cross the ocean from the Spains to the Indies *paucis diebus,* in
comparatively few days; and Strabo, the Greek geographer who died
about A.D. 25, hinted that it had actually been tried.

So it is that common experience became formal common knowledge,
painfully and slowly accumulated over many years, at a rate that
reached typhonic speed in recent decades.

Well then, the earth is round—but how wide? Since we all know that
there are 360 degrees in a circle and that the earth is circular it is as
simple as multiplying one degree by 360.

But again, *how long* was a degree?

"That problem," Morison tells us, "had been bothering mathemati-
cians for at least eighteen centuries. Eratosthenes around 200 B.C. made
a guess at it that was very nearly correct: 59.5 nautical miles instead
of 60. Columbus, however, preferred the computation of Alfragan.
That medieval Moslem geographer found the degree to be 56 2/3rds
Arabic miles, which works out at 66.2 nautical miles; but Columbus,
assuming that the short Roman or Italian mile of 1480 meters was used
by Alfragan, upon that false basis computed that the degree measured
only 45 nautical miles, roughly 75 percent of its actual length, and the
shortest estimate of the degree ever made. Arguing from this faulty
premise, Columbus concluded that the world was 25 percent smaller
than Eratosthenes, 10 percent smaller than Ptolemy, taught." Moreover, Columbus, who of course thought he was headed for the Indies,
assumed that six sevenths of the world was covered by land, and no one
knows whether he went any further in this deduction than his single
citation of the Book of 2 Esdras 6:42, "And on the third day Ye united
the waters and the earth's seventh part, and dried up the six other
parts."

How did Columbus measure the passage of time? (I give you thirty
seconds . . .) "In Columbus's day, and until the late sixteenth century,
the only ship's clock available was the *ampolleta* or *reloj de arena* (sand
clock), a half-hour glass containing enough sand to run from the upper
to the lower section in exactly thirty minutes. Made in Venice, these

glasses were so fragile that a large number of spares were carried—Magellan had eighteen on his flagship."

How could he tell the speed of the boat? The same way I did, taking my schooner one season to Bermuda when the Kenyon speedometer stopped working and our second taffrail log was eaten by a shark: by tossing out a cork at the bow and, with a stopwatch, noting how long it took to reach the stern. Columbus didn't have a stopwatch, and his grandfather clocks, as we have seen, all ran a set half-hour, but I warrant he had some *little* "hour" glasses, perhaps gauging the time down to as little as thirty seconds. I can't imagine that he didn't, is a better way to put it.

"At night, whenever the weather was clear and the latitude not too low, Columbus could tell approximate clock time from the Guards of the North Star. The Little Bear or Little Dipper swings around Polaris once every twenty-four hours sidereal time. The two brightest stars of that constellation, Kochab and γ, which mark the edge of the dipper furthest from the North Star, were called the Guards; and if you knew where Kochab the principal Guard was stationed at midnight every two weeks of the year, you could tell time from it as from a clock hand. The early navigators constructed a diagram of a little man with Polaris in his middle, his forearms pointing E and W, and his shoulders NE and NW . . . etc." The stars are funny, with their odd but useful little rigidities. For instance, depending on your and the star's declination, a star you see rising will set 270 degrees from where it came up, so that the star you saw for the first time exactly east of your course will sink, when it goes down, northwest of your course. Play with that a while and little exploitative things come to mind, especially if you are struggling to find out where you are using only such rudimentary tools as had to suffice for Columbus.

But Columbus's apparently paradoxical idea, best designed to irritate by his formulation that "he wished to go west in order to be east," was not considered entirely eccentric at the time he set out. "It was in the air for eighteen years before he put it into execution; and if he had faltered or failed, another was ready to embark on the same bold adventure." How did Columbus know in which direction to point the ship? Answer: He had speculated that the Indies he was looking for

began at a point about where Cuba is, and the idea was therefore to move down to that hypothesized latitude, and then to head due west. During his passage he never knew at what longitude he was because this you can't know without a timepiece accurate enough to give you the exact time, permitting you to lock in the angle of the sun and deduce a line of position. But by measuring the altitude of Polaris with whatever version of a sextant you had at hand, you could know that you were heading due east, or due west; which is how navigators mostly fared: Get up to, or down to, the latitude that corresponds with your home port, and maintain that latitude until you hit home.

In one respect, not widely known, Columbus was unburdened. His three boats, though things went wrong with each, were thoroughly seaworthy. They were toughly made and could stand dirty weather. As for dictating your course, true—"a ship in Columbus's day could not sail nearer to the wind than five compass points (56 degrees) even with a smooth sea." That means a spread of 112 degrees. Well, my schooner *Cyrano* could do no better than 110 degrees, and it was built four hundred and sixty years after the *Pinta*. A racing boat can point 30 degrees away from the wind direction, giving it a marvelous advantage in maneuverability. And you can improve the dull schooner's point 15 degrees by turning on the engine. It suffices to say that Columbus was not, in respect of his vessel, as disadvantaged as popularly assumed after you accept his basic limitation, namely that he had only the propulsive power of the wind.

Aboard a motor sailer the preceding July, cruising off Yugoslavia with Pat and Van and another couple, I made some calculations which interested me on the matter of sail propulsion. Unlike many motor sailers, the *Fei Seen* actually sails. She is 100 feet long and has a mainmast 110 feet high which (again, for the unacquainted) is very high, implying many square feet of canvas. They didn't have the figures sitting about on board, but you would not be far off if you estimated 4,500 square feet of mainsail, 6,000 of genoa, and 1,000 of mizzen. That is a *lot* of sail—understandably, if you reflect on what it is that the sail is required to propel, namely 149 tons. I like fiddling with these ratios and hope you do. We are talking about moving three hundred thousand pounds of weight over the water, so what it comes down to is that one square foot of sail is pushing twenty-six pounds; not bad. Doing so, moreover, at speeds as high as thirteen knots. If you have nothing better to do, contrive a little kite one foot square, attach it to a roller skate, dump five five-pound bags of sugar plus a one-pound can of coffee on it, take it out to the sidewalk in a fair breeze (make certain no other adult is in the area) and see if it scoots off at thirteen knots (14.95 miles per hour), in which event you will need to chase after it with a bicycle. Using this ratio, and assuming his vessel was as seakindly as *Fei Seen,* we would estimate the sail area on Columbus's flagship, which weighed 201.7 tons and traveled as fast as eight knots, at 31,076.9 square feet. The trouble with that figure is that, looking at the reconstruction of the vessel done by conscientious scholars, it's hard to believe the *Santa María* carried that much sail. I don't believe it, for one. One professional's estimate is 2,700 feet.

Columbus's son recounted the six arguments used in court in the effort to discredit Columbus's proposed voyage. It is important to keep in mind that these were arguments employed by wise men, or at least by men who believed themselves to be wise, and were thought to be wise. Their analogue today, one might contend, is those wise men who counseled so vigorously and still do, many of them, against building a defense system adequate to cope with hostile missiles coming in through the atmosphere. These six arguments were:

(1) *A voyage to Asia would require three years.* This was an especially risky argument to make given that Bartholomew Diaz, sailing under Portuguese patronage four years before Columbus set out, had reached the Cape of Good Hope, beyond which, sailing east, it was now inevitable that Asia would be discovered. Indeed it was Diaz's voyage that prompted D. João II of Portugal simply to abandon Columbus (why bother to sail west, if all you had to do was go to South Africa and sail east?), in whose project he had once been keenly interested, causing Columbus to turn to Spain.

(2) *The Western Ocean is infinite and perhaps unnavigable.* A very strange position for wise men to take at a time when the roundness of the earth, discountenancing earthly infinity, was a quite general postulate.

(3) *If he reached the Antipodes* (the land on the other side of the globe from Europe) *he would not get back.* This was a reasonable objection, to be answered only by an ipsedixitism, nothing ventured, nothing gained.

(4) *There are no Antipodes because the greater part of the globe is covered with water, and because Saint Augustine says so.* Augustine didn't say exactly that,* besides which, to reason that there was nothing at the opposite end of Spain was itself a mere postulate.

(5) *Of the five zones, only three are habitable.* Another hypothesis, nothing more. Not inherently foolish, since much territory we now know of as habitable, for instance the South Pole—where I have been and was made entirely comfortable—would not have been habitable in the fifteenth century. And, finally,

(6) *So many centuries after the Creation it was unlikely that anyone could find hitherto unknown lands of any value.* The trouble with that argument is that it rested on an insular fallacy, namely that all that was

---

*St. Augustine said that there was no "rational ground for such a belief." (*The City of God,* Book XVI, Chapter 9) His analysis was motivated by his presumptive reaction against any surmisal that there were two species of men on earth, in which case there were no common parents nor Original Sin. The Portuguese, anxious to make the case for slavery, argued the existence of a subhuman race. Spain, citing Augustine, never condoned slavery.

explorable had been explored. A major empirical ineptitude in a season crowded with burgeoning discoveries, reaching (as noted) as far south as the Cape of Good Hope.

The evolution of sea lore goes from naïve extremity to naïve extremity, ancient and modern. Where did Columbus's crew of thirty-nine sleep? Wherever they chose: on deck, below, more or less anywhere. Given the pitch and the roll of any ship, this was extraordinarily unresourceful, to be compared with the incomprehensible failure of the great Incan empire, discovered by Pizarro in Peru thirty years after Columbus's discovery, to conceive of the wheel. But it wasn't until Columbus observed the sleeping habits of some of the naked Indians he came upon in the New World that he observed how men at sea *could* sleep: in hammocks. This simple exploitation of the law of gravity promptly revolutionized seagoing sleeping habits, from that moment to the present moment. At the other hand, we are assaulted with ostensibly self-evident formulas which are in fact anything but self-evident, of which one of my favorites is the observation by the editor of Columbus's log (*The Log of Christopher Columbus*, Robert H. Fuson, International Marine Publishing Company, Camden, Maine, 1987): "A convenient rule of thumb for obtaining distance-to-horizon is: the square root of the height of the observer (above sea level), added to the square root of the above sea-level height of the sighted object, and multiplied by 1.3 for nautical miles, 1.5 for statute miles." That convenient formula inevitably reminds us of the old saw about the admiral and his strongbox, opened upon his sudden death, wherein lay another formula, written out in the admiral's own hand: "Port equals left, starboard equals right."

But I must not ignore my paper work, and so went below to tackle some of the mail Christo had brought me from my office.

—The Oklahoman who ran unsuccessfully against David Boren for senator writes to rebuke me on a column, published in October, in which I had criticized his record. He makes certain points about the victorious incumbent that I feel Boren should comment on, given that it was he who gave me the material on which I had based my column. "Dear David: Here is a letter I just now saw. It is a spirited defense of himself by Stephen Jones but he also makes a few direct criticisms of you and before I write a column of clarification I'd appreciate word from you on any inaccuracies in Mr. Jones's letter."

I first encountered David Boren when he was a junior at Yale. He was a member of the Conservative Party and the president of the Political Union. It was time (he wrote me) to redeem my promise to appear with the Political Union, of which, as an undergraduate, I had been a member. I had said okay, suggested a topic, and a week or so later received a schedule of the speakers for the fall season. I learned that one week after my appearance, the P.U.'s speaker would be Gus Hall, Secretary General of the American Communist Party.

This was 1962. I called David Boren on the telephone. I told him that I did not a) debate with Communists; b) appear on programs with Communists; or c) appear on any lecture series in which Communists also appeared. Young David Boren was appalled. What could he do, Gus Hall having been invited, and Gus Hall having accepted? I had a suggestion: If the invitation to Mr. Hall were reissued as contingent upon the vote of the entire Political Union at the end of an evening's debate on the question, "Resolved, That a Communist functionary should not be invited to speak at Yale," then I would appear—to defend the affirmative of the resolution. David Boren gasped. "Mr. Buckley, you'll lose the vote nine to one on that resolution!" Okay, but I would be holding fast to my threatened principles. Until the vote of the entire Political Union was taken—only *after* I had spoken—the vote to invite the Communist would not have finally been confirmed.

It turned out to be the most exciting night of my entire political life. The students convened in numbers so large the debate had to be removed to the mammoth Woolsey Hall. I began the affirmative argument by recalling that a few years earlier, students at Hunter College had invited the Nazi leader George Lincoln Rockwell and the Communist Gus Hall to speak on successive weeks. The president of Hunter, Dr. John Meng, distributed a letter to the students and faculty. He reaffirmed the students' administrative right to invite whomsoever they chose to address them, but recommended to the faculty that while the two men were addressing those students who were curious to know what they apparently didn't already know about Nazism and Communism, faculty members might appropriately convene at a neighboring synagogue to make common cause with the dead victims of Nazism and Communism. I went on, using in full my allotted twenty minutes, to say that the head of the Communist Party would not be telling the students anything they did not already know, that the students would not be able to reason with him to further the common understanding, no more than Anne Frank could have collaborated with Goebbels in a dialogue on race relations. A Communist functionary was a fit object of curiosity for students of disciplines other than politics—for students of sociology, perhaps, or serious students of psychology who seek to examine the reflexes of a man who, for the sake of his truth, will utter and defend every necessary untruth, every necessary depravity. The courtroom at Tel Aviv was crowded with professors of the specialized social sciences, but they were not men who would have invited Adolf Eichmann to their college to defend the regime of Adolf Hitler. But in Gus Hall's case, the special difficulty the students would face would derive from their need to deal with a human being. "What will you do when Gus Hall, the human being, comes here to defend the cause of what you know ahead of time to be the cause of organized in-humanity? Will you show that shudder of polite disgust? [I quoted the phrase used in Dr. Meng's letter to the Hunter students.] Is this a new social skill we need to cultivate, a part of the social equipment endowed upon us in virtue of our great good fortune as recipients of a Hunter or Yale education? (Did *your* son learn at his college how to give off a shudder of polite disgust?)"

An alternative was to jeer him—"some of you may treat him with that terrible coldness that is the sign of the intellectual foreknowledge that you cannot, at your level of attainment, take seriously the man who speaks and works for a kingdom which it is the very purpose of your education to know to despise. . . .

"Fight him, fight the tyrants everywhere; but do not ask them to your quarters merely to spit on them, and do not ask them to your quarters if you cannot spit on them. To do the one is to ambush a human being as one might a rabid dog; to do the other is to ambush oneself, to force oneself, in disregard of those who have *died* trying to make the point, to break faith with humanity."

There were four student speakers, representing the four political parties within the Union. Only one sided with me. But when the vote was taken—we *won*! There was tumult in Woolsey Hall when the verdict was announced. The Associated Press carried the story. The sweetest polemical moment of my life.

The appropriate motion was duly introduced, and the president of the Yale Political Union, young David Boren, was instructed to send a telegram to Gus Hall canceling the invitation to appear before the Political Union.

The following day, Yale chaplain William Sloane Coffin issued an invitation to Gus Hall to visit Yale's Dwight Hall.

—In my folder, a clipping from the *New York Post:* "MCGOVERN GOES BELLY-UP ON CONN. HOTEL." I knew that George McGovern was having a very difficult time maintaining the inn he had bought in Stratford, Connecticut. We had had three or four professional encounters during the year on the lecture circuit, and he kept me current on the vicissitudes of the white elephant he had purchased. He asked me, during the winter, to go to his inn to give a post-brunch speech, a feature by a public figure sponsored by the hotel on the last Sunday of every month. I complied. That was in June, and George told me, in private, that he wished that before he had entered public life he'd had the experience he was now having—trying to make out in the private sector. George McGovern had gone from faculty life to Congress to the Senate to a presidential campaign, back to the Senate. It was only after his defeat for reelection to the Senate, in 1980, that he went to the private sector. So I write now to extend condolences on the unhappy end to his life as a hotelier, and to suggest that he write a book on his experiences. He is a most charming man, and if he had been elected President in 1972, the United States of America would probably have ceased to exist along about, oh, 1973, '74.

—My beloved baby sister Carol writes to me. I remember the drama of her birth. One reason why I and two of my sisters were sent to England to boarding school in 1938 was that the doctors thought it possible that my mother would not survive the birth of her eleventh child. We had been told only that it would be a difficult birth, not that it was perilous. My concern, combined with my isolation, caused my father to consent to my importunate request that I be the godfather of the next child: and, at age thirteen, in South Carolina for the Christmas holidays, I proudly officiated at the baptism, saying all the correct things in my soprano voice. She has not had a happy life, divorced from the father of her four children, whom she left college to marry; then divorced from his successor; years of hard academic work to become an alcoholism counselor; encouraged by a major publisher to revise a novel, on which she is proceeding to work diligently. She writes that she is having difficulty mastering word processing. And then, quite suddenly, a few words of such acute and tender affection, with references to the Thirty-Fifth Anniversary Dinner. How fine to open such a letter in mid-ocean. How many godfathers get such treatment? I shall deed her everything I own.

—And from another relative, my late sister Aloise's ninth child, Timothy. He writes to say that he is leaving South Carolina, where he has been teaching school, and will come north and stay for a while with his older brother, who also teaches school. "John and I were discussing how nice it would be to get together with you someday. Is there a chance of that?" Indeed, and I will call him after we land. Whenever I think of Tim, I think of a few lines written about him by his mother in one of the fleeted Christmas stories she wrote every season for *National Review*. ". . . Timothy is seven years old [1965], and the subject arises, among the children, of World Affairs. The Communists, Timothy thinks you ought to know, are against us, and we're against the Communists, and they plan to beat us up, but, man, are they going to be surprised, because they don't even know about Timothy Heath yet! And with modest pride, Terrible Timothy sticks one skinny little leg in the air, and shows you his heavy brace and boot [Timothy was born with an impediment]. *'One kick with that foot,'* he grins from clenched teeth, and while you ponder the appalling fate in store for the Communists, Tim smiles, and the serious little face breaks into whole galaxies of twinkles and dimples."

There were sounds on deck above, and I go up. The wind, dead down, doesn't permit us the course I had specified. Either we have to head up fifteen degrees, or jibe. Jibing is a little bit of an operation, and the mood is not lively, so I opt to come up—there is plenty of time to regularize the course. I detect a look of relief on my son's face as he resumes reading his book. There is a little ennui creeping in.

I let my mind ponder, during a low point in our passage, six reasons *not* to undertake Ocean4, in the style of the dissenters in the court of Ferdinand and Isabella:

1) *It is dangerous to travel 4400 miles across the ocean in a small, self-sustained vessel.* Comment: Yes, it is dangerous in the sense that the sea is made up of a substance in which people can drown. You can capsize; the ship can burn and sink; you can run into a whale; someone can fall overboard and be lost; a freak hurricane can do to you what something like it did to Captain Slocum. But you can get run over in New York City.

2) *Such a passage consumes a month's time.* Comment: One month is only one 840th of one's biblical lifespan. Can you be absolutely certain that alternative means of spending one 840th of your life will prove more . . . interesting? . . . rewarding? . . . exciting? . . . memorable?

3) *You are separated from your loved ones for one month.* Comment: Yes, and it can transpire that that absence actually made the heart grow even fonder.

4) *You might be seasick and miserable.* Comment: If you fear that this might be the case for the entire month, you should avoid long ocean passages, by all means.

Or, 5) *You might have a burst appendix while at sea.* Comment: Such afflictions are rare, and these days it is probable that by radio you could raise a ship at sea with a doctor on board who would get to you ahead of the grim reaper.

And 6) *The whole thing is very expensive.* Comment: Yes, but that is WFB's problem.

Against all of which you have to ponder all the implications suggested in a single paragraph from Admiral Morison:

> This leg of the voyage must have been almost pure delight to the Admiral and his men. The fleet sped along, making an average day's run of 183 miles. In the trades, vessels always roll a good deal, but the steady and favorable wind singing in the rigging, the sapphire white-capped sea, the rush of great waters alongside, and the endless succession of fat, puffy trade-wind clouds, lift up a seaman's spirits and make him want to shout

and sing. The old-time Spanish mariners called these broad waters *El Golfo de las Damas,* The Ladies' Sea, so easy is the navigation. As Von Humboldt wrote, "Nothing equals the beauty and mildness of the climate of the equinoctial region on the ocean." Occasionally a black rain squall makes up from windward, but passes harmlessly with a brief lash of rain, and a slight change of wind. For days on end the sheets and braces need no attention, flying fish and dorados play about the ship, and the pelagic birds, petrels and the like pay brief visits. On moonless nights the sails stand out black against the star-studded firmament; and as the ship makes her southing, every night new stars and constellations appear—Canopus, Capricorn, Argo with her False Cross, and the true Crux Australis. Most of his men were new to southern waters, and one can imagine them, as in Hérédia's sonnet, leaning entranced over the bulwarks of the white caravels, and seeing in the phosphorescent sea an augury of the gold of the Indies.

· CHAPTER TWELVE ·

Life at Sea

I had on board a software program for the computer called PC GLOBE, around which Christopher and Douglas huddled the first evening and again on the second day, until curiosity and amazement wore out, which can happen, after all, even with Shakespeare and sex. PC GLOBE is one part plaything but more than that for a sailor with ambitious plans, and also a superb traveler's, or even researcher's, aid.

It gives you, first, a map of the world, much as you would see one in a map store. It then invites you to focus on the continent, region, country, or city you are looking for. "Watch," I told Christo, depressing "7" for "Select City." Once inside the catalogue of cities I marched the cursor highlight over to "Bridgetown," which is where we're headed, the capital (and only) city of Barbados. A one-inch square appears on the screen at the center of which is Barbados, too small to be discernible. Move the cursor once again to the right and a zooming process begins: Barbados is now a visible dot in the center. Cursor again to the right and an outline of the island of Barbados fills up your screen, together with the legend on the right, "Population 257,000, Area (sq mi) 166."

You keep asking for more data, and they come at you. Features of the island, its population—dating back to 1975 and projecting forward to 2000—population growth, age distribution, growth rate, GNP, lan-

guages spoken, ethnic groups represented, per capita income, health
statistics, telex access code, ham radio prefixes, type of government,
names of leaders, major political parties, currency exchange rates ("Barbados dollar, January 1990: 2.01 equals $1 U.S.") and: latitude and
longitude of its principal city.

But the payoff is coming. The city of Puerto Rico in the Grand
Canaries, from which we set out, is not among the five hundred cities
listed. But you don't much care. You merely flash to the screen labeled
"User Defined City/Point," and highlight *"Change Point of Origin."*
You are told, *"Enter Name of City/Point of Origin."* You type "Puerto
Rico," and, when asked, feed in the latitude and the longitude of
Puerto Rico, taken from the chart.

Then you push RETURN and, I swear it, *in less than one second* you
see on the screen:

		Latitude	Longitude
Origin:	Puerto Rico	28.00N	15.20W
Destination:	Bridgetown, Barbados	13.06N	59.37W
Distance:	3,022 miles		
Bearing:	259.4 degrees.		

And yes, highlighted on the map is a wiggly line stretching from
Puerto Rico in the Canary Islands to Bridgetown in the Caribbean, to
give you the graphic feel of the journey you are undertaking.

It is mind-numbing to reflect that this little program will give you
the distance and bearing from anywhere to anywhere in approximately
one half second.

Stop to think of it. PC GLOBE accepts coordinates up to one mile apart
(e.g., as above, 13.06 degrees North, 59.37 degrees West). If you placed
somebody on the South Pole, another person one mile north of him,
and so on, all the way up to the North Pole, at 00.00 degrees Longitude—i.e., on a line running through Greenwich, England—you would
have sixty people between 90 degrees South and 89 degrees South. You
continue the exercise on up to the Equator, at which point you would
have used up 60 × 90 people, or 5400. Continue all the way to the
North Pole, and you have double that, 10,800.

Now start down at 1 degree West Longitude until you reach the

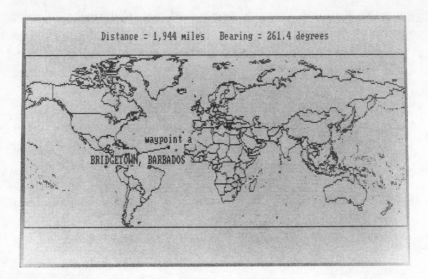

PC GLOBE, strutting its stuff

South Pole, then up again at 2 degrees West Longitude until you get
to the North Pole, and so on. By the time you get back to where you
started, you will have multiplied your figure of 10,800 by 360 degrees,
that being the circumference of the earth. That means: 3,888,000
people; or, if you prefer, 3,888,000 isolatable longitudinal coordinates.

But of course any longitudinal coordinate is also read as a coordinate
of latitude. At the Equator, 00.00 degrees Longitude, you are also at
00.00 degrees Latitude. *Now* imagine a calculator that can take any one
of those 3.8 million dots and give you the distance and direction to any
of the other 3.8 million dots in a half second. . . . Do you see the wonder of it all?

It fascinated Christo and Douglas, but more so the revelation that
the distance we were traveling was 3,022 miles.

"Plus," I said.

"Plus what?" Christopher was clearly alarmed.

"To make sure we stay in the trades, we're not sailing a straight
hypotenuse. We'll go south-southwest for four hundred miles to Point
A (another Point A), then head west. So that whereas the PC GLOBE's

figure 3022 is on the order of a hypotenuse, instead we'll be following the other two legs."

"That's a long way to go," Christo would later muse in his journal, "when you are traveling eight miles per hour."

Columbus didn't know about this navigational precaution—heading south to be sure to catch the trades—either. Morison wrote, ". . . Lord Dunraven, the English yachtsman who made a study of Columbus's navigation of the First Voyage, declared that if a modern sailing vessel wished to make a voyage from Palos [in Spain] to the Bahamas and back, she 'could not follow a better course out and home than that adopted by Columbus.' [But] This northern limit of the trades is variable, and the variations are unpredictable. Some years you can catch them further north, as Columbus did, and in others further south; our *Mary Otis* [Admiral Morison's sailboat] did not find them until she was below latitude 20° N in November 1937. Any sailing vessel proceeding from Spain to the West Indies today, whether or not calling at the Canaries, would be well advised to drop down almost to latitude 15°, 500 miles south of Tenerife, before straightening out on a westerly course." It is good to know this. And, of course, your Pilot Chart gives you this advice diagrammatically, by telling you where the trade winds predominate.

Christo and Douglas played with the program for an hour, trying to find a point in the United States separated from another point in the continental United States by as much as 3,022 miles. They failed. They accomplished their design, finally, by contriving an imaginary car journey that began in Boston, traveled south to Atlanta, then turned west to San Francisco: making for a 3,000-mile trip.

On the fifth day at sea, Christo looked up unsmiling at Douglas: "I think we're getting near to Atlanta."

"Of course we are. I can smell it in the air."

Our trip—by their coordinates—had begun in Boston. They scorned my latitudes and longitudes, they dealt in *American cities*. As far as Christo and Douglas were concerned, the *Sealestial* that morning had reached . . . Atlanta. And would proceed to Birmingham . . . Little Rock

... Tulsa ... Wichita ... Denver ... Salt Lake ... Reno ... Sacramento
... SAN FRANCISCO!

I went below for another belt at the correspondence Christo had
brought me from New York.

—A tortured soul (evidently met in passing after I gave a speech in
Allentown a few weeks ago) writes with throbbing heart and mind. "I
shan't be fully wedded to my bonds, those bittersweet painful bonds
of Vietnam, until my death. Before I go, however, I shall do my best
to see National Service become a reality. I came from a strange world
where the three pillars of society, home, school, country, were far
removed from your elegant wit. Home was a civil war of blue against
gray. School was a frightful drama. Vietnam was a dark, cold, blue rain.
It touched the violence of my soul. The sword drew the blood of
terror—Vietnam. As the self-proclaimed fool raised his right hand and
sang the Oath to Horatii (David) the blood oozed vehemence for the
deaths of Nam. In the long silences, before a hundred of the muses,
I reaffirm my oath to the fallen: God nattle my soul with fear that I
may know Your Grace."

Not entirely clear to me, his meaning, especially in that last sentence.
But the letter was touching, including parts not here quoted. I reply:
"If Vietnam did that to you, I am driven to the paradox of wishing that
everybody had had such an experience."

—A fascinating letter about the ongoing search for Whittaker
Chambers; from Sam Tanenhaus. He is a young scholar who has
undertaken to write a definitive book about Chambers. Definitive in
the sense of exploring the whole man, not just the-most-famous-spy-in-
American-history, who hid the evidence against Alger Hiss in a pumpkin one melodramatic night in 1948. I have tried to help Sam get the
backing to pursue a very demanding work. It isn't only that Whittaker
Chambers was mysteriously associated with many people (most of them
dead), it is that he was himself mysterious. I knew him very well (and
published a book of his personal letters to me), but in the years since
he died (1961), I keep learning about him, mostly from the scholar
Allen Weinstein, who wrote the book *Perjury,* in which he found for
Chambers although he had begun his researches thinking Chambers

the liar. I had asked Professor Weinstein please to give Tanenhaus some time. . . .

A.W. [Professor Weinstein] tardy (errands), but efficient when he appeared. He promptly set me loose at stacked boxes in a room of indeterminate function. His papers are less of a mess than I had been warned; the files are sane and alphabetized. I found the gems quickly: the Meyer Schapiro letters (including the postcard from Russia), the Herbert Solow letters (plus W.C.'s unpublished mss, c. 1938, containing his Notes from the Underground). There is also precious miscellany: A.W.'s chapter outlines, notes, related articles, virgin material (thought toward an unwritten play, *The Hearing*). A.W. himself most gracious: "I can tell you're a serious scholar, and Bill thinks you're okay. You can look at everything I've got." He also invited me back to Washington this week: The PP [Pumpkin Papers] Irregulars. I cannot afford this visit but cannot afford not to make it. A.W. will introduce me around. [The Pumpkin Papers Irregulars meet once a year, on Halloween, to celebrate some aspect of the Hiss–Chambers controversy.] Best of all, we talked— snatches of conversation, five minutes here, ten there—then a serious dialogue.

Within moments it was clear that on this topic, in all its proliferating complexity, A.W. has no rival He knows what routes CPs [Communist Party members] took to get to Russia, the port of entry (Riga). He knows the inner workings of espionage—the spiraling duplicities, the dense layers of aliases, the disclosures entwined with concealments. He knows W.C. "I've read every word Chambers wrote, at least that was available as of 1980" [the year *Perjury* was finished]. He takes an "agnostic" view of W.C. in Moscow. [Did Whittaker Chambers secretly visit Moscow while he was a spy? There is considerable scholarly interest in the question.] There is evidence, none conclusive. A.W. is, I saw, Oedipus, doomed to solve tragic riddles. At one point he said, "I haven't touched this stuff for a dozen years. It follows me—people call, ask questions. I try to avoid them": but then, once we pushed into the intricacies, "I can talk about this for days. My wife is having dinner out tonight. How late can you stay and talk?" The case is a snare; no one knew it better than W.C. ("Alger and I are archetypes.") A.W. described, with bravura flourishes, his own discovery, made in Sylvia Salmi's Mexican house, that W.C. had told the truth. No doubt you know the story: A.W. locked up in an "aerie" with Solow's papers, the mocking lisp of the water outside the window. Sifting through evidence that even Solow had forgotten about (is this Poe or Henry James?)—the careful log of dates, the meticulous chronicle of W.C.'s break with the Party. All of it proving W.C. hadn't lied. This discovery tipped A.W. into confusion, almost despair. Of course he recovered: only survivors tell such stories; for the rest, the cold comfort, the retreat, of silence.

I read on with mounting excitement. The exoneration of Whittaker Chambers was formally accomplished first by the courts, then by Allen Weinstein. Sam Tanenhaus is engaged in a more ambitious mission, and was proving in this letter his competence to understand the whole of this complicated man, whom I had grown to love and revere during the years I knew him and we worked together at *National Review*.

A.W.'s own journey strangely parallel to W.C.'s, though he wouldn't say so. Instead he said—with a kind of hush—"Chambers contains multitudes"; also, "I didn't do him justice"; finally, "After I finished *Perjury* I was going to write the book you're writing now." A.W. is brilliant. He looks rabbinical but you feel the heat of a skepticism so pure it seems a kind of faith. I don't mean to be fancy. I mean this: I have met the admirers, the foes. Here was the demystifier. His discipline, his pride, is never to flinch. Oedipus again. I said: "Ralph de Toledano [a close friend of Chambers and author of *Seeds of Treason*, the first book published about the trial] thinks it possible W.C. committed suicide. Is it possible?" "Yes, but it wouldn't change how I think about him." Later I asked, "When did you discover that W.C. was so encompassing, so large?" A.W.: "I knew that from the start. But I also thought he was a liar." He added: "And he did lie. To his wife and family. To his comrades in the Party. To his friends. To HUAC [House Committee on Un-American Activities]. They all lied. It's in the title of my book. *Perjury* refers to everyone involved." He told me his first title had been "Alger and Whittaker." It wouldn't do, but the thought stayed with him and shaped the book he wrote—the chapters that juxtapose their careers, again that fateful parallelism. A.W.'s most remarkable comment: "I don't care what you make of all this"—that is, of his archive. "You may come away thinking W.C. was a fantasist—that he invited it, everything. It doesn't matter to me." I repeated a remark of R.D.T.'s about W.C.'s "compartmentalized life," how suddenly it would emerge that he had a correspondence going with Thomas Merton or Marjorie Kinnan Rawlings. A.W., with a quick nod: "He thrived on having multiple lives. You'll never get to the truth. It was his business to keep it secret."

This was his unstated theme: all preconceptions must be stripped away. It's like entering a dark forest; you see flitting shapes and assume they are birds. But they may be drifting leaves. They may be flying bats. They may be something that isn't supposed to exist. Whatever you happen to think you must be prepared to disavow.

I'll leave you in peace, but first some lines of verse I read the other day. They come from Auden's poem on the death of Freud but apply, I think, to W.C.:

> . . . But he went his way,
> Down among the Lost People like Dante, down
> to the stinking fosse where the injured
> lead the ugly life of the rejected.
>
> And showed what evil is, not, as we thought,
> Deeds that must be punished, but our lack of faith,
> Our dishonest mood of denial,
> the concupiscence of the oppressor.

"I can't begin to tell you," I wrote to Sam, "how grateful I am for your extraordinary kindness in writing to me in such detail. Not only because I find what you say engrossing, but because I read it with enhanced appreciation knowing how it must drain you to bring it all together. I am increasingly excited by your subtlety, and the compass of your curiosity. . . . I write from a boat, after a bad preliminary passage. Three thousand miles to go." I closed the letter confident that I might have been let in on the makings of a masterpiece.

Daniel Kornstein (Esq.) writes to tell me he approves of my national service proposal and to enclose a blast he has published against a rather thoughtless sentence in *Time* magazine, ruminating over the appointment of David Souter to the Supreme Court. "A Supreme Court Justice's fondness for books strikes some people as a threat to the Republic. According to *Time* (Aug. 6) the more serious question" about Judge Souter is whether a man who seems to prefer books to people can empathize with and understand the problems of ordinary people. Kornstein chews over that fear until there is little left of it except pity for the man who framed those thoughtless words. "It is quite amazing what Judge Souter, by saying nothing before the Senate Committee, has elicited in others," I wrote to Mr. Kornstein, "including me."

My exchanges with Kornstein have been interesting. He was the lawyer for the author Joe McGinniss when Joe was being tried not exactly for libel, but for "contract fraud." He had been induced by Dr. Jeffrey MacDonald, a former captain in the Green Berets, to become his confidant during the doctor's trial—he was charged with murdering his pregnant wife and two children. Dr. MacDonald was found guilty of murder, and, having exhausted all appeals, went off to spend his life in jail. Meanwhile, his confidant, McGinniss, after a few weeks of the trial, became convinced that the subject he was writing a book about was indeed guilty of murder, and he wrote to say so in a best-selling book, *Fatal Vision*. MacDonald filed a lawsuit—not because McGinniss had made any commitment to write only an exculpatory account but because, MacDonald said, McGinniss had defrauded him by *pretending* to be convinced of his innocence at a time when he had actually concluded that he was guilty.

During the trial in Los Angeles, McGinniss had called and urgently asked me to testify, as a professional writer, on the subject of an author's ethics. I arranged to do so, while perplexed that a convicted murderer could sue a writer who had arrived at the same conclusion as the jury. But, it slowly transpired, the question *this* jury cared about was whether Joe, in his letters to the doctor, had lied to him to the point of committing fraud.

After I was sworn in, Kornstein asked me on the stand whether in my judgment a journalist is bound to reveal his conclusions about somebody he is writing about, and I said no, I didn't think so. For instance, I said, suppose I was writing a biography of Senator Cranston and discovered that he was a bigamist with a second wife living in Florida. And he were to say to me, halfway through the project, "Bill, you've heard that crazy rumor about my having another family in Florida—you don't believe that, do you?" I'd probably say, "Of course not, Senator."

On cross examination the murderer's lawyer said, "Aha, Mr. Buckley, you believe in lying!" So I said, Easy does it, Mr. whatever-his-name-was, there are critical gradations in defining a lie, as you may know even if you haven't read Sissela Bok's book on the subject. If in my little cottage in the woods I had seen a refugee from a Nazi posse run off on the left-hand road and the gang leader five minutes later, in hot pursuit, asked me, *"Where did he go!"* and I said, "That way," pointing to the right-hand road, I wouldn't think of myself as a liar, any more than I would if my wife were to say, "Darling, am I still the most beautiful woman in the world?" and I were to say, "Yes."

Incredibly, the McGinniss trial ended in a hung jury, with only one woman sticking by him, the others concluding that his misleading letters to the doctor amounted to fraud. Moreover, several of the jurors, interviewed after the trial, commented that they had found me "arrogant," a conclusion obviously indefensible and probably unconstitutional. At any rate, rather than risk another expensive trial, Kornstein was given no alternative by the insurance company than to go along with a costly settlement of $350,000. That money went to the murderer, with the interesting reservation that he can't spend it because California says you can't spend money made as the result of the commission of a felony. (If Dr. MacDonald hadn't killed his wife and children, there'd have been no book, and no profits.) One of these days in my spare time, when I am about ninety, I intend to read that entire trial transcript to find out just what it was that caused a jury to side with a man they knew had murdered his wife and children (the judge had instructed all parties that the earlier verdict was not to be challenged nor, in connection with arriving at a verdict on the points here under contention, relied upon), on a question that had primarily to do with journalistic technique rather than basic morals. Joe is Irish, and I gather that in those letters he probably went overboard, in the judgment of the jury, in blarneying MacDonald into thinking that Joe considered him a really nice guy.

A column by James Jackson Kilpatrick (I receive all of his columns from the syndicate). He begs all readers to write to Governor Wilder of Virginia to plead for the commutation of the death sentence given to Joe Giarratano. "On Oct. 1 the Supreme Court turned down his last appeal. His legal roads have run out. If Gov. Doug Wilder refuses to intervene, Joe will be executed before the end of the year. . . . I learned of the case three years ago. I spent hours reading the record and came away deeply troubled. I am not sure that Joe is guilty; I am not sure he is innocent; but I have spent fifty years covering courts and I am certain of this: He was not convicted beyond a reasonable doubt." I write to the governor: ". . . It seems to me a case that cries out for executive clemency and I urge you to give thought to Mr. Kilpatrick's eloquent plea." (The governor commuted the death sentence in February 1991.)

Helen Waitkevicz complains about the clearing of [my] throat on *Firing Line* "in an effort to take care of a post-nasal drip which can be helped by taking medication to eliminate this problem. You may confirm this observation by listening to a tape of the 9/1/90 program. Another observation is that, often, you wear shirts that are too small to encompass your neck size, making your collar wrinkled and unkempt. I hope you can accept these comments from a septuagenarian who is sensitive to negatives about public figures that are seen and heard on television." "Dear Miss Waitkevicz: Believe me, I am most flattered that you should take the trouble to write to me. I'm also very glad you don't have to pay my bills at my doctor, who has attempted to cope with that problem for years. Sometimes I seem to have it licked, other times it drives me—and others—to distraction. On the matter of the shirts, they are good and large, but I seem to have protruding tonsils. Perhaps the effect of the apoplexy I am so regularly given by my guests."

And then to this season's most charming letter—requesting something. The writer, a student in law school, wanted from me nothing less than a profound essay in which I would take the affirmative on the question, Should drugs be legalized?—for the writer's quarterly publication, which he serves as co-editor, along with a liberal. It is a three-page letter, and Tom Kennedy will certainly make a persuasive lawyer. "This correspondent has been an admirer of yours for over a decade, though more particularly since September 1981 when, while awaiting my flight from La Guardia to Washington, I bought my first copy of *National Review*. In a short time I became a subscriber. I promise to renew my

Sealestial (71 feet) berths up alongside a water-
supply boat in Lisbon and takes on 1,600
gallons. The transfer takes about an hour.
Other arrangements, one assumes, are made
to water the Golden Odyssey.

Ready to go on the first leg: Tony Leggett, Dan Merritt, Christopher Little, Dick Clurman, WFB, Van Galbraith

Powering out of the Tagus River

Routine harbor bustle

We're off.

"Everyone agreed it was either the worst night or second worst they'd ever spent at sea…"

WFB: 'A bloody nightmare.'…Danny: 'Just pure nasty.
I counted thirty-five hours.'…Tony: 'I've never been
in that strength wind, trying to keep things safely
in control.'

"…Somewhere, over the rainbow, lies Funchal."

We are heading in to the dock at Gomera. It was from here that Columbus set sail for the New World.

The church still stands where Columbus prayed before setting out.

WFB, *praying to the same God.*

A *final walk before the long stretch at sea.*

This was the little house Columbus stayed in while preparing to set sail. The building is now a monument and an art gallery.

The centerpiece of the public park in Gomera: a mosaic of Columbus's transatlantic route.

Dinner, below

Lunch, above

Departing Funchal. The harbor lights cavort about an open shutter.

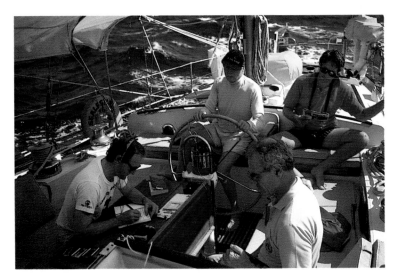

Carefree

2,600 miles to go

Jibe ho

A halyard is tangled.

"It was mid-morning and very hot—'Let's swim,' I said. The swimming ladder was put in place, and we all had our last, blissful swim off the Sealestial *and I thought briefly of the sweetness of life."*

subscription after I extricate myself from the rubble of a $50,000 law school debt. I must say that the greatest revelation of the biography by Mr. Judis, which I read in the summer, was the critically harsh reception received by [your book] *Overdrive*. I recall that on an unusually chilly evening in the late autumn of 1983, while serving as the Officer of the Day at Fort McClellan, Alabama, I enjoyed that fine work in a single sitting. You introduced me to a notion of achievement, service, and motivation which even Marine boot camp and Army officer training had inadequately addressed. I now measure myself against those high standards. Since then, I have pursued graduate studies in political science and English literature, taught high school, and—at this writing—am completing my third year at Syracuse University College of Law."

And so on, endearing and generous, leading to his request. To which I reply, "Dear Mr. Kennedy: To begin with, my answer is no—it will be five years before I am caught up with my commitments, and to say yes to you means to forfeit on one of these—no fair. But I truly enjoyed the wit and charm of your letter and rejoice that you are involved in that journal [copies of which he had enclosed]. I thought your piece on pornography especially effective. If you are in New York any time I am there, I would be happy to lunch with you." I didn't hear back from Mr. Kennedy, but I expect to hear of him, one day: He will be a winner.

I learned quite by surprise soon after the death of my friend, Fernando Valenti, that I had been named his executor. A lengthy telephone conversation with his son confirmed what I already knew, that poor Fernando died indigent. "If you act as his executor," my lawyer had told me, "what it means is that everybody who writes you with a claim against Fernando or even a question about his estate you will refer to me for a reply. I will make that reply, and bill you for it. If you withdraw as executor, the state will appoint one, and you will receive no bills from me." His son, Miguel, had agreed, in a long phone call, that there was no point in my acting as executor of a nonexistent estate (of which Miguel is the sole beneficiary), and worries instead about finding the money to reimburse his uncle for his father's funeral bills. I write now to Fernando's lawyer, to the effect that as soon as I get back from my trip I'll execute the withdrawal papers my lawyer will bill me for designing. There was nothing I could do for Fernando now. I tried very hard to help him while he was alive.

Ah, a note from my beloved Chaucy Bennetts. I remember when she first copy-read one of my novels, four or five books back, the hair standing on my head as I noted her fine meticulousness, the corrections and suggestions done with the total reserve of the copy editor who seems temperamentally to prefer anonymity. But this I would not permit, and effected a brief meeting at which I poured out my admiration for her. I have laid eyes on her only twice, but I feel very strongly about her, and invited her to the Thirty-fifth Anniversary dinner. She was sick, and dispatched, instead, her son. "Dear Bill: Somewhere I read that you will be sixty-five on Sunday the twenty-fourth. Having been sixty-five for two years now (and who knows how many years to come), I can only say that I wish I could have reached that milestone with the sparkle and grace you bring to it. I think I envy even more the elegance with which you will—eventually—become an elder statesman. It was so sweet of you to write inquiring after my health (it was a long recovery but yes, I am better), but I appreciate even more your evaluation of my son, Bruce, as an engaging presence. That he is, and I concur wholly objectively. Stay well and enjoy your birthday. Love, Chaucy." How splendid to come upon a letter like that in the middle of the ocean; as though a falling star.

Watch time. I am called to the cockpit.

The wind was taking us at a good eight knots, and we were using the mainsail and the MPS (Multiple Purpose Sail), which is a light, deep-chuted sail like a spinnaker, though its pocket is not so pronounced, and its tack is fastened down at the bow, permitting the genoa to go up simultaneously when you are headed pretty much straight downwind. The weather was bright and the sea surges bracing. We were well into the rhythm of the voyage and took to betting every day on distances we would travel in twenty-four hours, between 1300 (lunchtime) and 1300 (lunchtime). We were, in fact, averaging just over 180 miles—the daily distance traveled by Columbus, according to

Van, skiing at sea

Morison—on those days that he had wind, which was most of the time.

Van had been busy during the morning, finally setting up his exercise machine in the aft cockpit. He had considered bringing along a stationary bicycle, but decided that the ship's motions favored something with a lower center of gravity, and so brought aboard one of those contraptions supposed to simulate the motion of the body in cross-country skiing . . . Right-hand-right-leg-forward, left-hand-left-leg-aft, then reverse the movements, and so on. Van and Douglas spent much of the morning assembling the machine, and Van then fashioned a harness of sorts to hold him steady. It worked only in that he was able to get up a good sweat, but his exertions were primarily the result of trying to remain upright rather than of skiing cross-country.

After he was through he went forward to the bow where the anchor shower reposes: a hose with a spray at the end of it, permitting as protracted a (saltwater) shower as you want, no drain on the ship's freshwater supply. He joined us for lunch, lively with the pleasure he gets from exercise.

"Van's joke at lunch," Christo wrote, "is that 'Willie Horton is now saying that he and Dukakis were really never *that* close.' " Van picked up the latest issue of *Laptop Computer,* a magazine in which an interview with me is carried. He comments, "That is the last magazine in existence that Bill hadn't given an interview to. He's finally closed the loop." Which crack reminded Christopher, in his journal, of a line "WFB used a couple of years ago: 'I have something extremely rare, an unautographed copy of Edward Heath's sailing memoirs.' " Only it wasn't I who said it—I was quoting to Christo something Malcolm Muggeridge had told me. The lunch was good, spicy, and relaxed, the boat was charging ahead with pride and pleasure. The watches dispersed.

"While reading about Dukakis and Bush in my cabin this P.M. after a lunch of grilled cheese sandwiches with jalapeños," Christo wrote, "I heard the cry 'Dolphins!,' scrambled up on deck to find everyone gathered about the bow. There must have been a dozen of them, keeping pace with our prow in that effortless way of theirs, leaping out of the water, once five at a time in teasing synchronicity, exhaling loudly through their blow spouts, diving back under, crisscrossing back and forth, ramming through the cerulean blue with their bottle noses. Bill Draper ventured that it was 'a scene and a half,' and yes it was, a Thanksgiving all in itself."

Bill Draper was on duty. And later wrote, "Happy day. Time passes quickly. A lot of action. I am getting to feel comfortable at the helm. In fact I set a new speed record at 10.7 knots. Speed record immediately broken by Doug 11.7 knots." Below, Liz had given Christopher the advertisement for seasick prevention I had told the crew of Leg One about in Lisbon. Christopher read about the device. In his journal: "When Liz showed me the ad, I looked down at this elastic manacle I've been wearing on my left wrist since we left Grand Canary, this 'Nei-Kuan' bracelet with a small round plastic nub that presses a spot between the flexor tendons, thereby (allegedly) staving off *La nausée.* (Liz says she is going to write the manufacturer an angry letter about how they weren't worth a damn.) The first time I saw one was on

Reggie's wrist, in the hospital. I asked him if it was working, counteracting the effects of the chemotherapy. He gave me one of those Reggie-esque answers, endlessly deliberate, considered, scientific, ambiguous; then showed me his pot pills, extract of tetrahydrocannabinol in a suspension of sesame oil (to kill the high; God forbid that Calvinistic American pharmacology should allow dying people a little buzz on their way to the graveyard), with a certain risible pride: 'They're not easy to get.' Two months later the bracelet was still there, only now it was loose around the skeletal wrist. The morning he died I closed his eyes and removed his wedding ring, gave that to Margo, who had placed it on his finger at Trinity Church only three months before; then I took the band, slipped it off, put it in my pocket, left Reg for the last time and closed the door. It's in the small cedar chest that he and Pup buried in the sand at Treasure Island so many years ago."

Christo was, back then, six years old. Reggie and I designed a pirate's map which gave directions in "blood" to a little spot of sand at Eaton's Neck ("Treasure Island," we would ever after refer to it) where we had furtively buried a small chest that contained jewelry from Woolworth's, the discovery of which had transported Christo and his seven-year-old companion.

On board that night, we saw the movie *Harvey*. I had quite forgotten what an enchantment it is, or at least for me—some of my companions were not especially taken by it. I found the good nature of the protagonist (James Stewart as Elwood P. Dowd) and the affection he felt for his imaginary companion, the six-foot-tall rabbit, Harvey, something to which at first I condescended, then patronized, then egged on, then exulted in. There is one scene of heartrending suspense. It is the movie's climax, really, and what it does is pit the relentless good nature of Elwood P. Dowd up against his dependence on Harvey. The same doctor who had conspired to put Dowd away on the grounds that he was committable—a man who imagined the existence of an invisible rabbit with whom he converses as with an adult friend!—himself becomes hypnotized by the delusion and forms an attachment to the rabbit. As Dowd prepares to leave the sanatorium—with Harvey—the doctor stops him, and addresses the invisible rabbit: "Harvey, would you consent to stay with me?" Harvey evidently turns to ask Dowd what he thinks about this, and Mr. Dowd replies, *"It's entirely up to*

you, Harvey. You do exactly as you like." The doctor smiles triumphantly and opens the door for Harvey to go back in with him. The
camera catches the face of Elwood P. Dowd and we are allowed to
intuit the agony he feels over the impending loss of Harvey, his best
friend. Suddenly he looks up brightly, a radiant smile on his face.
*"You've changed your mind, Harvey? You want to come with me? Well,
that's just fine, now! What do you say we go down to Elmer's and have
a little drink?"*

Elwood Dowd was rewarded for his adamant disposition to sacrifice
uncomplaining. Later that night when, halfway through my watch, it
was Christo's turn to come on duty, he told me he had been reading
my book *Gratitude* and by coincidence had come across the sentence,
in a passage ruing the grip of drugs in America, that read, "The only
happy alcoholic I ever knew was Harvey." I had evidently remembered
that much about *Harvey* from seeing James Stewart doing a revival of
the Pulitzer-winning play years ago. It is a wonderful fairy tale and with
it G. K. Chesterton could have made yet another case for the triumph
of spirit. There are lots of very good reasons not to drink alcohol, but
there is no denying that the total absence of it can dry up those little
capillaries of bonhomie and light-spiritedness that accelerate gregarious
contact, and contact with Elwood P. Dowd was a magical experience.

I thought back with amusement, and tenderness, on the *Sea Cloud*'s
stop at Pitcairn Island, whose inhabitants turned during the last century to Seventh-Day Adventism and are pledged not to touch demon
rum. There are fifty-eight people who live there. During the day we had
poked about the two-square-mile island where, the same year that our
John Adams left the White House, their John Adams (the only surviv-
ing mutineer of the mutiny on the *Bounty*) had taken charge: a minus-
cule colony that mysteriously survives notwithstanding two corporate
attempts (1831, 1852) to move it lock, stock, and barrel elsewhere (to
Tahiti, and the Norfolk Islands). Forty-eight of the "islanders" now
came to us in the late afternoon, boarding the *Sea Cloud* for a visit.
Four generations, some haphazardly offering this and that artifact for
sale, all of them talking, laughing, listening; the children were obsessed
with the toilet (they have VCR television on Pitcairn, and outhouses).
They don't drink, as I say—unless you offer them a drink.

The time came for the *Sea Cloud* to leave. Three quarters of the

entire population of Pitcairn went down the gangway and packed into
one of their two sturdy longboats. But before casting off they paused
alongside our great bark and sang to us. Four hymns; I swear they
sounded as good and as full as the Mormon Tabernacle Choir. The last
words of their apopemptic hymn were:

> In the sweet bye and bye
> In the beautiful land beyond the sky . . .
> We shall part, never more, when we meet
> On the be-yoo-tee-fool shore . . .

Returning to their little acre in the South Pacific, the islanders
managed to leave our urbane company of sixty sailors and sixty passen-
gers, headed out on our luxury vessel toward civilization, feeling lonely.
Christo and I felt no loneliness in our little ketch, in the dead of night,
in mid-Atlantic.

CHAPTER THIRTEEN

The Birth of the Satcom

There is the allure, for many who sail avocationally, of being inaccessible when at sea. When, late in the summer, I first told Christopher about our proposed Satcom unit I could sense the sniff of disdain. When I told him that besides being useful for receiving and transmitting messages at sea it could also: a) give us some idea of dangerous weather ahead; b) give vessels in our area some idea that we were about to sink; and c) perhaps transmit, from his hearth in Washington to our saloon in *Sealestial,* a goo-goo-Daddy from little Caitlin, his daughter. Christo's interest sharpened.

I wasn't always convinced myself. We have known that ships have telexes since the Day of the *Titanic,* so what is so very new about—I looked down at the notepad to make sure I had the name straight—COMSAT's Inmarsat-C Store-and-Forward Satellite Data Messaging Service? Danny told me that the satellite transceiver was a miniaturized model of the large unit used by commercial boats. This unit is designed for the small boat, boats as small as our own; little fishing boats would be heavy users. And what would it do?

Using your own laptop computer you could, prospectively, transmit messages to any telex number in the world. And since telex units are equipped with relays to other electronic systems, we would be able to communicate regularly with my little network of MCI users, most importantly my own office; and they in turn could communicate with us.

It was with great zeal that I waited for Danny to bring in, from his obliging friends at COMSAT Corporation in Washington, the Thrane & Thrane unit they were going to lend us to try out on our passage. Several manufacturers had promised to lend us one, but evidently got caught up in production snags or were busy perfecting their instruments, which were to hit the market imminently.

COMSAT was willing to lend us one of the units they were testing. The system was still in what they called a "pre-operational" phase, and they were anxious to get some real-life experience on the various models being manufactured before the system came up to full service. COM-SAT doesn't actually manufacture the equipment, but is the service provider through its coast-earth stations for people who will be sending messages from these terminals into or out of the United States.

What Danny brought into the office was an eye-catchingly small suitcase, about three feet long, eighteen inches wide, eight inches thick, weighing fifty pounds. In the presence of a proud COMSAT engineer we opened the case—we were going to test it there and then. All that he required was a southern exposure and we would find that at my sister's apartment, facing the East River.

On lifting the lid of the carrying case you see a blue bubble bath, protective plastic macaroni designed to shield the three imbedded units. The first is the antenna. It is about ten inches tall, eight inches in diameter at its widest point, near the base, and weighs five pounds. Then there is the terminal unit, the heart of the system. It is the size of a laptop computer. The third unit is exactly that, a laptop computer, whose principal service to us would be to print incoming and outgoing messages.

We entered a car, motored to Fifty-first Street, and went up to Priscilla's apartment on the fourth floor, facing the East River. Getting ready to transmit was as easy as perching the antenna out on the balcony, i.e., facing south, and staring at a gauge on the right end of the unit. It showed five vertical black bars. You would stare at them for a minute or so and suddenly one or more would grow in height and in girth. When they reached triple the size of the passive little bars we first saw, that would mean that they were in communion with a COM-SAT satellite. There are five bars and three of them need to be enlarged before you can transmit.

All five of ours were now alive and I was invited to plug in my laptop to the unit. To transmit, you work through several questions posed in menus on the laptop. You need to indicate that you wish to transmit, then feed into the unit the document you wish to transmit, indicate which ocean you are transmitting from, and to which addressee you are sending the message. For your convenience, several of the most frequently used addresses are already programmed, waiting for you to pick one out, much as an automatic telephone can offer you FIRE, AMBULANCE, or PIZZA by pushing the coded numbers.

We had entered Tony Savage's number in my office, so that I needed only to point the cursor to it. Now I faced a screen that said, "**Message?**" I could extemporize the communiqué if I did not have a packaged message all ready to type out and send him. I tapped out, from my reserves of originality, "What hath God wrought?" We waited—Danny, the engineer, and I—exchanging not a word, waiting for the telephone to ring. In about five minutes it rang—Tony had our message!

This accessory would be seriously useful, for instance in dispatching my columns. But Danny wisely thought I should practice with it during the weekend, so I parked the antenna outside my garage-study door and hacked away, sending messages to my own modem. Because I was using a system not yet ready to be used by the general public, the results were—eccentric. I telephoned to the engineer and he cautioned me against sending messages more than 250 words long, for fear of "overcrowding the 'pre-op service.' "

Weeks later, at sea, we were exhilarated by our COMSAT Standard C service and the Thrane & Thrane unit, but also frustrated by its shortcomings, inevitable in prototypes.

Our experience taught us several things and we passed on our observations to COMSAT. The first is that the satellite in the sky that transmits shore-to-ship does not have, so to speak, a holding tank. It receives the transmission designed for *Sealestial* and shoots it down to the boat. If our computer was not in the receptive mode, during our experiment, that transmission was never seen again. Meaning?

Suppose that at 1532 GMT the satellite sends you a message from your wife. But on your ship, a) The antenna on deck at that moment is not shaking hands with the satellite world—its five tumescent bars have shrunk to the miniature size. Your message goes to the bottom of the sea. *And is never retransmitted.* Or, b) Suppose that at 1532 GMT your antenna is working all right but your transceiver is not—it has run out of power, as ours did a dismaying number of times. (You are not going to keep a sailboat's generator running night and day purely for the convenience of your Standard C unit.) You plug in the unit to the ship's inverter, which should give it the power it needs. But . . . you inspect it later and find that all the lights are blinking, which means *"I am completely out of power, do something about me."* It takes more than one hour to give it the reserves of power necessary to bring it back to life. And by that time? . . . Exactly.

Our experiences, along with those of others who helped test the system at sea, have persuaded COMSAT to develop a holding tank capability to alleviate this problem, and it is expected that this will have been done when their full commercial service is in place toward the end of 1992.

On the other hand, the transmission problems don't occur in the ship-to-shore direction. Because when your office, say, dials to check whether there are messages in the INBOX, it is going to say, "Yes, we have a message waiting for you," irrespective of whether the message came in at midnight or three days ago. On shore, storage facilities are ample. That is not true of the Inmarsat satellite itself which, as noted, has to discharge messages the moment they are received, or at most a few minutes later. This is not a shortcoming for a vessel that keeps its transceiver lit up day and night. But sailboats don't like to do that kind of thing, so we settled on three set hours in the afternoon during which we would be receptive to messages.

The following gives a flavor of our shore-to-ship experiences:

—RE YOUR PROBLEM WITH THE BATTERY I SPOKE WITH THE MANUFAC-
TURER WHO TELLS ME THE EARLY VERSIONS OF THE BATTERY CHARGER,
WHICH YOURS IS, OFTEN HAVE PROBLEMS RECHARGING DUE TO ELEVATED
TEMPERATURES AND LACK OF SUFFICIENT COOLING. SUGGEST . . .

. . . .

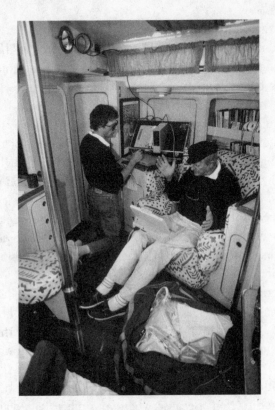

COMSAT's transmitting unit.

—BILL: UTTERLY BAFFLED BY YOUR INABILITY TO CONTACT CLURMAN. DOES NOT COMPUTE, INASMUCH AS THE NUMBER YOU HAVE FOR HIM IS INDEED CORRECT (338-8411). TO REPEAT THE OBVIOUS: DO *EXACTLY* WHAT YOU DO TO CONTACT ME, WITH THIS *SINGLE* EXCEPTION: INSTEAD OF USING THE NATIONAL REVIEW NUMBER (120-0058) USE 338-8411. THERE SHOULD BE NO OTHER VARIATION *WHATSOEVER*. IF YOU DO *EXACTLY* THAT, THEN IT IS SCIENTIFICALLY IMPOSSIBLE FOR YOUR MESSAGES NOT TO REACH HIM. MINE GET THROUGH TO YOU. CLURMAN'S GET THROUGH TO YOU. YOURS GET THROUGH TO ME. THEREFORE SOMETHING DIFFERENT IS BEING DONE WITH YOURS TO CLURMAN. AND IF YOU PLEAD INFALLIBILITY, I WILL SUBMIT AS EVIDENCE YOUR COMMUNICATION OF TODAY. WORD COUNT: 451. TYPOS: 310 . . . [We accomplished the scientifically impossible: We could never get a message through to Clurman.]

. . .

Holding out COMSAT's little aerial to test satellite reception

—RECEIVED ONE MESSAGE FROM YOU TODAY, SENT AT 1239 YOUR
TIME. *HOWEVER* IT WAS A REPEAT OF YESTERDAY'S MESSAGE—THE
FOURTH TIME THE SAME MESSAGE WAS TRANSMITTED.

Yes, that was a problem of another category. When all had gone well,
about five or ten minutes after a transmission the little Compaq would
clatter out on the paper roll, *"Message delivery successful."* But sometimes it would say *"Message delivery unsuccessful. Try at some other
time."* You would then go through the entire cycle. And sometimes a
third time. But it might prove that all four of the transmissions had
in fact been successful, leaving your office with four identical messages.

What we have here is what in the computer world is called "sludge-
time," defined as that period between when the operator and his
hardware first come into contact with each other and that time—a
week or a month or six months later—when the kinks are out of his
system and his machine's and the two of them are grooving together.
The system is already out of its pre-operational phase and basic service
is available, at this writing, through several coast-earth stations in the

Inmarsat system. COMSAT continues to conduct experiments and to pursue more sophisticated applications during what it calls its "interim service" period.

And when those applications become available—in the very near future—and all the kinks are ironed out, it will mean the end of the isolation of the small boat at sea. The advantages of the Standard C are overwhelming. There is no static, no (hypothetical) delay, and there is total privacy in the communications. The Satcom can be retained to give you printed news bulletins once a day, or twice a day, or more. And I have mentioned emergencies. By depressing a particular button, a distress message is given priority and all the ships at sea are alerted via the Coast Guard to your burst appendix or to your imminent capsize.

Cost? I have the feeling the accessory world is fiddling with the question. The unit we used will sell for about seven thousand dollars. As for the use of the satellite, no doubt there will be give-and-take depending on how many idle hours the Inmarsat satellite ends up with if it continues to charge users at the present price level. At the suggested one cent per letter there is no invitation to prolixity: a standard newspaper column (750 words) would come to (average number of letters per word, 5.2) forty-two dollars and fifty cents, forty-one dollars and fifty cents more than by simple shore-to-shore MCI; about three fifths of what telex would charge. Our own bill, over one month, was $282; perhaps we were given a discount owing to our travails.

But then, at sea (or elsewhere) you don't really want to encourage verbosity, at least not in ship-to-shore transmissions. Still, there is no substitute for reaching out to someone at home neatly and quickly when you want to. The usual radio (single sideband) is a never-ending pain in the neck, or perhaps that is so only of the *Sealestial's*—years before, we had very little trouble on *Cyrano* with our unit. And the big mastodonic SatComs are huge and unsightly, too big for a sailboat save of enormous length, and unbearably expensive. Anyhow, put the Standard C Satcom alongside Loran and Trimble GPS as aides at sea that will be deemed indispensable for blue-water sailors a few years from now.

· CHAPTER FOURTEEN ·

The Blues

Even when there are no storms, there is discomfort. This is so especially when the wind is behind you. The reason for it is that you don't get the kind of lateral stability that wind abeam gives you. The ship pitches, and it rolls; pitch-and-roll: we had had two or three thousand miles of this when crossing the Pacific five years earlier. The downwind scene is thought ideal by the uninitiated. It isn't. There's not only the pitch-and-roll but also the absence of good circulating air, since your own boat's speed eats up the first seven to ten knots of wind speed. The whole story is there in one paragraph from Christo's journal.

> I've got that mid-Atlantic lethargy, born of never really being able to fall asleep due to the following seas. Nights (and days) we roll and roll (*and roll*), sails set wing-on-wing, sliding back and forth on bedsheets, head wedged between a pillow and arm till the arm starts to itch from lack of blood; rolling over and trying again and again and again . . . Crash from the galley, Liz sticking her head in to say, "Don't walk barefoot in the passageway, a glass broke," slosh and dribble and the fish-warm Atlantic comes in the hatch, dampening the quarter of the bunk onto which the seas keep pushing you, dogging the hatch till the room starts to smell like the bottom half of the dirty laundry hamper, thumping on deck . . . sheets clammy, skin itchy, stomach sour from coffee and

antibiotics; really got to get some sleep before going on the one-to-five watch. . . . What time is it? Hold up watch dial, make out luminescent 11:45, too late for a sleeping pill, wedge pillow against cheek, try again, another crash of kitchenware into the passageway, clatter of plastic, muffle of voices.

Here our advantage—Van's and mine—was manifest. In the rear cabin there is less pitching and, except in foul weather, the glass hatch can be left open, admitting air. The noise from the galley is remote.

"Christo's and my watch," Tony wrote, "descended into a long list of questions such as, 'Why are we doing this?' 'Are we halfway yet?' 'Halfway from the Canaries? Or the Cape Verdes, or from Lisbon?' 'How much water do we have left?' 'How much beer?' 'How much mineral water?' 'How much longer do we have to stay cooped upon this thing?' 'When will we get there!' *'Why are we here?'* "

Tony, once again to the breach

And there are individual worries. Tony's has to do with his inventory of clothes. He is careful to ration his clean shirts, and comments on those worn by others. "Bill Draper has the most diverse causes to plug on his T-shirts: ExCom; UNDP commemoratives; the Vice President of the United States; but most cryptically, he wore a shirt that shows time zones all over the world and says, *'It's time to change your underwear.'* This led to Van's story about the attempt to boost morale, made by a Polish troop commander, who announced amid great cheering a change of underwear. 'Okay, Kowalsky, you change with Brozky, and you, Kozinscki, you change with Zamanski . . .'"

And, of course, the mind focuses on what one is missing back home. Tony wrote vividly on the subject. ". . . While I'm on the topic of Claire, I find myself thinking more and more about her, particularly while in my bunk. On the first leg, what with the storm, in a cramped, wet bunk, feeling a little seasick and sorry for myself, my thoughts were rarely about intimate details of my married life. But now, with the motion less violent, in a bigger and drier cabin, a crisp set of sheets under me, and an eyelet pillow case, my thoughts have turned decidedly amorous. It takes little to imagine Claire stretched out alongside me, perhaps sleeping quietly in my arms but preferably just waking up, moving, and turning toward me. . . ." (I draw the curtains at this point, recording only that Claire *is* enchanting.)

It is less distracting to think of homesickness in extraconnubial ways. Still, Christo had his own problem: "Thinking often of Caitlin [age two and a half]. Imagine her curled up beside me in bed with her penguin. Think of Van and Bootsie's terrible loss when Julie died, age eight. Not at all certain I would ever recover from that. I know life goes on, but I think life might go on without me in such a case. No point in morbid reflection; only wish it known (to myself primarily) how grateful I am for my little girl, how I want to express that by being a good father."

And homesickness and discomfort are made more acute by sleepiness. TONY: "Christo and I compared notes on the 1100–0300. The conversation started with the nature of our degrees of sleeplessness and the effect of that sleeplessness on everyone's mood and ability to function. It has been cutting into our journal-keeping and even into the reading of all those big books we'd been planning on getting through. In that disgruntled mood we wondered about long voyages in general.

After the first one, which is an important landmark in any sailor's life ('Looks good in the résumé,' as Walter Cronkite once said), subsequent passages begin to lose their allure. There might be one or two interesting events which make it somewhat worthwhile, like Kapingamarangi in the Pacific. [The five-star atoll we came across, described in *Racing Through Paradise.*] But in general, the two to four weeks away from home and wife become more trial than adventure. Christo had quite deliberately made the point that he would not do the entire trip, only a portion. I guess I've come around to the same point."

That mood is what I designate as *in partu* blues, the blues that come while giving birth. (There are no *post partum* blues in sailing.) They *always* happen. The trick is to anticipate them. Bill Draper wrote in his journal only a few days ago, "Tony is married to Claire now and fears some of his sailing days may be over. He doesn't expect to have a one-month stag cruise every year, but once a decade with Bill Buckley is like a chance to live two lifetimes. No bride could object. . . . Douglas's bride of one month, editor in chief of *Cruising World* magazine, when asked if he might go, said, 'I would, if I were invited.' Doug didn't ask twice."

Ah yes, Douglas had been keen to come. But then on Day 6: "Christopher and I on 1–3 and discussion was of how many days left, nine? ten? Who knows? [I knew, more or less. He should have asked me.] But the thrills abate as each of us finds we are missing our wives, soft curves and warm laughs. Each morning now after breakfast I check Bernadette's [trip souvenir] book to see what she has included. And that becomes the focus for my day. I'm feeling ready to get home now. And yet when will I be at 24 × 24 degrees again?"

The reference was to North Latitude 24 degrees, West Longitude 24 degrees—roughly speaking, nowhere; nearest land, Africa. Doug is likelier to remember the romance of his isolation than the homesickness.

Christopher has an explanation for much of it. A theory about me: "The 'no pain, no gain' element. I heard Pup in New Guinea express the belief after a relatively grueling thirty-day crossing of the Pacific— he said, if I recall, 'It doesn't feel this good unless there's some unpleasantness along the way.' Now I recall his beautiful obituary for Malcolm

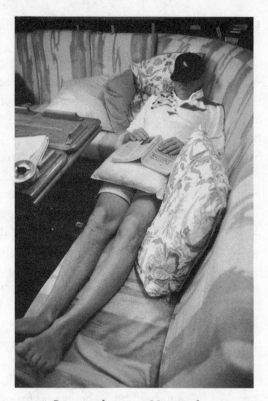

Some authors put Van to sleep.

Muggeridge of two weeks ago in which he alluded to Muggeridge's late-in-life Christian conviction that the central experience of life is, and must be, suffering. Now, Pup likes his creature comforts, it's true, so I don't think the object of his life is to suffer, exactly; but I've heard him extol in nearly sensuous terms the gorgeous feeling of climbing into bed after a day in which he wrote a column, taped three *Firing Lines*, gave two speeches, and closed an issue of *National Review;* or the feeling upon finishing [the writing of] a book."

So? Christo's perception is acute, though my attitude is hardly original. Shakespeare wrote: "If all the year were playing holidays, to sport would be as tedious as to work." Going to bed tired (after a useful day's work) is obviously more enjoyable than going to bed not tired. Moreover, like Christo and all of us, I have never encountered bad weather at sea when I didn't pine for a change in conditions.

And what I said about Muggeridge is worth elaborating at a little more length:

"When he died a week ago," I had written, "the commentators listed his affiliation with Christianity rather as though it had been his next post, after editor of *Punch*. He had been everywhere, doing everything, but his odyssey was not without purpose. He was moving toward Christianity."

"Why did this longing for faith assail me?" he once asked, on *Firing Line*. "Insofar as I can point to anything, it has to do with this profession which both you and I have followed of observing what's going on in the world and attempting to report and comment thereon, because that particular occupation gives one a very heightened sense of the sheer fantasy of human affairs—the sheer fantasy of power and of the structures that men construct out of power—and therefore gives one an intense, overwhelming longing to be in contact with reality. And so you look for reality . . . and ultimately you arrive at the conclusion that reality is a mystery."

I pursued the point in an exchange on a *Firing Line* program. Why did he relish the mystery?

"Because it leads you to God. . . . It's exactly like—Bill, it's exactly like falling in love. You see another human being and for some extraordinary reason you're in a state of joy and ecstasy over that person, but the driving force which enables you to express that and to bring it into your life is love. Without love, it's nothing; it passes. It's the same with seeking reality, and there the driving force we call faith. It's a very difficult thing to define, actually. As an old man, Bill, looking back on one's life, it's one of the things that strike you most forcibly—that the only thing that's taught one anything is suffering. Not success, not happiness, not anything like that. The only thing that really teaches one what life's about . . . is suffering, affliction."

I concluded the column, in which I quoted these words, "He suffered, even at the end; but throughout his lifetime he diminished the suffering of others, at first simply by his wit and intelligence; finally, by his own serenity, which brought serene moments to those graced by his presence."

Christo was right to suggest that I am kept busy by internal impulses of some kind, which reminds me with glee of Hugh Hefner. The godfather of Playboyism was asked, at about the time that his only daughter reached a certain age, whether he would consent for her to appear in his magazine as a Playmate? He stalled, and came up with the adroitest answer in contemporary polemical jousting. "Well," he said, "no. You see, there is still just *a little drop* of Calvinist blood in me. If I could succeed in draining it all into one little finger, I'd chop it off!"

If I'd been there, I'd have been tempted to ask, Would he chop off whichever appendage of his body the Calvinist blood drained into?

Well, I'm not sure the Protestant ethic is all bad, though I do not doubt that those who are good at putting it aside can enjoy more relaxation at sea, when the sea is disposed to oblige.

But speaking of Calvinist drives, I had to continue to tackle the correspondence Christo had brought on board. I went down to the cabin.

I was quietly infuriated (I mean by that that I didn't talk to any of my buddies about it when I first read it) by the note from the editorial page editor of the *Atlanta Constitution*. I had written the newspaper a detailed letter protesting an editorial proclaiming that I had suggested tattooing everyone suffering from AIDS. Now I have back an answer from the editor. He does not find anything in my letter to discredit the "facts" as the paper had reported these facts; our differences are purely "semantic," and so he will not publish it. I soothe myself now by typing out a reply to be sent on our arrival. I write:

> ... You began by asserting that I was a) a prime source of homophobia, b) that I once proposed to brand "gay AIDS victims" with a tattoo on the buttocks. And, lest there be any confusion about my motives, that I at times "dip toward the manners of Buchenwald."

I was able to show in my letter that what I had said earlier was that society should seek out "some sign that would alert anyone" who thought to engage in dangerous practices. And that I thought such a sign—whatever it might be—should be placed where it was likely to be seen by the other unwitting man or woman involved.

A matter of seconds before the specific suggestion first occurred to me, my guest on *Firing Line*, Professor Alan Dershowitz, had sought amplification. Would I, he wanted to know, advocate identical treatment for a rector, a priest, or a nun who got the AIDS virus through blood transfusions—would I require them, too, to carry that sign? I had answered: "I would be impartial in the application . . . I'd have a twelve-year-old child do it if he had gotten the disease from his mother." The idea was to protect people, not to stigmatize them. I suggested that a tattoo on the arm might have the same effect.

My motives were to defend those who do not have the disease. And if the Atlanta editor believed that the difference between what I said and what he said I had said was purely semantic, then we did not speak the same language. His cowardly and unrepentant use of misleading language reminds us that even the editorial page editor of an important newspaper is capable of dipping into the language of *1984*.

This second letter seeking fair treatment, born at sea, was not published either. Indeed, weeks later, the editor in question advised me that any letter of dissent should be limited to three hundred words. What I did do was publish my letter to editor Teepen in my column ("Notes & Asides") in *National Review*. The reaction was interesting, in particular one from a sharp-eyed lady in Pittsburgh who thought the letter something of a model for innocents mauled by editorial arrogance; and then a letter from a Georgian, who wanted permission to give it general circulation in the area to illustrate the unaccountability of the paper's editor. Permission granted.

. . . Which reminded me. I have always thought that Nat Hentoff of the *Village Voice* has a foot in dreamland with his opposition to all libel laws. His grounds are that in a free country, the victim can always take on the tort-feasor in public. Hentoff really *thinks* this, and once or twice cited my own editorial reach as a case in point. Why would somebody like me ever need the courts to set the record straight? But to cite me, e.g., in this example, hardly closes out the case, inasmuch as there are one hundred thousand-plus people in Atlanta who, having no knowledge of the libel committed, read the attack, picturing me as an antihomosexual crusader with branding iron in hand; besides which, what do we do about people who do *not* have their own magazine or column or television show? I hate to cite it because it is so often exploited by the redistributionists, but Hentoff's position brings to mind Anatole France's remark about how "the law, in its majestic equality, forbids the rich as well as the poor to sleep under bridges, to beg in the streets, and to steal bread." There are probably ten million people in America who believe that I came out in favor of tattooing all gays and nothing more and there is nothing I will ever be able to do to disabuse them of that conviction.

On the subject of homosexuality, a letter from Professor Harry Jaffa of Claremont. Rather severe. My learned friend writes to chide me for being too indulgent in my published reply to Marvin Liebman's "outing," as it is now called. Marvin, a very dear and old friend, and sometime conservative organizational entrepreneur, wrote in *National Review* during the summer an open letter in which he said that he was a homosexual and had always been one. He urged conservatives to be more understanding of the phenomenon. Professor Jaffa writes, "I enclose copies of the recent exchange with Liebman—which you initiated. You are a harder man to pin down than O. J. Simpson. I never addressed the question of whether Liebman should be excommunicated. I liked Jesse Helms's comment that if the United States continued on its present course, God would have to make an apology to Sodom and Gomorrah. I do not find in you as yet recognition of the fact that homosexuality calls into question, more radically than anything else, the idea of nature—and therewith of natural law—as the ground of morality. What possible *reason* is there to oppose abortion, not to mention slavery or genocide, if sodomy is not wrong *because* unnatural? Without nature, all moral judgments become ad hoc 'value judgments,' and relativism reigns supreme. Liebman seems to think that as long as he keeps yelling 'I love Jesus' he can bugger his way to eternal bliss."

He encloses a letter Marvin addressed to him. . . . "You stated in your letter to WFB that you 'write as a Jew.' I wonder, therefore, why—with your great knowledge and obvious admiration of the New Testament, which you quote so expertly to make your argument—you have not accepted Jesus Christ as your Savior as I have. In Him you will find the *infinite* love, mercy and compassion which neither you nor I can find in ourselves or in any man. If you so decide, I will be deeply honored to serve as one of your sponsors, if not your godfather. . . .

Finally, let me pose a question: who is closer to the throne of God—Torquemada or the 'sodomite' he had burned at the stake, who continues to profess his love of Jesus until the end?"

To this, Harry had answered: "Your kind offer to act as my sponsor or godfather, should I decide to convert to Christianity, is declined. I might have made a counteroffer to you, to convert to Judaism, except that I have made it a rule throughout my life never to tamper with another man's faith. As to the 'infinite love, mercy and compassion which neither you nor I can find in ourselves or in any man,' rest assured that the God in whom I trust is in no way lacking in those qualities. But while I believe God's compassion is infinite, I do not think it is indiscriminate—certainly not if Paul is to be believed. You ask me, 'Who is closer to the throne of God—Torquemada or the sodomite he had burned at the stake, who continues to profess his love of Jesus until the end?' If memory serves, Torquemada would have professed his love of the sodomite, even as the sodomite professed his for Jesus. Professions of love are not the same thing as love, however, as many a betrayed maiden (not to mention Jesus himself) has learned to her cost. I don't know who was closer to the throne of grace, Torquemada or the sodomite. But I am persuaded that the sodomite's hope of salvation depended upon whether he had repented of his sin."

I write to Harry, "You manage—somehow—to remain endearing even though you say utterly unendearing things. Besides which, surely you miss the point, since it is hardly possible to repent of unnatural inclinations, since inclinations do not disappear upon receipt of absolution." A few months later I'd have asked him to comment on a line I discovered on reading Ari Goldman's *The Search for God at Harvard*: "If a man cannot banish sexual thoughts from his mind, he should put on dark clothes, go to another town, find a woman and satisfy his lust, the Talmud advises. Just be discreet."

The American Academy of Achievement (no less) sends me a letter signed by Henry R. Kravis ("1991 Host Chairman"), Gerald R. Ford ("1976 Honoree"), and Edmund Morris ("1981 Honoree") inviting me to be a guest of honor at the Thirtieth Anniversary Salute to Excellence weekend program in New York City, June 27–29, 1991. "The occasion will culminate with a black-tie Banquet of the Golden

Plate on the evening of Saturday June 29, at the Waldorf-Astoria Hotel. Fifty eminent 'exemplars of excellence'—twenty-five of the Academy's illustrious past honorees now serving on the Golden Plate Awards Council and twenty-five new guests of honor—each a 'representative of the many who excel' in his chosen profession, will meet one another in a unique gathering of leaders and innovators." I write that, unhappily, on that weekend I will be in Australia (if necessary).

A woman in Seattle sends in the first part of a movie script she has undertaken, based on my novel *Mongoose, R.I.P.*, a fictional account of events in Cuba and how they led to the assassination of JFK. Her unfinished script, in my judgment, is very very good.

Six months earlier, in Switzerland, our cook, Julian Booth, had brought me a thickish manuscript. It was a full screenplay of my novel *Saving the Queen*, which script, Julian explained, had been written by a young second lieutenant in the antiterrorist battalion of the Marines with whom he had been corresponding. I smiled on the outside and groaned on the inside: clearly I would need, for the morale of our fighting men, to spend a fair amount of time on the work of a young amateur. I woke, for some reason, at three the following morning, picked up the ms. intending to read the first ten pages, and read it all. I found it superb. It is a frustration unique to the movie world that no matter how good a script is, this, in my experience, has *nothing* to do with whether a movie is going to be made from it. We have all heard about the scriptwriter (I forget his name) who earns $300,000 per script, does four or five a year (so much in demand is he) with this interesting lifelong record: No movie has *ever* been made based on one of his scripts.

The Hollywood people are utterly unpredictable and, in most cases, inscrutable—as likely to hand out a hundred thousand dollars in return for a paragraph that sketches a movie situation that captures their imagination as to reward a fine script by making it into a movie.

The nearest I have ever got, with nine best-selling novels, to getting into that door was in collaboration with Fraser Heston, son of Charlton and a professional movie producer. He was so enthusiastic about the possibilities for Blackford Oakes that he took off several months to write a screenplay of *See You Later Alligator*. He failed to crack that part of Hollywood that feeds the movie studios but told me exultantly one summer day over the phone that he and another producer, equally enthusiastic, had all but finally persuaded one of the networks to do a two-hour special on one of the Oakes books and, depending on its success, perhaps go on with a series. They wanted me to travel to Hollywood to meet with the five members of the top team. "They meet on Tuesdays."

I got this news while in Mexico and so I proposed to Fraser that I pop over to Los Angeles the following Monday, which was convenient to my calendar and geographically economical. A few hours later: No—next Tuesday was no good. What about the *following* Tuesday? But, I demurred, examining my calendar, that would mean leaving New York after a *National Review* closing on a Monday and flying back Tuesday afternoon in time to deliver a lecture that night. Why on earth do they need to interview me? They are going to make a special out of one of my books, I am willing to surrender artistic control, so what on earth is the *point* of my going to Los Angeles simply to chat with them for a half hour? (A half hour being the typical length of such interviews, I had learned.) It wasn't, after all, an audition, since I was not insisting on *playing* the part of Blackford Oakes.

They were set on it. I *had* to come.

So I did, breakfasting with the two producers before going to the large boardroom. There was nothing I had been warned either to say or not to say, and the youngish man at the head of the table, an agreeable figure, shook hands, introduced me around, and volunteered that he was the only Republican in Hollywood, on which I congratulated him, ruing his political loneliness; after which we all talked amiably about the Oakes series. I left it to the two professionals to exalt the television idea, answering here and there a question or two which really had no bearing on whether the proposed special would be or would not be a commercial success.

In due course I was thanked, left the room with the producers who, once outside the boardroom, glowed with enthusiasm about how well they thought the session had gone.

About two weeks later I called Fraser and asked whether a decision had been made?

"They decided to pass."

"To pass," v.i., means to turn a project down. I was of course disappointed, but for the life of me—to this day—I cannot imagine the point in getting the author of novels, one of which is being considered for a network special, to travel six thousand miles, nor imagine how the author could affect a network decision to "pass" or—the opposite of pass? (I don't know what word they use, never having experienced it—not-to-be-passed.) If I were Boris Karloff or La Pasionaria I *still* wouldn't understand what I could do to diminish (or enhance) the studio's commercial prospects.

Hollywood is most fearfully extravagant. On one sail to Bermuda with Reggie, Van, and Danny, I ground out a ten-page "treatment"— that is much less than a screenplay, merely an unfolding of a plot—for a highly successful producer whom I knew socially. He had called me on the telephone to say that his company thought it time to do a movie "featuring a lobbyist." He said nothing very much more than that: Sit down and write a movie-makable idea featuring a lobbyist in return for which they would pay me twenty-five thousand dollars. It was all in a day's work, and a few weeks after receiving my treatment the producer and his woman assistant scheduled a conference call in which they suggested that one feature of my plot might be improved.

Should I attempt the improvement or would they?

They would, and get back to me. Suffice to say, for the moment, that they both said, most cordially, that the treatment I had done was "highly professional," and the check was on its way (and in due course arrived). I never heard another word from them. That was eight years ago.

The poet Karl Shapiro is married to Sophie Wilkins, one of my friends most admired and cherished. They both came to my home at Wallacks Point in October. Rosalyn Tureck, the great Bach performer, had called to tell me she was going to perform the Goldberg Variations, this time not at Carnegie Hall but at Temple Emanu-El Synagogue, and would I like for her to come around and do a dress rehearsal at Wallacks Point?

This would not be the first time. Seven or eight years ago she called Pat and told her she would like to give me a birthday present—by performing the concert she would give the following week at Carnegie Hall, at our house.

It all happened. I introduced her to our thirty-odd guests by recalling a story that went the rounds at Yale when I was an undergraduate, gleefully repeated in at least one of my previous books. It is the story of a Junior Prom. A Yalie leaves with his date and says to her, "Would you like to come into my car and hear Guy Lombardo and the Royal Canadians?" She: "I didn't know you had a radio in your car." He: "I don't. I have Guy Lombardo and the Royal Canadians."

I felt that night as if I actually had them—her—right there in my car; and she played blissfully; and then played a second time in celebration of her own birthday a few weeks later; and then again, three times. We had the whole thing recorded by an amateur in Stamford and about a year ago the idea arose to listen to those recordings with a view to releasing them. This has been done to great critical acclaim ("transcendent playing, perfectly conceived, rendered with consummate artistry" . . . "gentle, contemplative and lyrical" . . . "seethes with intensity, heart and unalloyed love").

It was another triumph for Tureck, and Karl Shapiro sends me now a poem he wrote after hearing her again at Temple Emanu-El:

A jumbo jet could land in this vast space,
 This concert hall, this marble auditorium.
This temple of Fifth Avenue. On stage
 A concert grand the bigness of a toy,
A wee pink woman at the keyboard booming
 And tinkling Bach. Two tall menorahs wink
Their artificial flames, the lady's earrings
 Diamond-pink, and high up in the nave
The stained-glass windows exhale reds and blues.
 There are no images; one is forced to think.
The pews are hard. After an hour's sit

White heads begin to drift toward the doors.
 Time to go potty or the cocktail hour?
Was this Goldberg a Jew? How many more
 (Thirty in all) of these strange variations?

More and more white heads drifting up the aisles.
This is not "sewing-machine," this is *Romantic.*
The woman is transfusing female soul
Into the masculine Bach. She perseveres
To the closing variation, meant as a joke,
And plays it mournfully, almost in tears.
She stands, she bows to bravos and to cheers.

I congratulate Karl and send along my special love to his wife.

I hear sounds of sail slides coming down. The boat is slowing. I bound up to the companionway.

TONY: "It went. Finally."

"The main?"

"Yeap." Indeed. It was down now. Nothing to do but put up another headsail while sail repair went forward, which would be one of Allan's finest hours. Tony tells it with precision:

> While Allan was taking care of the damage, the cause of it was still there. Both sets of spreaders had to be rebandaged. Not having had much action recently I volunteered to go up. Given the way things were bouncing around on deck it was pretty clear it would be sick-making work up at the higher altitudes. At the top spreader I added the two pads per side and got down to the lower spreader, which needed much more work since the foam had already split and had to be carefully reapplied. While up at the top I noticed that the staysail halyard, which was being used as a pole lift, was frayed down to one strand! We caught it just in time. And I didn't get sick! In fact I was having a pretty good time except on the worst of the rolls. It was so much fun that I was somewhat embarrassed about all the attention that was heaped on me when I got back down.

Tony is modest about the ordeal of going up seventy or eighty feet in a bosun's seat and concentrating on anything other than staying alive, and he doesn't tell us that the operation took him a full half hour. Though that was nothing compared to the length of time required of Allan. The canvas material of the mainsail is so heavy, a needle can't

Tony prevails!

pierce it without the aid of a leather pad on the palm of his hand. The material is too thick for any kind of electrical sewing machine that could be operated on board, so it becomes one stitch at a time: a huge parallelogram to save that part of the sail that was frayed.

This is not—I exchanged thoughts with Van—a delinquency one can blame on the owner. It is foolish for a captain to permit a boat to set out across the ocean with less than fully insulated spreaders or, while we are at it, with less than robust halyards. It is one thing if the boat's owner refused to replace a dying cable—the fault then is his. But insulating the spreaders properly is not an expense, it is a chore. A chore that can save the entire mainsail, save hours of work at sea; and if the tear doesn't lend itself to stitching or even patching, conceivably save you from proceeding for the balance of the passage without the mainsail.

But after setting the two headsails and altering the course slightly, we were down only one and a half knots in our speed; so I went back to my clerical work.

Roger Stone, the political consultant, writes. He is concerned that Lowell Weicker, once a senator, has won the governorship in Connecticut. Roger thinks, as some others of us do, that Weicker is a blowhard, almost certainly a policy menace, and a very great menace to good rhetoric. Roger is very expensive as well as very smart, which made his volunteering to undertake an anti-Weicker campaign without fee all the more appreciated. He analyzes the reasons for the failure of our campaign for John Rowland, the Republican candidate. Roger had approached me in the first place because of my conspicuous role in the campaign in 1988 to unseat Weicker as a senator.

The idea of forming BuckPac (Buckleys Against Weicker) was my son's. Driving back from Thanksgiving dinner at the ancestral home in Sharon, Connecticut, we speculated on who might oppose Weicker in his race for reelection to the Senate the following year and how we might amuse ourselves at Weicker's expense. The following morning, I wrote out a self-interview based on our conversation. I released it as a column the following summer, and happily recalled it on reading Roger's letter . . .

A PRESS CONFERENCE

Q. What is the purpose of "Buckleys for Lieberman"?

A. To generate support for the defeat of Lowell Weicker.

Q. So that it is primarily the retirement of Weicker rather than the election of Lieberman [Senator Weicker's Democratic opponent then, now Senator Joseph] that you wish?

A. You can't have the one without the other. As for Joe Lieberman, he is a moderate Democrat, and it is always possible that he will progress in the right direction. There is no such hope for Lowell Weicker.

Q. Why do you call your organization Buckleys for Lieberman?

A. Within my own family there are a good many Buckleys grounded in Connecticut. An informal estimate suggests that there are about eleven thousand Buckleys in the state. Buckleys for Lieberman intends to devote its primary attention to mobilizing their support for Lieberman.

Q. What do you propose to do about Buckleys who advise you they are for Weicker, not for Lieberman?

A. That matter will be referred to the Committee on Genealogy. It is entirely possible that there are, in Connecticut, persons who call themselves "Buckley" whose birth certificates would not bear out any such presumption.

Q. You mean to say you would challenge the legitimacy of a Buckley who announced his intention of voting for Weicker?

A. This is a very serious business. The future of self-government depends on retiring such as Weicker from the Senate. Correction, there is no such thing as "such as Weicker." He is unique.

Q. How do you propose to establish that?

A. That is the responsibility of the Horse's Ass Committee.

Q. The what?

A. The Horse's Ass Committee.

Q. What are *its* purposes?

A. To document that Lowell Weicker is the Number One Horse's Ass in the Senate. The Committee, which is engaged in research, is absolutely confident that it will win any challenge, from anywhere, nominat-

DOES LOWELL WEICKER MAKE YOU SICK?

REPUBLICANS FOR WEICKER? YUCK

ing any other member of Congress: Lowell Weicker will emerge as the winner.

Q. Just how do you define a . . . horse's ass?

A. Oh, you know. The kind of person who says dumb things dully, you know—

Q. Well, what kind of research is the . . . committee you speak of engaged in?

A. Researching the speeches and public utterances of Lowell Weicker over the past eighteen years. We have a few specimens ready for release at this time, but many many more will be made public by the Degasification Committee.

Q. Excuse me?

A. Oh, yes. Well, the Degasification Committee is engaged in attempting to clean up the quality of public thought and intends to demonstrate that the bombast, murk, and pomposity of Lowell Weicker's public declarations are a threat to democratic ecology. Hence the need for a Degasification Committee.

Q. Does the Buckleys for Lieberman Committee intend to do any active work beyond research?

A. Oh my, yes. We have already formed a political action committee. The BuckPac. Contributions will be solicited from all Buckleys, state by state.

Q. Are you limiting financial contributions to people called Buckley?

A. No. Special membership goes to all Buckleys, whether Buckley is the surname, the maiden name, or the Christian name. There have already been inquiries from out-of-state Buckleys. Some of these will send money to BuckPac. Others actually plan to immigrate to Connecticut, become residents, and vote for Lieberman.

Q. Well, what happens when you run out of Buckleys?

A. Our Ethnographic Committee is compiling the names of Connecticut residents that appear most frequently in the telephone directories. We propose to encourage the formation of coordinate committees. You will not be surprised, I am sure, to know that "Smith," "Jones," "Gomez," "Guttman," and "Rosselli" are among the top forty in frequency that appear in the Connecticut phone books. But we do not propose to neglect any citizen of Connecticut, even those with unusual, not to say unique names. Our strategic objective is a committee representing every surname in any Connecticut phone book. It will take the civic lead from Buckleys for Lieberman to help in the campaign to liberate Connecticut, and Congress, from Lowell Weicker.

Q. Does the Committee have an address?

A. Indeed. It is P.O. Box 1464, Sharon, Connecticut 06069.

Q. And officers?

A. Of course. William F. Buckley Jr. is President. Christopher T. Buckley is Vice President. Priscilla L. Buckley is Secretary-Treasurer. James W. Buckley is chairman of the Horse's Ass Committee. Mrs. Jane Buckley Smith is head of the Genealogy Committee. James Buckley Heath is head of the Ethnographic Committee. And Bruce Buckley Smith is head of the Degasification Committee. Other appointments will be announced along the line. Good day.

"BuckPac gave Weicker fits," a reporter for the *Waterbury Republican* reminisced a few days before the election, "and it may have been a crucial factor in the campaign [of 1988] by legitimizing conservative and Republican support for Lieberman, who won by the slim margin of ten thousand votes out of nearly 1.4 million cast."

Roger now writes to remind me that he had predicted, in a letter sent to me and to others, a) what percentage of the vote Weicker would get, b) how many votes Republican John Rowland would get; and c) what percentage of the vote the Democrat, Bruce Morrison, would get. The first two were exactly on the mark. The failure had been the Democrat's—he needed more votes, and they would have come in from Weicker, enough to make Rowland the winner.

It was certainly the most Machiavellian campaign I had ever engaged in. Roger's strategy had been for me to make a series of radio pitches in Fairfield County trying to persuade Republicans to vote not for Weicker but for Rowland. *Bring the Republicans home*, was the idea.

Then I would broadcast, more or less simultaneously, a series of radio spots directed to the left-minded parts of the state—Bridgeport, northern Connecticut, and the New London area—giving the Democratic candidate hell for being so left-wing. Roger's idea was that liberal Democrats, hearing the Democratic candidate attacked by odious-conservative Buckley for being too far left, would support the Democrat—at the expense of Weicker. In the *New London Day* (November

Back to my clerical work

6, 1990) I would read, "Morrison said a negative advertisement by the columnist William F. Buckley, who criticizes Morrison as a liberal, will have no effect on the campaign, other than perhaps galvanizing Democrats to his cause. 'That's what decided me, when I heard those ads,' shouted one elderly gentleman who was listening. 'I heard them and I knew I was voting for Bruce Morrison.' "

Political commentators could not *believe their ears* when word of the broadcasts got out. "What can Buckley be up to?" I enjoyed especially the political commentator who picked up my most flagrant line and wondered whether I was insane. "Buckley said in his broadcast," he wrote, " 'A victory by Morrison threatens Connecticut with another Chris Dodd in the Senate.' *Doesn't he know Chris Dodd is the most popular politician in Connecticut?*"

But my conscience was absolutely serene. I uttered not one word in those broadcasts that I did not believe. That Republicans shouldn't vote for Weicker, and that Democratic candidate Morrison was too left-wing.

Politics can be fun, though not usually. "It was a wonderful idea,"

I consoled Roger Stone, replying to his letter, "and I greatly admire your ingenuity and your executive skills."

But it's boat time again.

Do I detect a change in mood? It was late afternoon, and there were three black shoelaces crossing the sun, on its way to sleep, slowly turning pink-pearl; and the boat's speed was a cool nine knots. Christo at the helm, visibly transported. A day later Tony would write, "While WFB worked on early morning sun sights and Bill Draper steered, I tuned in to 12095 to get BBC World News. It came in. It was one of those unexpected, perfect moments. My watch duty almost ended, some apple muffins baking in Liz's galley, the sun just coming up, the three of us in the cockpit a thousand miles from any land hunched over a radio that would put us in touch with the rest of the world."

And a day later Tony wrote, "I had been so exhausted during that day that Douglas offered to cover for me on the afternoon watch. Apparently my ebbing energy is palpable. Luckily I declined the offer and had an exhilarating four hours on the helm. The blooper was pulling like a full chute and we were making a solid nine with surges to the high tens. I know today will be a record run." And, the following day, "I take over from Christo and then swap with Bill through the next watch. It's glorious. What more could you ask for?"

An autopilot?

And then too, the company we kept continued to pay dividends. "Before you know it," says Christo, awakened from a deep sleep to go on watch, "Van was tapping on my head with his trademark, 'You don't have to stay in bed anymore!' Van. You got to love Van. And I do."

Douglas comments on the three older men. "Buckley, Draper, and Galbraith. Three little boys all grown up and enjoying each other. But still three little boys. Kids playing on this 71-foot toy in mother nature's liquid sandbox. Playing in a way that only old friends can manage. Cajoling, teasing, tweaking. Proud of each other's accomplishments, tickled by their own, grateful for good fortune, aware of the chaos and pain of life and despite that, perhaps especially because of the last two, happy to be together. Van so comical, but capable of being professionally serious and seemingly dogmatic. Draper is the loyalist, serving as devil's advocate, WFB the conductor, his sextant the baton."

And Douglas toward the end of the trip: "We could almost have read a book in the cockpit under this headlight-bright moon. But instead Christopher and I talked away the watch, sometimes laughing too hard to maintain course. At around four o'clock, as we were exchanging our favorite stories, I failed to pay attention to a shifting wind and managed to wrap the spinnaker around the forestay, a maneuver which required the sweat of three to help clean up my mess. After the adrenaline settled down we resumed our talk and laughter and I reflected silently how splendid it is to sail with such a friend under a full moon in the middle of the Atlantic. Despite my many complaints and my need for Bernadette, it is not lost on me that all the inconveniences of this journey are small prices for what we have got."

But hark! Christo writes a single dark sentence into his journal, giving it an entire page. *"Most ominous development of today: Liz says—casually—that WFB asked her if she would be available five years from now. [Apocryphal. This trip is almost surely the end of the affair.]"*

And very late one night, WFB picks up a battered copy of his first book about the sea, *Airborne,* about sailing in the opposite direction, Miami to Spain, and reads (to himself) the closing lines, taken from Christopher's journal:

> Last-minute observations: at 1330, the northernmost tip of Africa rose through the mist. During the afternoon, a hot hazy succession of sweltering hours, we saw: Cape Trafalgar, the Strait, a procession of ships and planes, and, at long last, Gibraltar.
>
> Rock of Ages . . .
>
> As we ate dinner, the waters of the Mediterranean seemed oily. To the south, Morocco: high cliffs rising out of the strait, forming the other Pillar of Hercules. To the west, Spain: desolate mountains and their foothills, a golden sun sinking fast . . . the first time I've seen the sun set over land in thirty days.
>
> Thirty days! For thirty days of happy sailing, thank you, Pup, from the bottom of my heart.

"Christopher and I talked away the watch, sometimes laughing too hard to maintain course."

And even though I've about had it with your logarithmic watch system (I figure I've been on duty four fifths of the time the last three days), even though the thought of a warm bath and a dry bed at this point is sexually stimulating, even though I couldn't take another gollywobbler [a quadrangular sail] setting or a fisherman dropping, even though the smell of the engine room makes me shudder, even though I'm restless for the touch of land, if you were to set sail tomorrow to cross another ocean, I'd sell my soul to ship out with you. Any day.

Ah, but Christo was only twenty-three years old back then.

WFB

Christo, 1975

· CHAPTER FIFTEEN ·

WhatStar

"Navigation is his intellectual relaxation. I'd guess he spends a quarter of each day at his plotting sheets, Air Almanac, Time-tic, sextant, WhatStar, calculator, GPS, looking for Fomalhaut, Rigel, Diphda, Deneb, et al. He loves the challenge of it, the (implied) precision of it. He likes to know exactly where, in the scheme of things, he is."

Christopher is half correct. The reasons for it all are my general interest in the subject, the satisfaction to be had from refamiliarizing myself with procedures half forgotten (as explained above), and the fascination with the potentialities of a program called WhatStar, to which several references have been made.

It's worthwhile to begin at the beginning. My guess is that something I wrote for *Yachting* magazine a year or so before the trip may interest more people than would think themselves inclined to read about an arcane science. When writing about celestial navigation, my ambition has always been to try to make it less than arcane, less than inaccessible. However, as is my custom I hereby serve notice that the balance of this chapter can be skipped by those who are resolute in their determination not to know about—WhatStar!

I find that the Q&A is especially useful when dealing with subjects inhospitable to casual encounter. The form stops you when you get too vague, or too technical.

THE "WHATSTAR"

AN INTERVIEW WITH ITS DESIGNER, WILLIAM F. BUCKLEY, JR.

Q. We hear you've designed some sort of navigation program.

A. No, that's not entirely accurate. It is true that I conceived the program and to that extent "designed" it. But its execution was entirely the work of Professor Hugh Kenner.

Q. Well, what was it you wanted designed?

A. I wanted to be able to take a star sight, or a planet sight, without having any idea of the identity of the star or planet, and yet score.

Now, I'm aware that a lot of this kind of thing is done at sea. Suddenly you see a tiny little nubile spark above you and you think, "That celestial body up there is just pining for a little navigational smooch." But there is no time (or inclination) for foreplay: Perhaps clouds are moving in. Perhaps there is overcast, and the star peeps out at you only for a minute or so.

You grab your sextant and shoot it; then you go below; then you struggle. You fuss with the Star Finder; or you diddle with the HO-249 tables, giving out your Assumed Position, the whole bit. And after ten minutes of paper work, maybe fifteen, you conclude, "Er, that star must have been Achernar."

Maybe it was—maybe it wasn't.

I wanted to avoid that kind of thing.

Q. You mean, when you say you wanted to avoid what you call "that kind of thing," that even when there are no problems of overcast you don't want to have to preidentify the stars you shoot? Even when you have plenty of time to figure out what stars should be where, and at what time?

A. As a matter of fact, Yes; guilty. It seems to me that the whole thrust of electronic navigation—whether through the use of signal waves, or calculators, whatever—is to reduce paper work. So I wanted to be able to say: I haven't the remotest idea what that object up there is. I never was any good at memorizing the eccentric configurations of the constellations. Ursa Minor looks to me as much like the opening notes of Beethoven's Fifth Symphony as it does a Little Bear. I was never an Eagle Scout. Sure, I know how to read the HO-249 tables but they are something of a bore. And if it's possible just to shoot the star and ask a computer to tell you what star it was you shot, wouldn't that be a blessing?

Q. So what did you ask Professor Kenner to do and, by the way, why him?

A. To answer the second question first, I tapped him because he is a personal friend and was willing to take the two hundred hours it required to dope out and write the program. Of course I needed someone who is a whiz with computers; but I also wanted a sworn enemy of clumsy and ambiguous prose. As one of the great literary critics in the English-speaking world, Hugh Kenner would devise pellucid instructions for WhatStar (catch—already—the simple beauty of the program's name).

Q. Let's get down to brass tacks. What exactly do you need in order to work WhatStar?

A. You need to have a computer. Aboard a boat, I assume we are talking about a laptop computer. It has to be MS-DOS, and it has to have a memory of 256K or better. And it must have a screen large enough to contain eight lines—which nowadays isn't very much. The little Epson Geneva, for instance, can do this. And so can one of Radio Shack's models.

Q. What else?

A. Well, obviously, you need WhatStar.

Q. What do you need to feed into the computer?

A. You need, obviously, the Sextant Altitude of the observed body. The "Hs," as we call it. [That is the whole purpose of a sextant: to measure the angle between the horizon and the celestial body.] And then you need the Greenwich Mean Time. And you need an Assumed Position good within about one hundred miles of your actual position. And of course you need your elevation above the water.

Q. Wouldn't it help if you had the azimuth of the observed body?

A. Yes, WhatStar makes room for those who want to furnish the approximate azimuth. You give it the azimuth and that narrows the search burden of WhatStar. And of course it reduces, at the same time, candidates for election. If you are looking south and note down the altitude of a star at a time that happens also to correspond to the altitude of another star that's sitting to your north at that identical time, you have a problem. That problem can be eliminated by feeding an azimuth to your computer which focuses its attention exclusively on the southern of the two stars.

Q. How many celestial bodies will it search, in toto, if you give WhatStar a free rein?

A. WhatStar will begin at the beginning, by asking you if you have

shot the sun or the moon. If you say Yes to either of those queries, it will go to work on the sun or the moon (or both) and simply ignore the stars. But if you say No to the sun and the moon, it will automatically canvass all fifty-seven of the navigational stars. Then it will go for all the planets. (Charting Saturn was a bitch, but Kenner did it.)

Q. Will it give you a fix?

A. If you ask for it. . . . Would it be useful if I were to give you an example?

Q. Okay. But make it fun.

A. How can you not have fun when you are sailing, as I was last November on the *Sea Cloud*—the largest private sailing boat ever built? It's 7:30 P.M., and a sumptuous dinner will be served in fifteen minutes or so. You had set out from Tahiti four or five days ago. The sun has just now gone down, and you are sitting there in the huge Blue Lagoon (as they call the after-cockpit), surrounded by South Pacific skies that are gradually consuming the sun's rays. Any minute now you're going to see one-two-three little diamonds in the sky—

Q. We didn't ask you to become poetic.

A. Listen, where I was, at sunset time on November 7, halfway between Tahiti and Pitcairn, a balmy northwest trade wind coming in at about ten knots, soft red-orange-yellow-amber sun line out there on the west side—hell, the Bureau of the Budget would have sounded poetic. . . . Anyway, I spot my star! Altitude 48–44, GMT 3:33:38.

Q. You had an assistant to write down the figures?

A. I am in favor of assistants in almost all situations. But, actually, they aren't indispensable for celestial navigation. They're like acolytes: you can, actually, pour the wine and water yourself. I jotted down the figures—

Q. Then?

A. Then I spotted a second body. Altitude 37–17, GMT 3:33:58. And then I spotted a third body, Hs 46–34, GMT 3:34:17.

Q. Then you went to the bridge?

A. No, to my cabin. I inserted my WhatStar disk into my laptop and at the prompt typed, WHATSTAR. Now pay attention to the wonderful spareness, yet unstinting generosity, of what then happens.

The first thing you see on the screen is:

We can search the whole list of stars and planets—or we can use a shorter list

Do you want the short list? (Y/N)

Let's suppose that you do want to limit the number of stars the computer will search out. In that event, you would push "Y"—and something like the following would flash on your screen:

24 Miaplacidus

22 Avior

21 Pollux

25 Alphard

28 Denebola

16 Betelgeuse

11 Rigel

19 Adhara

On the right side of the screen you would see:

If it's OK we'll use it; otherwise we'll make a new one.

Is it OK? (Y/N)

It's up to you. If it happens that you wish to search out only the favorites for that particular hour at that particular latitude as given in the star tables, or that you want to search out only your particular old friends up there, you could simply type in the numbers that correspond to the stars you want, and they would displace those perching in the system. After you have revised the list, you will see:

If this list is OK, answer "Y."

If not, answer "N" to begin again.

Then WhatStar will ask you:

Save for next time? (Y/N)

If you want the eight stars you just finished selecting to be those automatically consulted the next time you use WhatStar, say so now—write "Y." But whatever you do, the next time around you will still be given the option of choosing all the stars, instead of a selected lot. This is an option I regularly avail myself of.

Then you will get,

Greenwich DAY? (1..31)

Observe the wonderful clarity of this. The instructions within the parentheses make it quite obvious that the only satisfactory answer is going to be a number not less than 1 nor more than 31. If for instance you should type by mistake 301, you will hear a little ping, and there will pop up:

Too many digits! Try again.

The moment after you have given the day, you will see,

Month? (1..12)

Followed by:

Year (75..89)

There comes next:

DR Latitude? (D) DMM; [give up to two digits of degrees, give two digits in minutes—e.g., 308] if SOUTH, precede with "—"

Nothing could be clearer than that. I wrote in "−2350," to indicate that my Assumed Position was twenty-three degrees fifty minutes *south* of the Equator. Please note that Kenner does not ask for any decimal points. They are not needed unless one seeks out fractions of a mile. WhatStar doesn't bother with this, at the input level, although it yields a decimalized answer in the event you should desire it. There follows:

DR Longitude? (DD) DMM; if EAST, precede with "—"

I gave 13221, for one hundred thirty-two degrees twenty-one minutes
West Longitude. Then you are asked:

Height of eye? (feet) [and]

Hs of body (D) DMM

I gave respectively "50"—which is how many feet the "Blue Lagoon"
is above the water, added to my own height—and then 4844, for forty-
eight degrees forty-four minutes of Sextant Altitude. WhatStar instantly
rejiggers your Sextant Altitude to reflect your elevation from the water.
You will read on the screen:

Ho = 48:36.3

You are then asked in rapid succession:

Moon? (Y/N) [i.e., do you wish WhatStar to search out the moon?]

Sun? (Y/N) [i.e., do you wish WhatStar to search out the sun?]

Azimuth of body? (Degrees only!)

To omit, hit RETURN [At this point, if you wish to do so, you can
indicate the azimuth, and WhatStar will search an arc of thirty degrees, fifteen to the right, fifteen to the left, of the azimuth you gave
it.)

And, finally:

GMT of sighting (H) HMMSS [Give the hour, two digits of minutes,
two of seconds—I gave 33338.]

What happens then is one of the wonders of the world. You will see
scrolling down the screen in front of you the altitude (Ho) and azimuth
(Az) of every planet and every star, based on your Assumed Position.
They flash down at a dazzling speed, less then thirty seconds—*for the
lot*—if you can believe it. Suddenly you are left staring at:

Diphda. Intercept 3.1 Min. Away. Azimuth 91

The celestial body you show was Diphda.

Q. Is that 100 percent guaranteed?

A. Not with the certainty of death or taxes. WhatStar checks the sight
you feed it against the computed positions of the fifty-seven navigational
stars and four planets. It looks for matching altitudes. If the body you
sighted happened to have the same altitude as a star on WhatStar's list
(and by "same" altitude I mean within 2.5 degrees), you would get a false
match. Note that WhatStar reported an azimuth of 91 degrees for
Diphda. That is a ready check on plausibility; if you were sighting in a
different direction entirely, then you'd know something was amiss. By
the same token, if you were shooting the sun or the moon, which you

could hardly mistake for each other, or for stars, and you got a **No Match Found** from the computer, you could safely conclude that either your time or your sight was wildly off.

You proceed with the data for the second sight. WhatStar omits asking you the day, month, year, elevation, and assumed position, which are already logged in the memory. It takes you directly to **"Hs?"** The ensuing questions are identical to those already listed except that one is now added:

Fix wanted? (Y/N)

I said YES, of course. And what I now got was:

Star 5: Achernar. Intercept 8.2 Away. Az 145

Fix: 23:42:15.15

132:24.3W

I then gave it the data for my third sight, whatever it turns out to be. In seconds I had:

Altair. Intercept was 4.2 Min. Away. Az 3315

Fix 23:2.35.

131:22.3W.

It is easy enough to get a third fix, combining now the first and the third sights, Diphda and Altair. Which I did:

Fix 23:59.2S; 132:24.5W

It happened that all the sights were serviceable—i.e., believable, nonexclusive. But if one of them had been way off, that would quickly have been revealed by the anomalies so easily and quickly made conspicuous with a computer.

I am told by sailing's blasé community that the sextant is going out of fashion, that what with Loran in so many parts of the world, and GPS, the sextant is anachronized.

Yawp.

And cigarette lighters will anachronize the match. . . . So when you next use your sextant, avoid such pains associated with it as are avoidable, by using a calculator or a computer.

The last paragraph of my article the editor of *Yachting* declined to publish in the form I gave it, judging it to be commercially provocative. I had finished my piece as follows:

Q. Is WhatStar for sale?

A. Yes. Hugh and I feel tenderly about it and accordingly have set up a price schedule designed to encourage enthusiasts, and reward their enthusiasm. As follows:

Caribbean Enterprises Inc.
150 East 35th Street
New York, NY 10016

Dear Sirs:

(Please check one):

☐ I think WhatStar is a terrific idea. Please send me one. I enclose $29.95.

☐ Aargh. One more program. I am skeptical about WhatStar, to tell you the truth, but I'm willing to try it. Please send me one. I enclose $39.95.

What happened after the article appeared was that a youngish, French-born intellectual came around to see me. He was then the head of a small electronics concern. An avid sailor, he was fascinated by the idea of WhatStar, thought it might be successfully promoted among midshipmen of the world, etc.; all of this music to my ears, and to Hugh Kenner's. Between us we had spent considerable time in developing WhatStar, thus far with only the scant returns from the *Yachting* article (140 orders for the program came in).

But—Mr. Patrick Ciganer said—his thought was to add to What-Star other information useful to men at sea. When will sunset be at this location on August 9, 1994? What time will the tide be high, and what will be the tidefall, at Woods Hole, Massachusetts, on June 11, 1992? He had me drooling.

But in order to save computer space, he would have one of his technicians re-do WhatStar, from the PASCAL in which Hugh Kenner had written it, into C—which would consume only one tenth as much computer square footage space, leaving plenty for the other stuff as it was put into the floppy. Wonderful!

We turned WhatStar over to Mr. Ciganer's little company. A few months later he left the company to go to work for my old friend

Trimble, Inc., whose Geographical Positioning System I had celebrated in an article for the *New York Times Magazine* (May 19, 1985), and whose earlier Loran unit I published an ode to in *Racing Through Paradise.*

Trimble acquired Mr. Ciganer's one-third interest in WhatStar, but the whole idea—by the standards of Trimble, Inc.—is a potato so small as to be unnoticeable, and Patrick Ciganer was now busy with other matters, leading me to . . . the night, November 4, 1990, when I pulled out my old WhatStar—i.e., the one entirely designed by H. Kenner— shot a couple of stars, and went down to work them out.

I entered all the data and then came to:

Year (75..89)

89!!!! No!!!!

The year 1989 had ended ten months before, and here I was planning an entire ocean passage with the aid of a WhatStar that was obsolete. I tried applying the sight I had taken against several years between 1975 and 1989, hoping that I would find a pattern that would permit me to interpolate the correct readings for 1990. This took a while, but the answer was No. The only thing to do was to get word to Frances Bronson to rush me one of the Ciganer versions of What- Star, which obviously were dated forward perhaps to the end of the century or beyond. That was the express package I had been so anxious to pick up at the Canaries. We left Puerto Rico too late to take sights on Day 1, but on Day 2, I was ready and waiting.

There followed a series of disillusionments that assaulted my spirits (at star-taking time) for days. On these I shan't dwell except as they are especially interesting.

—If you do not know what "copy-protected" means, it means a software program that cannot be reproduced simply by copying it onto another disk.

—The Ciganer WhatStar was copy-protected. And my little laptop computer (Toshiba 1000XE), in order to reduce weight, doesn't have a floppy drive built into the unit. The floppy comes as a separate appendage, which you attach to the computer by a little umbilical cord, a clumsy 4 inches long. I say clumsy because this means that the little floppy unit needs to sit alongside the mother unit. Since your lap is made neither in the shape of a desk or table, nor is as long, you need to forswear the laptop advantage of a laptop and perch the computer on a flat surface. If the cable were 18 or 20 inches long, you could attach it to the computer while resting the floppy on the floor or wherever. In a heaving boat, such things matter a great deal. In order to operate the WhatStar I would need to huddle the two units, connected by the little cable, on the small navigator's desk.

What else was wrong with the new WhatStar, I described in a letter to my friend Patrick on getting to New York:

"I began with a few star sights. They were wildly off, five-, seven-thousand-mile errors. So . . . I went over every step carefully and discovered: That your programmer designated a minus (−) sign as required for sights taken in the Western Hemisphere. I mean, really!— 99.999 percent of users will be sailors in the Western Hemisphere.

"So I trained myself to put down a minus sign, throughout the trip.

"I then ran into your programmer's baffling additional refinements. Imagine being asked [by WhatStar] to give the azimuth of the sighted celestial body—*followed by a decimal and two digits!* You might want such specificity for landing on the moon, hardly at sea. Then they [the designers who took over my WhatStar] want *two extra digits* for your assumed position, a demand that is wildly ignorant, given that one of the virtues of WhatStar is that you always plot from generic coordinates. [No one who has ever sailed would give an Assumed Position of 39 degrees 20.48 minutes. For one thing, you couldn't enter anything that finely calibrated on a plotting sheet.]

"Then: not once on the trip did WhatStar acknowledge the existence of the moon or the sun. After staring the sun in the face, giving an exact Hs [Sextant Altitude] for it, the computer could come up: '**No Body Seen.**' Another unforgivably dumb thing is (I am writing from memory) to have the very first entry read, 'GMT . . . DAY (1–31).' I know, the information is there exactly, but every third time, on seeing 'GMT,' I would tap down on the computer—the GMT. Why didn't the programmer write, 'DAY . . . (1–31 in GMT)'? There were other anomalies that communicated to the user that the programmer had never been to sea or even used a compass. By contrast, Hugh's version is elegant, simple, unmistakably sure-footed."

To probe the question whether the Kenner-PASCAL-WhatStar differed from the Ciganer-C-WhatStar in computed result, I took Hugh's program for 1989 (the latest year I had it), and the C program for the same year, and gave the two programs six stars, in search of discrepancies. There were none. For that reason I would have to say that any failure in identifying the stars I was looking for would presumably have been a failure in both programs. I used WhatStar every day for thirty days. It was wonderfully useful—after I had myself identified the stars. (By that time I was accustomed to the stars I would run into at twilight.)

"One distinct disadvantage," I wrote to Ciganer, "is the apparent inability to ask the computer for a fix on stars sighted out of sequence. For instance, you shoot star A and get a plausible LOP [Line of Position]. You then shoot star B and get a highly implausible LOP. You then shoot star C and it is plausible. Ah, but you can't get a fix on stars 3 and 1 unless you reenter all the data of #1 after #3. That is a nuisance. It would be very nice if the machine were to ask, **Indicate Which Star LOPs You Wish to Combine for a Fix: Check 1 2 3 4 5 6 7 8.**"

As I got into the swing of our southwesterly course I would get to know the four or five celestial bodies that circled enticingly about us at sunset. I can still remember them, beginning at approximately 9 o'clock on *Sealestial*'s left, Fomalhaut. At 1 o'clock, Altair; at 2, Vega; at 3, Deneb; at 5, Alpheratz; at 7, Mars. Getting those sights and working them out on WhatStar was delicious—I mean, the speed with which they came in. If WhatStar could be devised to give you varying fixes without needing to replot, that would be splendid.

With which I conclude that the idea is tremendous, its mechanical failings (greatly reduced in the original Kenner–PASCAL version) perplexing. But its performance is good enough, enough of the time, to make it a primary aid to celestial navigation. What is missing at this point is to account for its occasional listing of the wrong star. Obviously this can be the result of bad sights (or wrong times), and the incidence of such errors could be minimized if one exercised the option to supply the azimuth of the body sighted.

What remains to be done, in the high laboratories of astronomy, is to give us an almanac of hypothetical misidentifications. One night I should have got Vega, and did so; should have got Deneb, and did so; should have got Mars, and did so; should have got Diphda, and got

"**No Match**"; should have got Fomalhaut, and got Fomalhaut; should have got Peacock, and got Rasalhague. Was this last sight, for instance, bad? Or is the proximity of Peacock to Rasalhague less than the tolerable distance between the navigator's Assumed Position and his actual position?

Such questions are intriguing, and perhaps one day I (or someone else) will rap on the door of the Hayden Planetarium in New York and ask the kind people there please to leave me alone for a couple of days with their wonderful inventory of man-made stars, precisely positioned in respect of one another, even as though God had put them there also, and let me figure it out.

CHAPTER SIXTEEN

Discomfort

Douglas is upset because I flouted a rule honored (mostly) in the breach. He is very good at making the sounds of sternness in his journal, better than when he attempts this mode in talk, where his good nature tends to take over.

> Had minor words with WFB at 1:00 this morning. Himself launched himself forward in the darkness—unnecessarily, I thought, and without much warning—to rearrange something on the foredeck. No harness, no lifeline, something of a pitch to the seas. He returned to find me galled and noisy. It is *his* trip, and I have little right to give him instruction. But that seemed reckless, and I didn't want him fucking up *my* trip by sloppily letting his own damn heinie sink out here on my watch. I had visions of having to go below and wake Christopher with some gallows good-news/bad-news. "Christopher, the good news is you are now quite rich. The bad news is . . . well . . ." WFB did not much cotton to an attempt at a dressing down, but seems to have heard my genuine concern for him. Not that I think it will do much good.

Man-overboard is deadly serious stuff. But experience is pretty reliable on the subject. If you are limber, and if you crouch as you move forward, your knees will absorb anything the boat is likely to do to you short of running into a whale. And even then, come to think of it, you would almost certainly be able to grab a handrail, or whatever, as the ship rose and descended again. The rule about putting on your lifeline before you go forward is theoretically sound because it has to do with habituation, a word clinical psychologist Douglas is familiar with. But experienced men (and women) at sea usually know when they should wear a lifeline and when they don't need one; and I am one of these. To be sure, Douglas has had extensive experience as a single-handed sailor. (When there is only one of you, extraordinary precautions are in order.) There are circumstances at sea in which I would never go forward without one. This is especially the case when you know that the duty you are going forward to perform requires the use of two hands, robbing you of one hand to grip the lifeline or handrail; or that you will need to stand up and reach for a sail or a halyard.

Doug reminds me here of the quite ancient philosophical argument, allegedly separating the rationalist French from the prescriptively directed American. If you are driving down a road in your car in a desert and can see miles to the right and to the left of the crossroad you are approaching, do you feel you should stop at the stop sign? The American says (typically) yes; the Frenchman, no. For the American the idea is to *obey the law in every situation*—that way you become accustomed

Douglas is upset . . .

to the law, and habit protects you from any temptation to decide, ad lib, close calls, which you may one day end up calling wrong.

The Frenchman tends to believe that *Homo sapiens* can goddam well see when there is *manifestly* no reason to stop—i.e., he knows when the stop sign is discharging *no useful function*.

The only man-overboard I've ever had was dear Bruce Lee (now R.I.P.), aboard *Cyrano,* nosing out past Ambrose Light in New York one night en route to Bermuda. Wind? Zero. Waves? Zero. Bruce was forward, where the lifeline descends on a diagonal to the beginning of the ship's prow. Somebody then tossed him a flashlight, he stepped back, to catch it against the lowered lifeline, which hit him not at knee level where lifelines should hit, but a few inches above the ankle. No black-belted karate champion could have maneuvered him more deftly into the sea. After we scooped him up, he thought his going into the drink all very funny, which it was—in those serene circumstances. In other circumstances, it could have been very deadly; but in other circumstances, he wouldn't have been postured as he was.

And one bright morning, off Watch Hill, skippering *Patito* on a trip to Newport, Reggie lost a friend overboard, swept off the deck by the boom on a jibe. Quite scary, because it took a full five minutes to turn the boat around (the spinnaker was up, lines fouled, the whole bit). And then they cruised right by the nineteen-year-old victim without seeing him (the sun was directly above him); another five minutes went by before he was picked up by a fishing boat. Ever since, I've been rigid on the matter of fixing a preventer in place to hold back the boom. The preventer I have is a joyful contrivance with two blocks and four sheaves, with a grip-lock and two large snap hooks, the combination making it wonderfully easy to secure the boom in a matter of, oh, fifteen seconds; we refer to it as "the Stoops Preventer."

At this point in the trip, I'd have worried more about falling inside the boat than outside it. There had been creeping complaints about smell. Every day, Martin and Denis tried something new. Nothing worked. There has been (this was a deduction) a leak into the bilge. Not, I say in quick relief, from toilets: offal gets pumped overboard. But much that goes to the bilge from the galley, or from seawater sloshing about, or whatever, is designed to be collected and tossed overboard by a sump pump. The pump was working but it was not collecting whatever it was that produced whatever that odor was that (happily) didn't reach the master cabin but brought misery to the two forward cabins. Douglas wrote: "We seem to be sleeping in the thermals of a factory spillway, a veritable shit sluice. We are inhaling noisome airs, the source of which has so far eluded me. I do know Christopher has been sick for a day from it and I have a headache."

Problems at sea have a way of proliferating, and dear *Sealestial* seems to collect problems. About eight days out, with six or seven still to go, Liz announces a water shortage. *But how could that be?* We had sixteen hundred liters, a liter per person per day, and we were all scrupulously careful, showering in salt water only. The generators on *Sealestial* also make water, up to 900 liters (237 gallons) per day. I calculated that our consumption rate, added to that of the crew, was 650 liters per day. That sounds awfully extravagant, but then I remember two poles by which to judge it. Racing to Bermuda in my 40-footer in energetic years gone by we used to carry 65 gallons of water for eight people. With that supply, we managed a spartan shower per person per day, and would arrive in Bermuda in five to six days with about 25 gallons unused. That is the austere end of water usage. Five years ago a technician from the Army Department of Engineers was telling me at Kosrae in the Caroline Islands that to his despair he could not persuade the natives to use less than one thousand gallons of water per person per day.

Now Liz sent out the word: *Stop using water.* It upset most people more than it did me, since I don't drink water (except in coffee). It upset water-nut Christo, for instance, when Liz told him not even one glass per day.

> "*No no no,*" I say, "*not possible.*" I beg. "All right," she relents. I promise in return to shower with my used toothpaste water. She looks at me. "You're brushing your teeth with water?" she says. Very successful upmanship, this. Stephen Potter would be proud. Ten days of treating H$_2$O like liquid diamonds, and this! Here's what's happened: The freshwater pumps were turned off as a conservation measure, then accidentally flipped on at the switch panel. (An honest error: *Sealestial's* electric

instrument panel is anagrammatically labeled; for instance, if you want to turn on the spreader lights, just flip on the switch saying "Steam." Logical, no?) Resulting in profligate streams of—heated, for heaven's sake—water pouring into the bilge. You watch, before this trip is over we're going to be lavving ourselves with beef broth and cooking with orange crush.

I feel very bad about not having been in the saloon when the following exchange took place, recorded by Christo after he ventured, "Be nice to have a desalinator."
MARTIN: We have one.
ME: Oh, well, great!
MARTIN: Doesn't work.
ME (to myself): Of course not.
MARTIN: It's brand-new.
VAN: Is it Japanese?
MARTIN: American.
VAN: Hm.

I felt very bad and very helpless—Christopher had suffered from cluster headaches into his early twenties; indeed they and his asthma kept him from being drafted during the Vietnam years. In this sense, a providential affliction that resulted in a valuable ineligibility, the implications of which he wrote about years later for *Esquire,* a heuristic essay; the first, I think, from a member of the Vietnam generation who did not go. He lives having escaped the Vietnamese snipers but not his own conscience, never mind that it was the medical examiner who said no. Still, he suffers, though now one stage reduced from the dreaded clusters: as recently as a couple of years ago he spent an entire week in the hospital, suffering from asthma.

But this morning Christopher was worried about lesser afflictions: "Stumble up onto deck, feeling unusually grungy. It makes a difference when there isn't enough water to splash on your face, and no milk for the coffee which itself tastes like battery acid. But the night is beautiful, glorious, even: a bright full moon balanced above the masthead, an easy northeasterly swell, and enough wind to keep the great MPS [Multi-

Purpose Sail] filled. At breakfast Martin asks me if I want ice in my pineapple juice in such a way as to make me think he wants the ice cube back after it has cooled my juice."

I remembered a passage in Morison, so piquant under the circumstances. Five hundred years of technological advances at sea and we read about a morning aboard the *Santa María*—the morning of September 16, about halfway through his trip from Gomera to the Bahamas. Columbus's amanuensis transcribes the admiral's feeling on rising and coming to the deck in the morning—*era plazer grande el gusto de las mañanas* ("the savor of the mornings was a great delight"). "What memories," wrote Morison, "that phrase evokes! A fragrant cool freshness of daybreak in the trades, the false dawn shooting up a pyramid of grayish-white light, the paling stars, the navigators bustling to shoot their favorites in the brief morning twilight of the tropics, rosy lights on the clouds as sunrise approaches, sudden transformation of the square-sails from dark gray to ruddy gold, smell of dew drying from the deck, the general feeling of God's in his Heaven and all's right with the world. 'The weather was like April in Andalusia,' said Columbus: 'the only wanting was to hear nightingales.' "

It was not so aboard *Sealestial* during the noisome hours.

—It is not a bad idea to have a little place of refuge from general discontent of the kind you can't do anything about, e.g., the facility to make (drinking) water. So I went back to my correspondence. Letters here from, of course, Charles Wallen. It is five years since he got his computer, and now he is able to count up without difficulty the number of letters he writes. Last year, he told me, he wrote me 169 letters but he intends to do better in 1990. Charles, retired from a trucking company, father of three sons, lives quietly with his wife and sister-in-law near the airport in San Francisco. I have never known anyone who reads so prodigiously, purely for the sake of pleasure, and to pleasure others. He writes to everybody, in a diction that rolls and ripples like King James fondling the Old Testament. His best friend is retired jeweler and cosmopolite Harold Berliner, whose occasional versifying Charles delights in belittling. "Harold's poetry cleaves the general ear with horrid speech:

> Have you been to Kuwait, of late?
> For Hussein has put out the bait.
> But it's surely our fate,
> That he'll never be sate,
> Can we give him the gate? Great!

"Harold lives in a high meadow in Marin County under the shadow of Mount Tamalpais and this stimulates his rampant morality and fertility rites. He also dresses like a whiskey drummer." And a second letter: "As Harold grows older he grows worse, but he has a kind of seraphic look as he composes, and he cleaves the general ear with horrid speech with his haikus. Here Harold is uninnocent and he presents us with a pleasure so great that even when it seems unsharable it stands for gladness at living. He roams over unplowed fields"—whereupon another Berliner poem is quoted.

A third letter regrets that he, Charles, has hurt Tom Wolfe's feelings. "I first came across *The Bonfire of the Vanities* in the antinomian pages of *Rolling Stone* magazine where it was partially serialized. When later on I got the book, I found it un-laydownable. Tom & I wrote to each other for several years. I started reading him in the early sixties. Then came his great *The Right Stuff* about the astronauts. Then the movie . . . Then having dinner with Tom and you and Van and Harold at the Washington Square Bar and Grill in San Francisco. Then a few years later I was incautious enough to write Tom that I thought his book *The Right Stuff* was incomparable (he is the world's greatest reporter) but in the same letter I told him that I thought the movie did not live up to the quality of the book. I never got a response to that letter—and I must have offended him, but I did not intend to. Historians will be poring over *Bonfire of the Vanities* ages hence as they will be with Flaubert's *Madame Bovary*. Tom was inflamed in the same manner that Flaubert was inflamed. But, of course, Tom is a Southern gentleman and does not flourish his inflammations."

I write to Charles to tell him I am certain that Tom did not take offense over criticism of the movie of *The Right Stuff*. I myself had thought it awful, and had the bad luck to be seated next to Tom's wife, Sheila, at the screening of the movie. When the lights came up I sensed her disappointment, and she sensed mine, but it was hardly the occasion to express it, since about seven hundred people were staring at her and Tom to evaluate their reaction. I had once told Charles about the wonderful occasion when Hollywood promoters, in 1934, brought in, all the way from India, the head of the Bengal Lancers to view the premiere of the famous movie *The Lives of a Bengal Lancer.* Major General Sir Gerald Fitzgerald, height six feet six, sat stiffly through the entire film, at the end of which the cameras whirred on him, a dozen microphones thrust up at his face.

"Well, General, what do you think of the picture?" the producer asked, beaming expectantly.

"Oh. Verrie nice. But nothing like Inja, you know."

—Hank O'Neal, a producer of music LP's and cassettes, approached me a dozen years ago to write the liner copy for an LP featuring Dick Wellstood, piano, and Kenny Davern, clarinet. I did so, and we are irregularly in touch, but the death of Wellstood, whom I revered, brought our correspondence to life. Would I like to join him on a cruising jazz festival? "This year's will be held aboard the S/S *Norway* (the old S/S *France*), the dates are 27 October through 3 November; a Saturday to Saturday sailing. The ship stops at St. Maarten, St. John, St. Thomas and a private island in the Bahamas. There will be sixty great jazz musicians on board; Illinois Jacquet and His Orchestra, Clark Terry's group, Lou Donaldson's band, lots of extra instrumentalists, and many pianists. . . . We have a nine-foot Baldwin that will be played by Dave McKenna, Ray Bryant, Ted Higgins, John Bunch, John Varro and Dorothy Donegan all night long, each night." What an invitation!—except that I'd be cruising elsewhere. I wrote to thank him, and I hope he'll invite me the next time around.

—Herbert Kenny is one of my oldest friends, a scholarly Catholic liberal who was for years in charge of the cultural section of the *Boston Globe.* Herb tries to look after any animal, vegetable, or mineral in need, and writes now to say that a fund is being established to break ground for a Center for Photographic Art in honor of his friend Arthur Griffin, "now in his mid-eighties. He is a sweet and noble man besides being an eminent artist, and dear to me." I reply sadly, because doing a favor for Herb Kenny is a wonderful experience. "I don't have money on anything like that scale [$200,000] and with fifty nephews and nieces, some of whom have problems, I must pass on photographic art. Forgive me."

Perforce I document also that it is firmly and irrevocably fixed in the mind of responsible people that—one night we ran into a whale. Christopher permits a trace of skepticism, but not much: "On the 1 to 5 watch last night, no doubt about it. Just as I was relieving Van, we struck something. Douglas and I both felt it (so did Bill Draper, below) and *Sealestial* shuddered from it. It felt soft, not like striking a log, more of a bounce. Too much for a dolphin—unlikely in the first place, as they're so agile; large shark? But they don't sleep, as I seem to recall, having to keep water flowing through their gills. That leaves: a whale? We know that they sleep, we know they're in these waters (from the VHF conversation two days ago with that boat five hundred miles ahead of us). Not sure what else it could be. We don't mean to be hysterical, understand, and are wide open to countersuggestions. In the morning, Douglas, up before me, is greeted at breakfast by survivors of the whale-bump as if the 1 to 5 watch had been visited by Martians. 'Must have been a log,' suggests one of the nonbelievers."

Tony told us about cruising alongside a whale, between Monte Carlo and Sardinia, a dozen years ago, that was distressingly cozy with his sailboat. Finally, as Christopher recorded, "Twenty yards away, it sounded, and Tony saw the long gray shape disappear.

"Funny, but I couldn't shake it for the rest of the watch, this spooky feeling that I was going to surf 79-ton *Sealestial* down a moon-shimmery swell at ten knots onto a slumbering cetacean, thereby annoying it mightily. Next day I find myself perusing *The Atlantic Crossing Guide*, specifically the section, 'The Whale Hazard.'

" 'At night, little can be done to avoid accidentally hitting one; but steer clear, if you see one in daytime; and if a whale seems interested in the boat, start the engine which, according to some people, tends to scare them off. The wrong-colored bottom paint is thought to be conducive to attack; opinion seems to favor blue or green rather than red or white.'

"Today I lean over the rail and check our under-color. *Blue.*

"I wonder if a blue-water version of those ultrasonic deer-alert thing-amajigs you put on your fender would be feasible. Find myself thinking, 'Ask Reggie.' Dear, dear Reggie. Reggie would know."

I am willing to believe it, and since there were three witnesses I see no reason not to indite it as The Truth:

We were hit by a whale.

Bill Draper tries to enliven the mood

· CHAPTER SEVENTEEN ·

Music on My Mind

Back to the sack of correspondence. . . . Beekman Cannon, professor emeritus of music history, writes. My teacher forty years ago, he remains a pillar in the music establishment at Yale. His idea, a year or so earlier, when he learned that I would perform a harpsichord concerto in Phoenix, was to get me to do the same thing for the benefit of the Yale Music School's Library. With the Yale Symphony Orchestra, I would play the F Minor Concerto of Bach; then, as a soloist, the Chromatic Fantasy, and finish by reciting the Ogden Nash verses designed to accompany Saint-Saëns's *The Carnival of the Animals.*

Two days before leaving for Lisbon, I did the concert and now was heartened to have such a letter from the gracious if austere musical scholar. "That your performance yesterday gave us all a lot of pleasure and edification was clear from the enthusiasm of the audience. Much more than that was the modesty and dedication of your devotion to JSB. Naturally this was most clearly demonstrated in the Chromatic Fantasy because it provided an opportunity and a challenge, too, to your own personal love and understanding. You surmounted whatever hazards were involved and won a whole batch of new friends to help in our many musical causes, most notably the Library."

He didn't say, nor could he truthfully have done so, that my performance had been of professional quality. But it was a nice ending to a very

*With great gratitude to William F. Buckley, Jr.
whose "exiguous musical resources" brought us
prodigious pleasure and profit*

Marcia Stevens
Buchanan Cannon
~ Charles Pickands
Eugene M. Ewald
Craig Wright
Mejro BAckus
J. Merrill Knapp
Kathrin Salmon
Luca Plaudingss
Sonost & Puschot
Zany J. Bun
Ayne Durand
Harold E. Samuel

*The Council
The Friends of Music at Yale
October 28, 1990*

short and bumpy public career. Three weeks before, I had done the same thing at a benefit for the North Carolina Symphony. (One critic wrote that "whatever the chaos preceding the coda, Mr. Buckley and the symphony finished neck and neck." I thought that very funny.) It was good to know that the anti-stage-fright pill I took (Inderal) had done some good at New Haven. My memory went back a year to the Phoenix concert.

I had written about that upcoming event for the *New York Times* Arts & Leisure section, as a sort of conversation, while cruising Sardinia and Corsica aboard a majestic old 100-foot Rhodes ketch, *Dolphin,* owned by a friend, Parker Montgomery. It was published simultaneously in New York and in Phoenix:

What made you decide to play a concerto with the Phoenix Symphony Orchestra?

That's easy—I was invited. The interesting question is, What made the Phoenix Symphony Orchestra decide to invite me?

Well, do you have the answer to that?

After my first few months of shock, little hints drifted in on the disorderly beach of my correspondence. Yes, I now know how the idea began. In one of my autobiographical books I apparently made some reference to the singular pleasures it must give a musician to be able to play, night after night, masterpieces written by great composers, by contrast with the fate of the contemporary public speaker who needs to be satisfied with reiterations of his own invention. But that blissful alternative, I commented, is available only to the artist, which is what I hoped to be up until about the age of fifteen when I was precocious enough to recognize that I didn't have the talent to become one.

But you decided at age sixty-three that you had enough talent, after all, to play with a symphony orchestra?

Well put. But we need to make distinctions. If the letter I received from the managing director of the Phoenix Symphony in September 1988 had invited me to take up a career as a performing keyboard artist, I'd have replied without any difficulty.

But he didn't do that. His challenge was excruciatingly finite. What he said, and the words are engraved in my memory, was, "Would you play any Bach concerto any time in 1989 or 1990 with the Phoenix Symphony?"

That was not an invitation for me to take on a profession at which I knew I would be a failure. It was a challenge which, transcribed into the language in which I read it, said: "Do you think you could manage to cultivate the technique and the savoir faire to play any one Bach concerto with a professional orchestra on a public occasion if we give you two entire years in which to practice?"

That was a very different invitation.

What was your immediate reaction?

At first I thought, No, it is quite simply impossible. My fingers have been rusty for generations, the butterfly-in-the-stomach problem is not one I could predictably overcome, and anyway, the endeavor would consume entirely too much time. I wake up and, roughly speaking, work until I go to bed—there is never any time just "left over," let alone the kind of time it takes to attack the keyboard at a professional level.

So then what did you do?

I called Fernando Valenti. You don't hear his name as a recitalist so often nowadays as he has retired from the professional circuit because of health problems. But I first heard him play when he was a senior at Yale University, only a few years before *Time* magazine made a casual reference to him as the "best living harpsichordist." Years later we became very good friends, so I called and told him about this crazy offer. I had the advantage of talking to someone who knows a) that I revere music, and b) that I am lucky if I get through chopsticks without playing a wrong note.

What did he say?

Well, he said it was a very "interesting challenge"—nobody was going to say anything different from that, by the way, right up to the present moment. So then I asked him which was the briefest concerto Bach ever wrote, and he said, "The F Minor takes only eight and one-half minutes."

Eight and one-half minutes! I was being given, potentially, twenty-four months to discipline my fingers to play eight and one-half minutes, which comes down to about three and a half months per minute, or about one week per note. Hell, figuring it out that way, I could perform the "Flight of the Bumblebee" in a couple of years!

What was Mr. Valenti's reaction?

He said: Why don't you try working on it for a month or two and see if anything happens? . . . Well, that is exactly what I did, only first I called Rosalyn Tureck, who is also a very close friend. She knows by heart everything Bach ever wrote for the keyboard and is as incomparable at Bach as Valenti is at Scarlatti. And I said: What do you think about the F Minor Concerto? And she said, "Well, everybody knows the famous Largo, the slow movement from the concerto. But my advice to anyone who sets out to conquer it is: Start with the third movement. Then go to the first movement. If you can manage those, you can manage the second movement."

Did you follow her advice?

No, actually. I lined up my teacher. Rick Tripodi is an organ virtuoso at a local church whom I had come to know and who is a very gifted musician. Together we listened to a recording by Trevor Pinnock, and I decided the first movement was as difficult as the third. So . . . we set out. My idea was to give the experiment a two months' trial, practicing one-half hour a day and taking a one-hour lesson every week. Getting to hit the right notes was sheer hell.

But, obviously, you didn't give up?

No. But I came close to doing so. After I'd been working on the first movement for about three months a friend told me about a musician who lived in the neighborhood with whom my friend was studying. "The wonderful thing about Mrs. Josephson," she said to me, "is that every five or six lessons, she just stops me and reteaches me how to practice. She's great on teaching you how to practice."

This I needed special training in, because over the years, when your technique is quite awful, you get used to slurping your way through whatever little piece you are engaging, and time after time you make the same dismaying errors. I needed someone who could coach me in the correct gymnastic basics. So I finally prevailed on Mrs. Josephson to give me a lesson.

She was genial and quite stern and told me to practice the first movement no faster than speed 90 on the metronome until New Year's Day—that was six weeks off. I had been playing it at about speed 110.

I persuaded her to give me a second lesson during which I played the first few bars of the third movement. She listened patiently. And then she said, "Have you made a commitment to the Phoenix people?" And I said, Well, I had a telephone conversation just a week ago with the managing director and I told him I was practicing every day and I had a premonition that I would be accepting his challenge. I told her rather excitedly that I had asked him one specific question: How late in the day could I actually pull out? His answer was: "Ninety days." They would not schedule the concert until ninety days before. If I said Yes at that time, I would need to go ahead with it. So, I said exuberantly, I've decided I can't possibly devote two years of my time to learning the F Minor concerto, so I am going to perform it in mid-October, thirteen months after first attacking it, which means that I have until mid-August to say yes or no definitively to Phoenix.

That was in January.

"You may as well say no now," said Mrs. Josephson.

"Oh?" I asked, probingly.

"You will never be able to play the F Minor concerto. Not ever. Not unless you stop everything and practice three hours minimum per day, for two years."

That was a very sobering statement, and I recounted it not only to my first teacher, Rick Tripodi, but to my second teacher, Barbara Cadranel (Mrs. Fernando Valenti #2), herself a harpsichord recitalist, who had undertaken to coach me an additional one hour per week. She was indignant at this sign of negative fatalism and flatly contradicted it. The following day I had a telephone call from Fernando in his sickbed—he too was passionately aroused by the categorical pessimism of Mrs. Josephson. I felt suddenly as though I were listening to Knute Rockne during the half of a Notre Dame football game.

So what did you do?

I persevered. I resolved that a day would not pass without my giving the concerto at least the half hour. Now this, for a peripatetic Modern Man, was a considerable commitment. I had to buy, of course, a Yamaha portable five-octave keyboard instrument, which is designed for rock bands but which will give your fingers the requisite daily workout. Let me see. In the months ahead, I played bits and pieces of the F Minor Concerto in Antigua, St. Lucia, Martinique, Bequia, Switzerland, England, Mexico, Greece, Turkey, California, Hawaii, Tahiti, New Zealand, Australia, Sri Lanka, Kenya, South Africa, aboard my little sloop en route to Bermuda, and on a ketch touring Corsica and Sardinia. As I say, not a day went by—

Had you at that time decided whether to perform on the piano or the harpsichord?

I was amused early on, struggling through the first movement in front of my original piano teacher, age eighty, whom I adore. She suggested I play it on the harpsichord. When next I played it for my harpsichord teacher, she suggested perhaps I ought to play it on the piano. Fun. But I came early on to the decision to do it on the harpsichord, for two reasons. The first that Bach wrote it for the harpsichord, which is also the instrument I love beyond all others; the second that my fingers, which are structurally weak, can handle the muscular requirements of the harpsichord with less strain—the harpsichord key depresses more easily than most piano keys. The disadvantages, on the other hand, are manifest.

What are they?

There is less room for dynamic interpretation when playing the harpsichord with a chamber orchestra than when playing the piano. You cannot control the volume, and your articulation of the notes is less easily discerned. You are entirely at the mercy of tiny gradations in timing which the listener needs to struggle to detect, when there are other instruments playing. I discussed the whole question with Trevor Pinnock who came to lunch one day and is a great performer and scholar. He had recently played the F Minor in Berlin and had recorded it. He dismayed me by referring to it as "a treacherous body of music." Which it is, by the way: your fingers never get any time off, and if your fingering goes askew, it can only be compared to your parachute failing to open. And then Mr. Pinnock, whose (very brief) cadenza, by the way, he was kind enough to copy out and send to me so that I could use it—it comes in just a few bars before the end of the concerto—told me that he has no hesitation in using the sixteen-foot pedal during the *tutti* passages, i.e., when the harpsichord and the chamber orchestra are playing simultaneously. On this point the musical world is furiously divided. The purists say, No!—Bach did not even know of the existence of the sixteen-foot (which gives you a register one octave below the register you are playing). Others say: Nonsense. He might well have known; and certainly he would have availed himself of it had it been around.

And then there is the question of amplification. Mr. Pinnock agrees that his own recording of the F Minor underplays the harpsichord sound to the point where it sometimes just gets plain lost in the ongoing commotion. The idea of one of my precious eight and one-half minutes getting lost is more than I can bear, so that I have put in for plenty of amplification, and hope this will not become a point of contention between me and Mr. James Sedares, the distinguished conductor who is indulging all of this.

An interesting point. What is in it for Phoenix?

I have pondered that. There are two extreme possibilities, from either of which Phoenix would profit. Suppose I go out there and—freeze. Or, perhaps, hit a few notes and then dismember the rest. Just turn in an absolutely memorable, god-awful performance.

Now that wouldn't be all bad for Phoenix, frankly. People would remember it, and write about it: "Were you there when the Phoenix Symphony Orchestra gave Buckley that chance-in-a-lifetime and he fell on his right-wing arse? It was speck-*tac*ular!" You don't really get mad at Barnum and Bailey when one of its trapeze artists misses and goes down, down, down to . . . Exactly.

Now the other possibility—I'd say the first possibility is infinitely more likely than the second—is that the local critic will say that last night was definite proof that all those years spent by Mr. Buckley writing and speaking were wasted, given what he might have given the world as a harpsichordist.

Now even if I perform creditably, no critic is likely to say this who knows what I have been through, because it would take me longer than I expect to live to be able to perform Bach's other half-dozen concertos, at the rate at which I learn, let alone the whole of the harpsichord literature.

In between the two extremes, if I hit most of the right notes and prove that I understand what Bach was trying to do, people will say: That was a nice little stunt Phoenix pulled off. They ran risks, granted; but they weren't embarrassed. And it was fun finding out that a lapsed amateur can, if he is willing to spend lots and lots of time on the problem, manage to draw on a lifetime of devotion to a composer and play creditably for eight and one-half minutes one of his beautiful concertos. Besides, think of all the books and articles and speeches Buckley might have done in the hundreds of hours otherwise devoted to solitary practice! We may have been spared the equivalent of another six months of Reaganomics.

Who knows? The Phoenix Caper might become an annual event. If anybody wants to start a scholarship that would make it possible for John Kenneth Galbraith to devote all his spare time to mastering the Minuet in G, why I will contribute to that fund, and maybe even organize a picket line around his house in Cambridge to guard against any distraction. You know, don't you, that he has pledged never to cross a picket line?

Great fun, I think, but the dread hour was approaching and in preparation for it I went to Phoenix five days early, in time to hear the symphony play a regularly scheduled concert. The following day I was to meet the press. They were there in dismaying numbers. I had written out a statement:

> I arrived in Phoenix yesterday in the late afternoon, just in time to attend the concert at the Scottsdale Arts Center by the Phoenix Symphony. The experience was appalling. During the past thirteen months, since receiving the invitation to perform with the Phoenix Symphony, I have supposed that it was a competent body of instrumentalists. I had no reason to suppose that the forty musicians I heard under the baton of James Sedares would sound like ten Stradivarius quartets celebrating a joint concert in Vienna. To meditate that I am to appear as soloist with those musicians next Tuesday would drive me to drink, except that I have no time to drink, only to practice.
>
> I am not altogether surprised that the literature distributed in the concert hall about the musical season of the Phoenix Symphony made no mention at all of my own appearance with them. It gave out the feel of a church calendar omitting any mention of the forced wedding on October 17. Well, I bear them no grudge: given the musical standard they maintain, they are right to treat me like Jack Benny.
>
> Unhappily, I am not as funny as Jack Benny. But nobody in the history of the world has attacked the F Minor Concerto of Bach as I have done, extruding my exiguous musical resources with the kind of care you would take with only one quart of water embarking on a life raft across the ocean. But I rejoice that I have three days ahead of me in which to redouble my efforts not to sound, next Tuesday evening at Scottsdale, like a stuck horn on a Rolls-Royce.
>
> I very much regret that students from ASU are underrepresented. Perhaps that is because they are being charged ten dollars, and usually they get to hear me for nothing. But on those occasions when I am lecturing to them they have no alternative than to listen to discordant political themes, rendered with singular wit, passion, and eloquence. I cannot imagine a Democrat at ASU missing the opportunity to hear me on Tuesday in a medium I do not master. I suggested to my sponsors

that we should invite ASU Republicans for two dollars per ticket, Democrats for ten dollars, but there was vague talk about the possible unconstitutionality of such a suggestion. I was surprised by this, having been schooled to believe that Arizona's constitution was a wonderfully supple instrument. [A fight was raging over the constitutionality of the impeachment of Arizona Governor Meacham.] I look forward to my debut as a harpsichordist in Phoenix, and beg the sufferance of the fine artists I heard last night.

The critics were merciless, though two or three of them conceded that the performer's nervousness might have been a significant factor in his performance. "Yet even the brave, nervous smile [the conductor] shot at Buckley near the beginning of Bach's first movement was not enough to keep Buckley from hitting many wrong notes. Too many to ignore. It is clear Buckley wishes fervently to express himself with music. Otherwise the idea of a concert like this would not have burned

WFB and the Phoenix Symphony

within him. However, before there can be art, with its fervor, there must be cold technique." Absolutely right.

Another critic wrote that the performer "was cheered unabashedly by an appreciative audience; [however], the musical results, all said and done, were less than inspiring . . . the nervousness behind his smile was immediately detectable upon his arrival onstage—perhaps the result of what he knew to be a decidedly premature standing ovation from a few listeners—and from the onset of the concerto it was apparent that the entire undertaking was an overwhelming challenge. To his credit, Buckley displayed a keen understanding of the concerto's stylistic demands: the moving lines were pleasingly understated, while the concerto's more reflective moments, noticeably in the Largo, emerged with consummate musicality. Buckley's most obvious shortcoming, then, was a lack of the sufficient technique: Considerably more than a handful of wrong notes were detected, and his pacing of what should have been steady tempos, particularly in the opening movement, was erratic.

"For all of its shortcomings, Buckley's performance was greeted with a standing ovation that surely reflected audience appreciation of the man rather than the musician. In response, the erstwhile harpsichordist turned to a brief, unannounced encore. Unencumbered by the need to collaborate with an orchestra, he fared considerably better.

"One must applaud Buckley's good will, adventuresome spirit, and courageous willingness to endure the uncertainties of the concert hall. Nevertheless, the evening's most compelling lesson was that, at least for Buckley, the odds are considerably better when the challenge is John Kenneth Galbraith rather than a Bach harpsichord concerto."

A television critic wrote, "Mr. Buckley is obviously a risk-taker, as anyone who watches *Firing Line* or reads his work knows. This is different somehow. He is risking not just himself, but in some sense the danger of doing a disservice to the music that he loves so much. It is strange to see someone who usually seems completely unflappable actually look nervous and vulnerable. His courage is impressive."

And one more. ". . . Music not only is fun, it is necessary for a full life, Buckley had said at a press conference Friday. By continuing to play—even if only for home consumption—Buckley has set an example for all. And by appearing in public with a professional orchestra, he not only fulfilled a lifelong wish but also hoped to convey his message loudly and clearly.

"The audience did not fail to notice that the fun part of the musical experience also requires hard work and courage. On Tuesday, not even a diehard, kneejerking liberal could have enjoyed the brave columnist's squirming on the keyboard hot seat. Buckley, whose articulate semantics have made him the ideal of intellectuals of all political persuasions, tackled the concerto with stubborn determination. He did not always hit the right keys or play in the correct rhythm, but none of this mattered. James Sedares, in accompaniment, broke out in a cold sweat more than once as he teetered on the brink of disaster. The conductor, however, did a masterful job of holding soloist and orchestra together; he even encouraged the soloist with a reassuring wink from time to time. Quickly granting an encore to reward the sincere ovation from the audience and the orchestra's musicians, Buckley played the difficult B flat Gigue with nimble fingers and considerably more self-assurance, shrugging off such technical trickeries as crossed hands and seemingly endless virtuosic runs."

The despondency of a failed performance is what you carry away that evening and the next day, but there are wonderful ancillary moments, such as warm telegrams, some incomparable. One from Christo, "KNOW IT WILL BE A NIGHT TO REMEMBER—AND NOT THE WAY WALTER LORD MEANT THAT. CAN ALREADY HEAR THEM SHOUTING ANCORA ANCORA. VERY PROUD OF YOU. ALL LOVE."

And the great Fernando Valenti rose from his sickbed in New Haven to attend a special rehearsal for the Phoenix concert in Stamford and submitted the following day "for publication"—needless to say, his paragraphs were neither forwarded to any paper nor would any paper have run them. He must have known this, intending them for my own eyes. His words have remained private until now. And they can no longer embarrass him, since, as observed, he died two weeks before we started our ocean passage. His words were touched by a singular grace.

On the evening of September 8, 1989, a few of us witnessed an event that illuminated an aspect of the musical arts too rarely seen in our day. Too rarely and by too few of us. We watched and heard a performer motivated entirely by his love for the music at hand. Not so very rare, you say? Reread the word "entirely." Here was no ulterior desire to impress. Self-aggrandizement is an unlikely motivation in the mind of one already so aggrandized in other fields, enough, perhaps, for several lifetimes. No desire for mere attention can explain a carefully premeditated swan dive into the tricky musical performance field. William F. Buckley, Jr., is not a fool. He is quite simply enamored. The object of his affection goes by the name of Bach. Mr. Buckley has for years been stung by him and it shows. Even when imparted through the mechanisms of hands and fingers unpracticed for years, not to speak of an unfamiliar string orchestra snapping at his heels, the fearsome tiger of *Firing Line* made clear a message that came from somewhere inside his ribs. Technically, if a few moments of disorder crept in, it is best to say that they happen in every household. What cannot be changed, or measured or taught by any teacher is the devotion to Bach Mr. Buckley is willing to share with his listeners.

It comes across the footlight without cunning, without showing the seams of a treacherous craft, and all of this by a man whose humility must be very carefully rationed before the public. Is all this not a lesson to be relearned by most of us who have spent a lifetime in an ice-cold limelight that made us forget? I think it is.

Not as a personal friend but as a harpsichord teacher of some thirty-five years' experience, I say, "Play it again, Bill."

How does this sort of thing begin, this music appreciation? When in 1933 my father returned to America after three years in France and England, he brought with him a large household: his wife, nine children, a French governess and three Mexican nurses. The youngest of us was a year old, the oldest, fourteen. The time had come, my father decided, for his children to "learn music," as he put it. Before the summer was finished, the regimen had been institutionalized. On Tuesdays and Fridays, Mr. Peláez came to us from Poughkeepsie. The voluble and lighthearted Spanish-American, about forty years old, was a professional violinist, I suspect of the Phil Spitalny type, but, for reasons never explained, none of us was burdened to study the violin with Mr. Peláez, which of course meant that no one had the derivative burden of having to listen to any of us practicing the violin.

Mr. Peláez taught many other instruments and, pursuing no musical schematic that comes easily to mind, we found ourselves divided into mandolin players (two), banjo players (two), guitar players (two), and ukelele players (one—my six-year-old-sister). We were taught individually, and then made to perform jointly. Mostly we played traditional American songs ("But re*mem*-ber the Red River Vall-eee . . .") and Mexican folk songs ("Ay, ya, ya yaaaa. Cantaaay-no yorrres") because my father, who had lived many years in Mexico, simply loved Mexican folk songs. We were as a matter of course regularly entered in the local Amateur Hour competitions, which were everywhere during the thirties, in the little country towns of New England. We gave ourselves the name "The Cannot Be Better Orchestra," an evaluation not regularly sustained by the judges, some of whom gave higher marks to the dancing sequences of our neighbors, Jayne Meadows and her sister Audrey, in those days Jane and Audrey Cotter, and to a twelve-year-old violinist from nearby Armenia, New York, a dirty little sneak who, we discovered after it was too late, was a protégé of Nathan Milstein.

My father was a retiring man who, however, saw no reason why his children needed to be retiring, and I remember even now the mortification with which, during a Christmas holiday in Grindelwald in Switzerland, we learned that Father had volunteered the services of The Cannot Be Better Orchestra (he never knew we had so named it, and if he had learned of it, he'd have quite simply forbidden it) to the management of the Palace Hotel for a little concert at teatime. There were times when we hated Father, who was the most admirable man I ever knew.

But teaching us the piano was the major strategic undertaking of my father, and to the end that his children should have that opportunity, he engaged the services of a twenty-six-year-old tiny, shy, pretty, witty, endearing young woman, herself a concert-level jazz pianist, a composer, an organist, and perhaps the most captivating creature I have known in my lifetime.

She would arrive at Sharon, Connecticut, in her convertible Dodge from Tivoli, New York, where she lived with her parents when not studying in New York City, on Monday mornings between eleven and twelve. She would leave forty-eight hours later. In between, she would have given six of us a forty-five-minute lesson every Monday, Tuesday, and Wednesday. The contract was that we should also practice forty-five minutes every day—not difficult to arrange, on Father's six pianos. Every day, except for the Fourth of July, Thanksgiving, and our birthday, when we were excused.

Now as anyone knows who has ever wrestled with young piano students, there are ways and ways of spending forty-five minutes practicing the piano, and the cognoscenti know that it requires inventive monitoring to see to it that the slothful student does not spend his time playing and replaying easy lush passages (say the languid early measures of the Minuet in G) over and over, neglecting his scales, his Czerny, and the tough new piece he is supposed to be working on. I remember vividly spending an entire half hour replaying the soft passages of the second movement of the Pathétique sonata at the end of which I heard a rustling of the Spanish shawl that covered the little grand I was slaving away at. Out came Marjorie Otis (we called her, still do, "Old Lady") who in the exercise of what the Securities and Exchange Commission calls "due diligence," had esconced herself behind my piano, out of sight, before my practice hour, precisely to catch me *in flagrante.* There is steel in that woman, and the inarticulateness of her middle-aged former students when at the piano is entirely the result of their lack of talent and/or application, rather than of her lack of diligence during those seven or eight years at Sharon, before Pearl Harbor and the ensuing diaspora. Two or three of us were so much in love with her that we resolved at one point to become concert pianists, more or less in her honor. And indeed my sister Patricia played the Grieg Concerto at Ethel Walker School and a Beethoven sonata at Vassar before highly appreciative audiences, and I, at age fifty-six, played "Twinkle, Twinkle, Little Star" (twelve variations, Mozart) before twelve hundred airborne campmates one summer evening.

But the absolute no-nonsense figure in our musical training was called Penelope Oyen. A tall Scandinavian of austere features (no makeup), Miss Oyen, along with a forty-year-old bachelor, divided the tutoring duties of five Buckleys and three friends, who came to learn along with us at our house, a curriculum that covered approximately grades one through eight.

Penelope Oyen loved music with passion. It is relevant to stress that the word as here used is not platitudinous. Penelope Oyen would *weep* when the Capehart was on. Not always; and not for every composer heard on our record player, but almost always for J. S. Bach.

The drill was four times a week. At four o'clock we came in from afternoon recreation and entered The Playroom, as we mistakenly continued, out of habit, to call the room over which Miss Oyen now had dominion. My father had bought a huge machine, a Capehart, which, if memory serves, was the first company that boasted that its instrument could handle records consecutively. This it did not by the simple device of dropping another record on the one just finished, but by actually taking the record, when finished, and convolutedly lifting it up, turning it around, and either placing its flip side on the turntable, or replacing it with the next record, a quite remarkable feat of engineering, executed at the cost of a broken record every two or three days—expensive fractures which, however, had as an uncharted social benefit the interruption of Miss Oyen's lacrimations.

The absolutely decisive feature of Miss Oyen's discipline was very simple: darkness in the room. Not total darkness, else we'd have ended up playing Sardines. Too much light and we'd have managed to read—anything, anything to avoid just . . . sitting there, listening to what I suppose in those days we'd have called "that darned music." There was simply *no escaping it.* We just sat there, while the Capehart blared away; and the ordeal lasted *one whole hour.*

And, of course, *it* happened. I'd say it took, depending on the individual child's latent inclinations, between four and eight months. One of my brothers (R.I.P.) left our tutorial system in the fifth month to go to boarding school, and the result was that he never ever got around to enjoying beautiful music. I am willing to bet that if he had lasted with Miss Oyen another two months, he'd have become an addict, which is what happened to the rest of us.

When I think back on musical education, I tune in on two landmarks. The first was when I came—gradually, inexplicably—to the conclusion (at, oh, age eleven) that the "Scheherazade," which had enthralled me a year earlier, was, really, a most awful bore. That is the equivalent of discovering, usually four or five years later, the same thing about much of the poetry of poor Longfellow.

The other experience was unusual. I was, at age thirteen, at an

William F. Buckley, Jr., soloist
Yale Symphony Chamber Players
James Ross, director

WOLFGANG AMADEUS MOZART: Divertimento in D, K.251
(1756–1791)

I. *Allegro molto*
II. *Andantino*
III. *Menuetto*

IV. *Menuetto [Tema con variazione]*
V. *Rondeau*
VI. *Marcia alla francese*

Mozart's K.251 septet, was scored for oboe, two horns, and strings,
dates from Salzburg, July, 1776 and was allegedly written for sister
Nannerl's 25th birthday.

JOHANN SEBASTIAN BACH: Concerto in f minor, BWV.1056
(1685–1750)   Chromatic Fantasy, BWV.903

Mr. Buckley, harpsichord

Christoph Wolff, the Bach authority, considers BWV.1056 an
arrangement of a lost oboe concerto, probably written for the
collegium musicum concerts in Leipzig. The slow movement was
later used as the *Sinfonia* to Cantata 156, Leipzig, 1729/30.

Bach's *Chromatic Fantasy (and Fugue)* is an early work from Cöthen,
c. 1720, revised ten years later in Leipzig. Mr. Buckley dedicates his
performance of the *Fantasy* to the memory of his late classmate and
friend, Fernando Valenti.

CAMILLE ST.-SAËNS: Carnival of the Animals
(1835–1921)

Mr. Buckley, narrator

*Introduction and Royal March of Lions. Hens and Cocks. Wild Jackass. Tortoises. The
Elephant. Kangaroos. Aquarium. Personages with Long Ears: Mules. Cuckoo in the
Woods. Birds. Pianists. Fossils. The Swan. Grand Finale.*

Written for a private concert in 1886, *Le Carnaval des Animaux* was
never fully performed in public until after the composer's death.
The original instrumentation is for flute, clarinet, 2 pianos,
glockenspiel, xylophone, and strings. Ogden Nash's poems were
especially composed for a Columbia recording by André
Kostelanetz in 1950, with Noel Coward reciting.

WILLIAM F. BUCKLEY, Jr., was graduated from Yale in 1950 with the
degree of BA (Honors) in Political Science, Economics, and History.
While still a student, he was chairman of the *Yale Daily News*, a member
of several clubs and societies, and Class Day Orator. Before and
following graduation, Mr. Buckley was for several years an assistant
lecturer in Spanish at Yale. An author, editor, lecturer, syndicated
newspaper columnist, periodical founder, essayist, playwright,
television host ("Firing Line"), and contributor to many publications and
magazines, he has earned honors and awards in every field of activity.
John Challis made Mr. Buckley's harpsichord in 1961.

English boarding school, and my letters went out, in equal volume, to my mother, and to Old Lady. I was studying the piano at school, one lesson per week, three practice sessions (there were two pianos, ninety boys), to which I looked forward hungrily. My piano teacher suggested he coach me in the first movement of the "Moonlight Sonata." I told him that though nothing would delight me more, I would need the permission of my American teacher because she had early on warned us that playing the "Moonlight" before one was ready to play it was, well, wrong. If we had been older, she would probably have used the word "blasphemous." I never quite understood her point, in those days, but my loyalty was complete; so I wrote, from the bowels of that remote little school, in the cold, cold days of the winter before the World War started, asking for permission to study the "Moonlight."

Permission denied.

In a sweet, loving letter from Old Lady. She tried to explain that music was very serious business, if one wished to be good in music, good in understanding music. No one, she said, who didn't have the technical ability to play the third (difficult) movement of the "Moonlight" had the moral right to undertake the first movement. And anyway, technique quite apart, to play the first movement of that sonata required . . . a certain maturity. Her phrases were kindly composed. I didn't fully understand them.

But they taught me that good music is a very serious business. As poetry is very serious business. As art is very very serious business: that which is sublime can't be anything less. My debt to her is eternal: to her, and to dear, strange Miss Oyen; and, above all, to my father.

Maybe all of that suggests that music is an obsession with me. In fact I don't think it is, though it is hard to imagine life without it. Something generally useful, I think, has issued from my year-long concert career. I devised a new notational system in which I have great confidence. It is designed to help amateurs such as myself. It is very simple: notes played on the black keys are printed in red ink, every note is fingered, and where a finger crossing is about to take place, that event is telegraphed by circling the finger immediately before the cross occurs. Already three volumes incorporating my system have been published, featuring Bach, Mozart, and Chopin.

But, crossing Columbus's Atlantic, I confess to have been discouraged on the general question of music appreciation. I had brought
on board a portable radio/cassette player and six boxes of cassettes, plus
a seventh, ceremoniously given to me by Fernando Valenti, in which
he brought together two or three hundred of the five hundred Scarlatti
sonatas he recorded during his lifetime. The six cassette boxes were
about 80 percent classical music, the balance jazz, of the melodic kind,
with heavy emphasis on jazz piano—splendid people like Dick Wellstood and Teddy Wilson; that sort of thing. These I played during
cocktail hour and supper; the balance of the day, classical music.

On the fifth day of Leg Two I determined surreptitiously to ascertain
whether either of the following two developments would take place
and, if so, how frequently.

Experiment #1. WFB inserts a cassette into the player, and turns
on the music. You are hearing now Side A, let us say a Mozart symphony, with a second Mozart symphony waiting to be played on Side
B. Now this cassette player, unlike many of the more modern sets,
doesn't automatically reverse the cassette when it arrives at the end of
a side, which was an okay thing, given my plot. How often would I,
having left the scene—left, say, the cockpit to go below for a while—
hear a continuation of the music after it had come to the end of the
first half of the cassette?

Experiment #2. The cassette player would be silent. Unactivated
by me. But, suddenly, I would hear: music. Somebody actually took one
of my cassettes, pushed the eject button, took the dormant cassette out
of its case, inserted the new one, closed the lid, and pushed PLAY. In
other words, how many times, in the succeeding four days, would I hear
music played which I hadn't myself initiated?

Answer to Experiment #1: 0.

Answer to Experiment #2: 0.

I have decided simply to give up. What is the point? I am sailing
with grown men, one of them my son, who has been exposed to good
music throughout his young years, had the usual piano and guitar
lessons, etc., etc. It is surely wrong to say that there is simply no
appreciation among them for music. It certainly would not be wrong
to say that, self-evidently, there was no operative appetite for it.
Whether, while I had the music box on—which was much of the

time—they occasionally *listened* to the music that issued from it, I honestly don't know.

The effect of this experience, after about twenty years on board boats, of trying to cultivate appetites I assumed to be merely dormant, not dead, has melancholy implications. (Classical) music is not a readily addictive drug. And you learn, reflecting on the inventory of cassettes that are the permanent collection of the *Sealestial,* that there are two very distinct musical cultures out there. The *Sealestial*'s collection is about the size of my own, and although the "Nutcracker Suite" may be there and maybe the "Best of Wagner," the balance of the tapes are all of the modern variety, or so I assume, having recognized the names only of the Beatles and the Rolling Stones. I like some of the Beatles' music (I don't presume that anybody cares whether or not I do, but there it is); but I had to confess something to Christo a few days later, on the final evening aboard the *Sealestial* when we came back to the boat from the hotel for the last meal, in the heavy heat of late afternoon Barbados, and I had begun packing my gear. Lo! there was *music* issuing out of the ship's stereo system. It wasn't my kind of music, but I didn't say anything, listening to it from a distance while packing up in my cabin. After about three minutes, I went to the main unit, removed the tape, inserted one of my own, and went back to my packing. Nobody noticed the change in the music—*nobody was really listening.* Christo came in and I blurted it out to him. "I got a problem with that kind of music. It isn't that I don't like it [hard rock]. It's that I *can't stand it.*" I say this having, several years ago, made a conscientious effort to hear it out. Well, conscientious by my standards. How many hours of listening would it require for someone of my age to take pleasure from hearing a disk featuring the Amazon Flyboys? I have problems with pre-baroque music. I've never really swung with Frescobaldi. I've given him many hours. There aren't enough left, in my lifetime, to make it with The Grateful Dead.

What haunts the musically isolated sailor is the inability to share. It is as though you were sitting there, hour after hour, repeating to yourself silently all the amusing stories you had ever heard, but husbanding them determinedly to yourself. This generates a masturbatory sort of sadness. I have in late years affected to be interested, when the subject is raised in my company, in institutional sport, because I have sensed the disappointment some people feel when my response is not as it ought to be to the intelligence that somebody or other has just won the World Series. (Should one pretend to be pleasured by music, simply in order to gratify the music player?) But I shouldn't be pushed too hard on the analogue, sports and music. Joe DiMaggio and J. S. Bach are not, really, competing in the same ballpark.

· CHAPTER EIGHTEEN ·

Christo

It was just midnight, and Christo turned his head momentarily to starboard, where I sat beside him, and said to me—we were alone in the cockpit—"Happy birthday, Pup!" I had at that moment become a senior citizen, and though I did not have my eyes on my watch I knew that midnight would come and go before my tour of duty was over.

"It's been a hell of a whirl, the last month," he added, keeping his eyes on the star by which he was steering.

"Yes," I said. I knew there was an affectionate smile on his face, but it wasn't light enough to discern it. Yes. For me, Christopher's father, it had been a high season, not even counting a fortieth wedding anniversary and a fortieth college reunion.

Two months later I would laugh with Pat about the point. What triggered it was a lunch with our dear friends James and April Clavell. We were saddened when they gave up their house down the road a little way, in Château d'Oex, which had made practical frequent meetings in years gone by. (We spend two months each year in Rougemont.) They have moved fifty miles east to a house that looks over "The Lake" (Geneva). Inevitably our encounters became fewer, more nearly fortnightly than semiweekly. Today they had motored up to lunch with us.

A spirited session, as always with James, about this and that, with heavy emphasis on his bad luck with his failed musical, *Shogun*. That evening I caught myself saying to my wife, as, that night with Christo at sea, I had thought about it,

"You know—James didn't ask what *I've* done since we last met. If he had, I could have said, 'Waal, James, let's see: In the ten weeks since I last saw you, I've played two harpsichord concerts; I've retired as editor of *National Review*, after thirty-five years; I've crossed the Atlantic Ocean on a sailboat; I've published two books, one fiction, one nonfiction; and I have become a senior citizen.' " (I am running no danger whatever that James will see these words—he doesn't read my books, and I haven't read all of his. And what I am recording is by no means intended as critical: mere social piquancy; curious, scientific bemusement over solipsistic social manners.)

Christo, by contrast, would not let five minutes go by without inquiring into a companion's recent activities. He of course knew the personal drama in my decision to retire as editor of *National Review*. And he knew something (but not everything) about what the harpsichord concerts had meant to me; and—most obvious—here we were, at midnight, in mid-Atlantic, sharing the ocean, a singular experience. He continued, with vigorous attention to the demands of the helm—"I'm doing all right on the steering, you know" (he permitted himself to acknowledge his adroitness in keeping us on a steady course in the roiling sea)—and we talked, talked animatedly about this and that. At one o'clock Van came up to relieve me. Generally we tend to be rigid about rotational movements at watch-relief time, which would have dispatched me instantly to bed. Tonight, instead, I went down to the galley and fetched myself a gin and grapefruit juice ("California Leg Spreader," Van bawdily calls this confection), and a little cigar, climbed back up to the cockpit and sat in on the late, late night chatter between Christo and Van.

An hour or so later I said good night and went below, but before going aft to my cabin I went forward to Christo's empty bunk and left him a note I had written out earlier that day, one of those father-son intimacies we had begun exchanging when he was a teenager.

At dinner that night he replied to it with a note of his own. It was taped to one of the birthday gifts he had come aboard with, brought in to the candle-lit saloon (on my sixty-fifth birthday, the seas were obliging) with the birthday cake at dinner that evening. What we said to each other in detail is not in the public domain.

Two years ago we were estranged. For a period of nine months, no communication of any kind passed between us.

The proximate cause of the rupture was his informing me over the telephone on returning to Washington from a summer in Maine, where he had struggled over the third rewrite of his novel, *Wet Work*, that he would not reconnect his MCI; that henceforward he would communicate with me over the telephone.

This seems trivial. It was a shattering blow. Although of course we regularly saw each other, often vacationed together, and talked often over the telephone, for five years it had been mostly by MCI that we—connected. (It had been so, I later reflected, with my father who, when he had serious things to say to his ten children, would write to them. As a matter of fact, it is so among his children, my siblings.) Four or five times every week I would MCI (v.t.) him—a note, sometimes a line or two; sometimes something lengthier, transmitting one of my columns, even an article. And he would reply in kind, simple notes recording his experiences, or more; sometimes documents of his own, drafts perhaps of an article he had written for *Architectural Digest;* or his book reviews; or accounts of travail with his work, or with life at the office, or at home.

For those who do not know about electronic communication it should be explained that there is no other way to transmit, with such gratifying and total facility, what is on one's mind (faxes, wonderfully useful, are more often than not creatures that fall into the view of more than a single person). The modem in the computer is brought to life by tapping out first the 800 number of MCI, followed by the name of the sender and the sender's (secret) password. The screen is then activated, onto which you are free to pour out your thoughts, in sentences diffuse or telegraphic. By touching a few keys, the word that you have a message awaiting you materializes in the addressee's INBOX in approximately five seconds. Whether at the same time every day (even as every day at about the same time one reaches for the morning paper, or checks one's mailbox) or on impulse, the addressee tunes into MCI and notes that there is a "document" there waiting for him from "WBuckley, New York." He types out, "Read 1," and your message scrolls onto the screen as also, if so desired, into your computer's memory, and from there to the printer. If you wish to react immediately to what has been transmitted you have only to type, "Ans" (Answer) after the "Command" appears on the screen, and proceed to type out what you want to say. Or, you can reply at your leisure. If I transmit, say from Switzerland, a message at 7:01 and Christo happens to consult his INBOX in Washington at (Swiss time) 7:05, and elects to tap out his reply on the spot, and I happen to consult *my* INBOX at 7:10, I will have back an answer to my message less than ten minutes after dispatching it.

I was wounded (there is no other word for it) by his decision. He was liquidating, I interpreted it, the operative vehicle of our intimacy; and doing so—I pursued my reasoning with fanatical concentration—on particularized grounds: he found the MCI, he had said to me, *"intrusive."* Never mind—I explained to myself—that one need consult one's MCI only when the mood is on you to do so, whereas by contrast one is summoned to a live telephone. (My reasoning was formally correct: An MCI message will sit in your INBOX for a year, if you do not trouble to fetch it up today, or tomorrow, or next week. I did not permit myself to reflect that regular users become accustomed to regular monitoring by their correspondents, and are put off by aggravated inattention to the INBOX. Not infrequently I would telephone Christo and, in effect, ask why-in-the-hell had he not consulted his INBOX?)

I was so incensed (so reckless) that I wrote to him that I found the telephone much more intrusive than electronic communication, and that therefore he was not to call me on the telephone except in emergencies.

The effect of that message, with ramifications, proved sundering: Suddenly we were no longer in touch, and even his mother failed in her attempt to bring us together.

There had been heavy pressures on him, over and above my abuse of the MCI. He was desperately discouraged about the unsatisfactory state of his novel. He had sent it to me to read. I had found it rich in descriptive and satirical prose (for which he has become justly renowned: I write these words on the very day the *New York Times* reviewer pronounces him something of a seminal satirist on the literary scene); but the plot, in that early version, was mortally wooden, a mere clothes hanger for his verbal talent, and I wrote and told him so, suggesting the means by which I thought he might, with minimal exertion, make the necessary changes.

My letter added to his depression. And it all happened just after his quite stupefied sense of loss at the death of Reggie Stoops. The terminal phase of Reggie's illness had begun only a few weeks after his marriage. Christo, summering in Maine with wife, Lucy, and newborn child, had identified Reggie as—after Reggie's wife—Christo's special charge. He traveled to Newport week after week to be with Reggie at his bedside. Christo had intimated his dismay at my own deportment during the period: I had declined to visit Reggie in Newport, reasoning that our telephone conversations, two or three every week, could do as much to comfort him as corporal visits. Granted, I was suiting my own inclinations here. I knew what lay ahead for Reggie; knew that if I visited him in the hospital I probably would not succeed with the you're-going-to-be-fine-tomorrow line. I could manage this gambit over the telephone, but not in person, as I had shamefully demonstrated when at his wedding party, at which I was the host, I had broken down on reaching the end of my toast to him, for reasons he of course penetrated though not, providentially, the great majority of the hundred guests, who simply assumed I had had too much champagne and was waxing sentimental.

And then—I would learn this in the trough of our estrangement—Christo had lost that Christian faith that had been so vibrant a part of him, so quietly and serenely defiant of secularist fashion. When he was twenty-odd and there had been a whiff of skepticism in the air I proposed a long weekend together in Mexico. We traveled to Taxco and during two or three days we read aloud to each other G. K. Chesterton's *Orthodoxy*, that buoyant testimonial to the intellectual and spiritual depths of Christianity (written by GKC after he had become a Christian, before he became a Roman Catholic). Christopher had twice remarked that experience in Taxco, once in an exchange with Kathy Cronkite, the daughter of Walter, about offspring of celebrities and how they coped. His words on that and one or two other occasions had given me acute joy unlike any I had ever before experienced. Then, suddenly (I learned of it through a friend), he had become an ex-Christian, rendering so much so convulsively irrelevant, so much of his background, training, education, fruitless, in the context in which I live, and hope to die.

In the early spring, six months after the curtain had closed between us, I received from him a copy of a letter he had directed to a close friend who served as captain of the little club, or "camp," in the Bohemian Grove. Christo and I had been together there for a few days every summer for almost ten years. He had been elected, and was by far the youngest member. He mingled with his characteristic ease and humor and benignity, giving evidence everywhere, to everybody, of his singular personal appeal. Perhaps in part because of his young age, contrasted with that of other members, he was not altogether happy as a "Hillbilly" (the name of our camp), however much he enjoyed the company of Van and Bill Draper, and Walter Cronkite, and his former boss, George Bush; and on one occasion he had even told me, *"Except for you,* I would resign." Now, I learned, he had resigned. As the family logician I had no alternative than to reason that he had resigned *notwithstanding* me.

My bereavement reflected primarily my failure to begin to comprehend, let alone fully to do so, that evolution of loyalties that accompanies marriage—and should do so. Christopher was now wedded and had a child. He is devoted to his wife, and understandably so; and about his daughter, he is quite simply cuckoo, also understandable. Day-to-day closeness of the kind we had had was becoming a drain, distracting to the primary emotional and psychological demands he was feeling. I was wrong in supposing that the nature of a relationship that had proved airborne in his teens and in his twenties could hope to continue into married life. The rift, however painful, almost certainly had to come, and had to be painful, there being no anesthetic for extractions of this kind, never mind that there were other factors bearing on our particular situation foreign to the essence of the affair that imposed an extra heaviness on the rupture.

. . .

In late May of 1989, the private telephone rang in my study in Stamford. It was Christo. We spoke, and conjugated our reunion. Again a few weeks later he called me, this time from Australia. Father's Day.

Now, on board *Sealestial,* in the note he passed to me on my birthday which I read hungrily in the privacy of my cabin, he told me in language extravagantly generous and eloquent and affectionate that I was still in a way central to his life. I know that this is true, as he knows it is true of him in my life. He added one sentence I presume to reproduce because it brought me joy not rightly confined. "My prayer tonight—and it will be that, a prayer—will be for you, my dear and beloved Pup." I have a devoted son, if no longer my old companion.

From Bill Draper's log: "Today is WFB's birthday, sixty-five—a big one! He qualifies for Social Security and no one lets him forget it. He spends his whole day as he spends every day, hunched over his computer swearing at his StarWhat [sic] program, angling for stars, sun, and moon with his sextant and charting his charts so we don't get any more lost than necessary. [It is never "necessary" to get lost, and if the sky is clear, there is no excuse for it.] If I remember nothing more of this trip I will certainly never forget the author and commentator perched cross-legged with the sextant pressed into his face calling 'Mark!' and then grinning from ear to ear, proud to have captured Fomalhaut, Vega, and Altair again. His chronometer was one minute off on the other leg and you would think a German U-boat had surfaced in front of us, from what I heard. All is well today and he is having a very happy birthday. Particularly pleased when he got through on the radiophone to Pat. Some static, but a great birthday treat to be able to talk to her. He then settled in with a gin and tonic and, later, champagne courtesy of Van. Great birthday dinner. Some presents including a very special clipboard from Christo and a photo of Christo and his baby and Lucy and his father, nicely framed. And a yummy chocolate cake with candles from Liz."

Christo wrote in his journal, "Thoughts on birthday. In 1975, he was fifty and I was twenty-three. Fifteen years from now, he will be eighty, and I, fifty-three. (The mind is boggling.) Caitlin will be nearly eighteen. (Is this possible?) I make these reflections without morbidity, much as it is inconceivable to imagine a world without Pup. I remember a Zen koan within a koan from years back.

"A lord summoned a monk and asked him to devise a koan celebrating his family. The monk went off to contemplate, and returned, presenting the lord with a scroll upon which were the words:

> *Grandfather dies,*
> *Father dies,*
> *Son dies.*

2 Buckleys Become Best Sellers

By EDWIN McDOWELL

Being on the best-seller list is nothing new for William F. Buckley Jr. — but being on the list with his son is. And that is what will happen this Sunday, when the 60-year-old Mr. Buckley, who has written nine best sellers in the past 10 years, is joined on The New York Times fiction best-seller list by his 33-year-old son, Christopher.

The elder Mr. Buckley's "High Jinx" (Doubleday), will be No. 10. Christopher Buckley's "The White House Mess" (Knopf), a satirical first novel, will be No. 14.

It's a rare first novel that winds up on the best-seller list. But publishing industry officials say they cannot remember another instance of a father and son having simultaneous best-selling novels.

"I couldn't be more pleased," William Buckley said about the success of his son's novel. "I wish I weren't biologically related to him so that nobody could suspect that my enthusiasm for his book is self-serving."

Much of that pleasure is rooted in obvious parental pride, but part of it may also be rooted in surprise. Mr. Buckley said that as a reward for his son's doing well in school one year, he took him with him on an airplane trip to the West Coast. "He was listening to that dreadful music on the earphones," Mr. Buckley said, "and finally I said, 'Christopher, have you ever read a book?' He looked at me with a languid expression and said, 'Treasure Island.' If anyone had bet then he had a literary future, I'd have guessed 1,000-to-1 he had not."

Christopher Buckley wrote only one previous book, "Steaming to Bamboola: The World of a Tramp Freighter" (Congdon & Weed, 1982). It generated respectful reviews but only lukewarm sales. By contrast, "The White House Mess," a madcap romp through the corridors of pomp and power, has been racking up strong sales and warm reviews. "The delight of Mr. Buckley's satire," Christopher Lehmann-Haupt wrote in his review in The Times, "is that it not only sustains itself, but actually makes us laugh harder as it makes its outrageous way along."

The novel opens in January 1989, with President Reagan declining to attend the inauguration ceremonies for his successor, President-elect Thomas Nelson Tucker (TNT), and for the next 224 pages it heaps good-natured, bipartisan ridicule on the functionaries who maneuver for power and perks. (The White House Mess is actually a restaurant in the basement of the White House, in which all the aspiring movers and shakers desire membership.)

The author's insights into the corridors of power were acquired during the year and a half he spent as a speech writer for Vice President Bush, starting in 1981.

"I had agreed not to write about my experiences at the White House," the author said. "But I'd read about 10 or 12 White House memoirs, and I was somewhat appalled. The themes are generally, 'it wasn't my fault,' or, 'It would have been much worse if I hadn't been there.' Then one day, bingo, one of those light bulbs just went off. I said, 'Let's write a fake memoir.'"

Mr. Buckley, who with his wife recently bought a house in Washington, sent copies of the novel to President Reagan and Vice President Bush, both of whom appear to have enjoyed it.

"I had a letter from Reagan, whose sense of humor is as secure as his phone lines," Mr. Buckley said. "He thanked me and said he was delighted to share my new endeavor. Bush, who gets elected in my book, wrote to me a few weeks after George Will's attack calling him a smarmy lap dog. He said he was sorry to unseat my President, but the guy was such a smarmy lap dog that he deserved it."

The younger Mr. Buckley — an only child and, like his father, a graduate of Yale University — said that his father has been a constant inspiration to him, although he did not directly influence his wanting to be a writer. "I grew up in a house surrounded by typewriters," he recalled. "I used to sit on his lap and he taught me how to touch type when I was 6. I guess some of that enters the psyche."

Now both have graduated to word processors, although they compose at different speeds: the younger Mr. Buckley wrote his novel in about a year, his father typically writes his in 150 hours. "When I was in the middle of my book," Christopher Buckley recalled, "my father called me and said, 'Well, I finished my novel in 12

Christopher Little

William F. Buckley Jr., right, and his son, Christopher, during a sailing trip aboard the elder Mr. Buckley's boat.

days.'"

William Buckley's best-selling novels — "Saving the Queen," "Stained Glass," "Who's On First," "Marco Polo If You Can," "The Story of Henri Todd" and "See You Later Alligator" — feature the exploits of Blackford Oakes, the intrepid American agent. In "High Jinks," Mr. Oakes sets his sights on the traitor who spoiled a plan to liberate Albania.

The Buckleys have often sailed together on the elder Buckley's yacht — William Buckley's nonfiction best sellers "Airborne" and "Atlantic High" are based on his trans-Atlantic voyages — and they telephone or write to each other several times a week. "It's a very brotherly relationship," the son said, "and now we can sort of talk shop."

Their one apparent disagreement is whether being William Buckley's son has been helpful or a hindrance.

"On the whole, I think his being my son negatively influenced his own chances, although perhaps not anymore, just as I think my novels have been negatively influenced by my having a political identity," the father said.

However, Christopher Buckley said that being William Buckley's son led to his being hired after college by Clay Felker at Esquire, where he is currently an editor at large, although he acknowledged there was a presumption that "because you're someone's son," a publishing house will publish your book.

"Martin Amis once told an interviewer he was pretty sure someone would have published his first book for being Kingsley Amis's son, but not for being William Buckley's son," Christopher Buckley said. "Maybe now that my book is on the best-seller list people won't assume it was published because I'm William Buckley's son."

"The lord was furious. 'I ask you to give me something to express my joy, and you bring me this?' He was about to order a soldier to behead the monk when the monk said, 'No father lives longer than his son. Therein lies truest happiness.'

"The lord ordered the soldier to sheath his sword."

CHAPTER NINETEEN

Final Days

As I looked about the cockpit on Day 29 it seemed that everyone was somehow busy. Or at least was doing something. As ever, always: We know that most of the crew accompanying Columbus were not literate and could not occupy themselves with writing or reading, but they gambled, and they talked, and they drank, and they slept. Bill Draper was playing chess with Van, on a small set magnetized for use at sea or for travel anywhere. Tony was writing in his journal, Douglas was at the wheel, Christo was somewhere below. That evening on late night watch Douglas told me how singularly attractive he found Draper as a human being. That afternoon Christo had come up with a Nintendo game. Douglas laughed. "Bill said, 'Oh no, not Nintendo! The invention of Nintendo cost me a quarter of a billion dollars!' Apparently when Nintendo came out, Bill Draper's company went belly-up." I confirmed that that was so, as I remembered, and told Douglas that he was hardly the first to find Bill Draper, so soft-spoken and self-effacing, an attractive human being; he was enormously popular at Yale where I met him. A few years out of college he borrowed ten thousand dollars from his father, our first Ambassador to NATO, a general during the war, a telephone executive who, however, lived on a modest income. Bill and his wife drove with their three little children to Silicon Valley, arriving there just in time. "He told me a few years ago," I said to Douglas, "that if anyone had ever told him he would be worth one hundred million dollars he'd have had him arrested for lunacy." Bill had laughed and then added, wryly, that those millions seemed ephemeral to him then, so much so that the loss of one-half of them during the preceding year seemed almost meaningless.

Douglas is scientifically interested in human reactions, of course, and particularly in the special circumstances of such a passage as ours. He wrote: "It takes considerable effort to get along on a boat. Perfunctory civility won't cut it. One needs, really, to become engaged on a more caring level, especially on the dark watches when there are only two awake. Conversations often seem to pick up precisely where they left off. With Tony it is often about racing his boat, his impending fatherhood, and his business ambitions. With Van, about politics, about the relationship between psyche and physical illness, and about our common backgrounds, growing up in Ohio. With Bill Draper, about various topics in business, politics, and psychology—Draper was fascinated by what psychological testing (Rorschach, etc.) can reveal. With WFB, about music and how clinical psychology actually works. There is a pleasing continuity to this process, rather like picking up a favorite book and going on to the next chapter. It is like psychotherapy, when

patients unconsciously return to themes they were exploring the week before. We all wish to complete our stories."

Douglas makes a wise point about the extraordinary civility required on a small boat, the japanization of workaday manners. Morison wrote pithily on the subject: "Only those who have experienced it, know what wear and tear shipmates inflict on each other's tempers during a long sea voyage. . . . But on a vessel like Columbus's caravels, where men even had to ease themselves in public, it is impossible to get away from your mates except by sleep; and even then they fall over you or wake you up to ask silly questions, such as, Where did you leave that marlinspike last watch?" But Admiral Morison had cited problems that didn't affect even the occasionally distraught company of *Sealestial*—unless my friends kept a set of secret journals they have withheld from me. (Bill Draper amused himself with a long mock log that was not, I hope, father to the thought, because in the very first chapter I am washed overboard and trail the vessel for the length of the journey on—no less—Van's exercise machine.) "In a really long voyage such as this," Morison continued, "which is full of anxiety and disappointment, especially if there is no stiff weather to keep them busy, the men invariably form gangs and cliques, work up hatreds against each other and their officers, brood over imaginary wrongs and unintended slights, and fancy that they are shipmates with some of the world's worst scoundrels."

Christo remarks on Draper's bonhomie, which he defines as a kind of "Reg Stoops cordiality." For "sweet disposition and all-around cheerfulness, the award goes to Bill Draper. He's been unfailingly upbeat, telling you as you wake him up to go on watch at 0300 hrs: 'Thank you! Great! Thanks!' He keeps our spirits up by putting on a new, exotic T-shirt every day. He never passes up a chance to compliment you on something, indeed anything. He showers Liz with (deserved) praise for her terrific meals; Douglas for his psychological acuity; WFB for his star sights; Tony for his agility at the bow; me for no good reason at all."

Ah, another reference to my sights. Well, let me light up the sky with a singular discovery. I suppose it has been remarked a thousand times before, but there is no mention of it in Columbus's journal or, for that matter, in any of the half-score books on navigation I have perused. It is this: Taking star sights in the early morning is easier and

more reliable than taking them at night. The reason is so obvious I cannot forgive myself for not having initiated it thirty years ago. After sunset, you are looking nervously for the tiny little one-sixteenth-karat diamonds in the blue sky. They begin to appear and some of them will grow to full karat size; but when you first see them they are maybe 20 percent as bright as they will be when dark sets in. But when dark does set in, the horizon disappears. You want to shoot them as near to darkness as you can, but this side of such darkness as obliterates the horizon and makes the sights useless. That is hard to do.

But hark! In the *morning,* before sunrise, you are looking at the stars at the plenitude of their strength. Yes, that is Altair, that Vega, that Fomalhaut. You have spotted them and then—and then they begin to get just a little dimmer. But as this happens, the horizon line materializes.

See my point? Much easier to have the stars presituated. . . . I thought to pass my insight along to my companions, but I had the feeling that one more bit of celestial lore would shatter that hyper-civility Douglas was celebrating.

Douglas is observant in all things, dress included. "WFB has again today scaled the height of sartorial indifference. Two belt loops hold air, his underwear reaches above his shorts and appears to be on inside out, the label in clear view. His hair has gone Sufi. His new socks each have plastic tags hanging off them, and his left thumb is circled with black electrician tape instead of a bandaid. My God, who dressed him?" I suppose I am a careless dresser, though I am comfortable and adamantly conservative: no combination of any of the clothes I wear would ever exacerbate a hangover. And my gloriously protective wife packs for me everything I'd need, were I to dress with care, to step into the pages of *Gentlemen's Quarterly.*

Douglas's eyes move along the fashion parade. "WFB wears only blue or white *National Review* golf-style shirts. A fresh one, it appears, each day. Van wears Yale T-shirts with the 1950–1990 logo. He also favors shirts with the logo of the Bohemian Grove and turtlenecks. Tony has some Brooks Brothers stuff but appears especially partial to blue golf shirts with the name and logo of his own boat—*White*

Bill Draper and salt water

Arrow—printed with the facsimile of an actual arrow facing to the heart side. The ideal logo for a man who is such a straight arrow. I have my usual collection of mooses and artichokes and Draper has apparently filched bodywear from every organization he was worked for and from each person at whose home he has stayed."

Clothing? There are three tricks to Dressing at Sea. They took me thirty years to learn, opsimath that I am in so many matters. The first is to put on a foul-weather suit *before* your clothes get wet, not after. The second is to take preemptive care to dress warmly when you have the slightest suspicion of cold coming in. The third is to bring along twice as many socks as you will spend days between ports. Simple. But the discipline takes time to assimilate. Though, come to think of it, Dick Clurman knew all of the above on his very first passage aboard *Sealestial.*

But I liked best Douglas's description of Tony's garb when going up the bosun's chair to insulate the spreaders. "Tony could have been a model for Yuppie garb: a photo out of J. Crew or Brooks Brothers. Uniformed correctly: Ray-Ban aviator shades, Top-Siders, a white button-down shirt (where in the name of God did he think he was going to wear that thing?) [Answer: Tony wears regular shirts to protect his arms from the sun—he is very blond. They are presumably button-down because he owns no non-button-down shirts, no more do I], khaki chinos. He looked more like a Washington attorney in the office on a Saturday than a man about to get a 500 cc. adrenaline rush, swaying 60 feet above a moving boat, hoping the lines are good and the crew holding him up there relatively attentive. . . . Am I the only one on this ship who wears moose T-shirts?"

A question I would answer, but cannot, until I am told exactly what a moose T-shirt is.

We were getting close. "Lovely watch last night with WFB, under a three-quarters moon," Christo wrote. "He speaks in the excited tones of a boy about the ocean we're crossing, how Columbus traveled where we are right now, Benjamin Franklin, on his way back from his diplomatic missions. . . . 'Everyone took this route to the New World after Columbus discovered it, until the age of steam. And nothing has changed in the five hundred years; it's exactly as Columbus saw it.' "

When Van relieved Christo we decided on the spur of the moment to listen to a spoken cassette. I go below and fetch up *Liar's Poker*, written and narrated by Michael Lewis. On a cruise there is a question of protocol that doesn't arise when you are racing. During a sailboat race you pay zero attention to the serenity of off-duty crew. It is absolutely routine to go below and haul out a sail, waking up three crew members while doing so; or to fiddle with a radio direction finder that emits shrieking sounds through the sleeping quarters; or to listen in for a weather broadcast in a hailstorm of static. There is something in the immune system that comes to the rescue of a racer: Even if he can't sleep through it, he manages to eke out biological rest; he is very tired when off duty. For one thing, a racing crew (at least this was so back when I raced) is on duty twelve hours every day, not the hedonistic eight hours on a cruise, when two men at a time take care of the boat and it doesn't matter whether it takes five minutes rather than three to bring down, or up, the sail. . . . Accordingly, Van and I try to mute the marvelously alluring and amusing voice of the author as he tells us about the skulduggeries of Wall Street.

I still have some of the old habits that stay with me from racing days

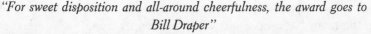

"For sweet disposition and all-around cheerfulness, the award goes to Bill Draper"

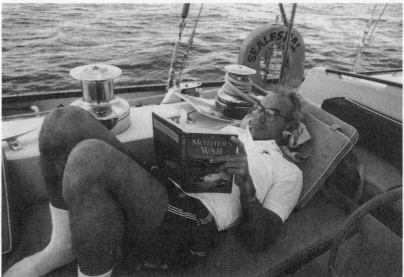

(1939–1965). Tony, who continues to race his own boat every weekend, is not put off by them, but some are—notably my son, who grew up just late enough to miss the racing routine with his father (I retired from the circuit when Christo was fourteen). He writes acidly about "WFB's latest"—

"This A.M. we're flying along at eight knots, keeping to course. WFB, his philosophy being if it ain't broke, by all means fix it, decides we must put up the spinnaker. Myself, whose philosophy is: if it ain't broke don't even *touch* it, demurs, pointing out true wind speed of twenty knots and these moving hills we're plunging in and out of, rolling everywhere. As usual, this makes no impression on him, and now eight of us are jibing the main, moving the running backstay, taking down the leeward spinnaker pole, dousing the blooper, grunting the spinnaker to the bow, dousing the genoa, which is now torn along the entire of its foot. I catch Allan, looking ever like a *fin-de-siècle* Prussian sergeant-at-arms. He is holding the spinnaker halyard, looking up the mast with an expression halfway between resigned and mournful. At the ultimate moment, he looks back at WFB and says, 'What's the true wind speed?' 'Twenty.' Allan makes the European hand gesture—palm down, sides up and down, indicative of uncertainty. This does register on WFB. (He has the highest regard for Allan, as we all do.) So?—It's jibe the main back, up again with the blooper, vang, preventers, etc., etc. The whole maneuver has taken an hour (equals eight man-hours); perhaps this was just his way of making sure we got our exercise for the day. With Pup, it is always an adventure. It's my theory that the great ones always have up too much canvas. They have no patience with the cautious norms. I'd be interested to know if Chichester, say, or JFK, J. P. Morgan, Jack London (yachtpersons, all) were always blowing out their sails."

Never mind. At sunset I told my itchy friends that if my labors were rewarded, we would see Barbados shortly after sunup. I left word to wake me in time to take the morning stars. I was confident. And, perhaps inevitably, just a little apprehensive. If the sky were overcast and we sailed north of the nine-mile-long island or south of it, we'd next see land in Puerto Rico. Two days later.

If such a thing were to happen to *Sealestial*, I could think of no melodramatic historical consequences traceable to my miscalculations.

Tony, undressed to make repairs

For Columbus, on the other hand, the consequences would have been ironic—

> Columbus's decision to follow these feathered pilots [playing a hunch, Morison informs us, Columbus slightly altered his course to head in the direction he deduced the land-birds had come from] rather than his inaccurate man-made chart was vital for the whole future of Spanish colonization. For when Columbus determined to follow the birds, his fleet was on latitude 25° 40' and fast approaching the area of zero compass variation. Had the due west course been maintained from that point, the voyage would have taken at least a day longer, and the landfall, provided Columbus had managed to keep down mutiny another day, would have been Eleuthera Island or Hole-in-the-Wall on Great Abaco. What then? Except for the unlikely contingency of the local Indians piloting Columbus south through Tongue of the Ocean, the fleet would have sailed through Providence Channel slap into the Gulf Stream . . .

Which would have carried him north of Bermuda—heading back toward Europe.

Christopher Columbus and I would have had in common only that neither of us would have survived our navigational misreckoning.

CHAPTER TWENTY

Finale

It was Tony, reaching around the lee strap of my bunk to nudge me on the shoulder. Some sailors need protracted jolting to wake up. I don't, though I found myself grunting, "What time is it?"

"Six o'clock—what you asked for."

I had time for a star sight, though not much time. Getting dressed on a boat in the morning in balmy weather is an operation that in my case consumes about three and a half minutes if it is your habit, as it is mine, to do your bathing in the late afternoon. That three and a half minutes even includes brushing your teeth.

By 6:05 (unbreakable force of habit: checking the logbook comes before even a hop up to the cockpit to take in the general situation) I was staring at the page for December 4. At 2400, I had written:

> *Log 2533* [nautical miles traveled by the reckoning of the ship's mechanical log, since leaving Puerto Rico]
> *LOP on Sirius plotted*
> *58 miles to Barbados*
> At 0100 I had written:
> *DR plotted*
> *Sunrise at 7:04*
> *WAKE WFB AT 6 AM*

Light characteristics in Barbados:

Fl 15 s, 21 m [The Barbados light is supposedly visible 21 miles away when it is totally dark. It flashes a white light every fifteen seconds.]

The only log entry between then and now had been by Tony:

0530 Course 270 Speed 8.1
Log 2580

I went up on deck. The moon was very full, lighting up the horizon so much as to make star sights difficult. The wind was fresh and warm without being humid and Bill Draper and Douglas were taking turns with the binoculars, scanning west in hopes of spotting the Barbados light. I think of the grandiloquent sentences of Samuel Eliot Morison when he evoked the tension on that great night almost five hundred years before. "Anyone who has come onto the land under sail at night from an uncertain position knows how tense the atmosphere aboard ship can be. And this night of October 11–12 was one big with destiny for the human race, the most momentous ever experienced aboard any ship in any sea." For us it would be momentous only if Barbados did not lie ahead.

The Spanish sovereigns had offered a substantial purse to the first sailor who spotted—the Indies, as Columbus thought them to be. And Columbus was already one week late, by his own reckoning, and his journal expressed near certainty that one more day without a landfall would kindle the mutiny he had only just succeeded in quelling two days before. Morison imagines the scene:

> Lookouts on the forecastles and in the round-tops talking low to each other—Hear anything? Sounds like breakers to me—nothing but the bow wave you fool—I tell you we won't sight land till Saturday, I dreamt it, and my dreams—you and your dreams, here's a hundred maravedis says we raise it by daylight. . . . They tell each other how they would have conducted the fleet—The Old Man should never have set that spritsail, she'll run her bow under—if he'd asked my advice, and I was making my third voyage when he was playing in the streets of Genoa, I'd have told

Van is serious. There is land ahead.

him. . . . Under such circumstances, with everyone's nerves taut as the weather braces, there was almost certain to be a false alarm of land.

An hour before moonrise, at 10 P.M., it came. Columbus, standing on the sterncastle, thought he saw a light, "so uncertain a thing that he did not wish to declare that it was land" (the words are those of Las Casas, who sailed with Columbus), but called Pedro Gutiérrez to have a look, and he thought he saw it too. Rodrigo Sánchez was then appealed to, "but he saw nothing because he was not in a position where he could see anything." . . . The light, Columbus said, "was like a little wax candle rising and falling, and he saw it only once or twice after speaking to Gutiérrez."

Admiral Morison has great sport with his withering exploration of what the light was that Columbus had "seen."

What was this feeble light resembling a wax candle rising and falling, which Columbus admits that only a few besides himself ever saw? It cannot have been a fire or other light on San Salvador, or any other island; for, as the real landfall four hours later proves, the fleet at 10 P.M. was at least 35 miles off shore. The 400,000 candlepower light

Christo, at the captain's mercy

now on San Salvador, 170 feet above sea level, is not visible nearly so far. One writer has advanced the theory that the light was made by Indians torching for fish—why not lighting a cigar?—but Indians do not go fishing in 3000 fathoms of water 35 miles offshore at night in a gale of wind. The sentimental school of thought would have this light supernatural, sent by the Almighty to guide and encourage Columbus; but of all moments in the voyage, this is the one when he least needed encouragement, and he had laid his course straight for the nearest land. I agree heartily with Admiral Murdock, "the light was due to the imagination of Columbus, wrought up to a high pitch by the numerous signs of land encountered that day." Anyone who has had much experience trying to make night landfalls with a sea running knows how easy it is to be deceived, especially when you are very anxious to pick up a light. Often two or three shipmates will agree that they see "it," then "it" disappears, and you realize that it was just another illusion.

Admiral Morison will not himself let us see land; not quite yet. The
great moment requires full histrionic development:

> At 2 A.M. October 12 the moon, past full, was riding about 70 degrees
> high over Orion on the port quarter, just the position to illuminate
> anything ahead of the ships. Jupiter was rising in the east; Saturn had
> just set, and Deneb was nearing the western horizon, toward which all
> waking eyes were directed. There hung the Square of Pegasus, and a little
> higher and to the northward, Cassiopeia's Chair. The Guards of Polaris,
> at 15 degrees beyond "feet," told the pilots that it was two hours after
> midnight. On sped the three ships, *Pinta* in the lead, their sails silver
> in the moonlight. A brave trade wind is blowing and the caravels are
> rolling, plunging and throwing spray as they cut down the last invisible
> barrier between the Old World and the New. Only a few moments now,
> and an era that began in remotest antiquity will end.
>
> Rodrigo de Triana, lookout on *Pinta*'s forecastle, sees something like
> a white sand cliff gleaming in the moonlight on the western horizon,
> then another, and a dark line of land connecting them. *"Tierra! tierra!"*
> he shouts, and this time land it is.

I decided to shoot Jupiter. A line of position on it would run roughly
east-west, and reassure me that I was headed toward the island, not
north or south of it.

0650 Star [planet] sight plotted.

No more plotting sheets. I was now drawing the sight line directly
on the sea chart, the left half of which contained the island of Barbados. We were, I figured—*e i g h t miles* from shore.

"Land ho!" It was Allan, and a half minute after the words rang out,
the cockpit was crowded.

I climbed the companionway, affecting total complacency. Good Bill
Draper shouted out: "Three cheers for the navigator!" Oh dear, what
a sublime moment.

It is my habit, as recorded, to take the helm when land is sighted,
and to stay on it until the ship is berthed. This (as I have also recorded)
is always—*always*—longer than even experienced sailors reckon with.
And today it would prove still longer.

Because after we rounded the southern end of Barbados, going north

Landfall

now, the wind from the east, on the beam, I had the guy eased forward until it was just short of resting on the head stay. The spinnaker was taking the full force of the wind. The boat began to heel hard to port as the twenty-knot breeze engaged the mainsail and the chute. I kept the helm steady, taking the full force of the wind, the lee rail skimming the water. Allan, standing on the starboard side by the mast, looked back at me, visibly concerned. Van, standing by him, came aft to the helm. "Allan says you'd better watch it. The boom. He's afraid of it."

Ah yes. The boom. It had split, a season or so back, and the owner had welded it together instead of installing a new extrusion.

"The hell with the boom," I said. We had come 4400 miles with an under-strength boom. If we had been a thousand miles out, or even one hundred, I'd have eased up, letting the mainsail luff a little, reducing the strain. But by God if the boom was not fit to stand a twenty-knot beam wind, let the damn thing split. Nobody was going to get hurt, and if we lost our boom and mainsail and had to come in on a headsail—even if we had to turn on the engine, powering in with a disabled rig—the hell with it. That was the owner's problem. I wasn't asking the boat to do anything such a boat oughtn't to be perfectly able to do: Let him get a new boom, along with a new sail.

I ignored the consternation, and we had a smashing half-hour sail, until we were perpendicular with the harbor entrance. Only then I altered course, facing the bow downwind to shield the chute as six sets of hands reached up for it, prepared to bring it down to the foredeck.

But, the halyard loosed, the sail stayed put, dangling lightly in the protected air. The halyard was jammed at the sheave up at the masthead.

Tony-time. He went up the bosun's chair. Indeed the wire halyard had slipped off the groove, and was now stuck between the sheave and the cheek. Tony needed to loosen the shackle and connect the sail to another halyard—the last we had in operating condition. They let the sail drop down on the foredeck.

This now meant powering dead into the wind the four miles we had traveled away from the harbor. One thing we were not short of was fuel. The logbook for December 5 reads, *Fuel consumption: 1282 liters.* We used just over three quarters of the ship's main tank. The extra barrels were unnecessary. Does it follow that we were heedlessly prudent in going to the trouble of getting them, filling them, and storing them? No. The winds might have been less obliging.

Thirty days, Lisbon to Barbados

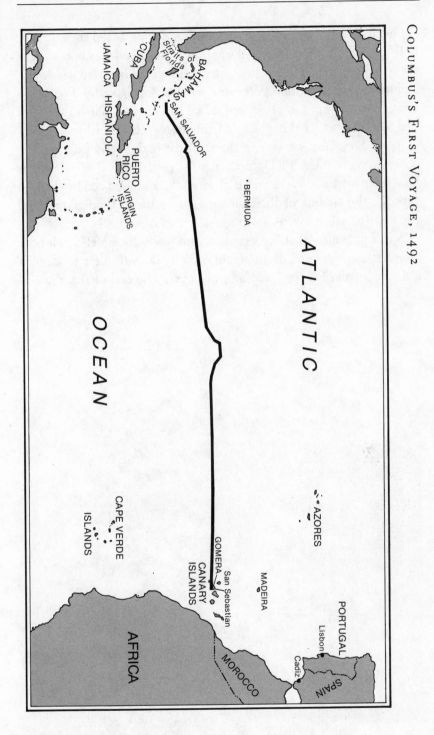

One hour later we had made our way, and approached the entrance to Bridgetown harbor. I said—it was midmorning and very hot—"Let's swim." We winched in the preventer, hauling the boom to windward, ending the ship's motion. We were more or less hove to. The swimming ladder was put in place, and we all had our last, blissful swim off the *Sealestial* and I thought briefly of the sweetness of life.

A half hour later we were in the still little harbor, and I docked the boat. On shore, all of Bill Draper's men—the Barbados United Nations Development Fund cadre and Barbados officials mobilized by them to expedite the landing of their director—were there. Immigration and customs formalities were, so to speak, informal.

A half hour after that, we were in our rooms in the hotel; a half hour after that, in the hotel dining room, making do with mere food, such a letdown from Liz-food. Ocean4 was over. The end of the affair.

EPILOGUE

I am asked by one or two of my friends who have been kind enough to read the manuscript why I thought to subtitle it "the end of the affair." I had in mind to externalize my mood when I sat down, in Switzerland, to write this, my fourth book about the sea, but to write also about other things, perhaps even primarily.

The voyage, as I have noted, began almost immediately after my formal retirement as editor of a magazine I had begun as a very young man; and I would, on this passage, enter senior citizenship. Practically the whole of my professional life had centered on that magazine, and when I left New York, having just then put the last issue away, I felt that certain sadness—a deracination, almost—one would expect to feel, even though at no point was it so keen as to make me wonder whether I had made an unwise decision in retiring.

And then, also, I don't know whether, five years from now, I will be in shape (physical, psychological) to crank up the energy required to organize a fifth ocean crossing. The odds are against it, I am told, never mind the buoyancy that continues to sustain me as I write. I am much struck by a passage in a letter I had from Whittaker Chambers, the more so since it proved to be the last one I'd receive from him. "Weariness, Bill—you cannot yet know literally what it means. I wish no time would come when you do know, but the balance of experience is against it. One day, long hence, you will know true weariness and will say: 'That was it.'" I have very little in common with Whittaker Chambers, having suffered so little by comparison, my link to the heavy machinery of history so greatly attenuated alongside his. He put it this way: "Our kind of weariness. History hit us with a freight train. But we (my general breed) tried to put ourselves together again. Since this meant outwitting dismemberment, as well as resynthesizing a new lifeview (grandfather, what big words you use), the sequel might seem rather remarkable, rather more remarkable than what went before. But at a price—weariness." Even within that weariness, Chambers found the exotic contentment he believed Sisyphus to have found, though consigned to labor every day to roll the huge stone up the hill only to see it roll back to the bottom again, requiring him to renew his labor, indefinitely.

Yes, said Chambers, he thought Albert Camus correct, that in labor, and in the "strangled cry" described by the John Strachey who had fought his way free of Communism, there was satisfaction—better than that: Katow, who in the novel of Malraux sacrificed himself by giving away his cyanide to a younger man, must now, without alternative means of ending his own life, walk into the fiery furnace prepared by his executioner. He "walks toward the locomotive through a hall of bodies from which comes something like an unutterable sob—the strangled cry. It may also be phrased: 'And the morning stars sang together for joy.' It may also be phrased: *'Il faut supposer Katow heureux,'* as Camus wrote: *'Il faut supposer Sisyphe heureux.'* For each age finds its own language for an eternal meaning."

I do not anticipate a Sisyphean end, except in the sense that all of us are condemned, always, forever, to renew our labors, and I have never courted, let alone been stricken by, the sadworldiness that afflicted Chambers. My life, on the whole, has been joyful, and my passages at sea have been pleasures so marked that I thought it imprudent to suppose that I might continue, as though it required merely the setting of the clock, to have another such an experience, with my friends, every five years.

And, as I have related, the nature of my companionship with my son is changed, as it ought to have done, and I have no clear sense of it that were I to suggest another passage to him, five years hence, he'd join me eagerly. At his age, one should expect that alternatives would be more beguiling. On the other hand, in the unlikely event of a prospective ocean passage, I might find his absence critically discouraging to the enterprise.

Oh yes, and there is the navigational point. About fifteen minutes after the appearance of this volume, we can expect that navigation at sea will cease to be more than an antiquarian exercise. Probably a couple of flashlight batteries attached to a Trimble hand unit will tell you exactly where you are, day or night. And when that happens, what shall I have to fret over on a long passage? . . . Ah, but the sea always has something lying in wait for you. Perhaps, in my declining years, I'll deny it the opportunity to vex me.

But if so, how can I draw from it those fleeted moments? You have shortened sail just a little, because you want more steadiness than you are going to get at this speed, the wind up to twenty-two, twenty-four knots, and it is late at night, and there are only two of you in the cockpit. You are moving at racing speed, parting the buttery sea as with a scalpel, and the waters roar by, themselves exuberantly subdued by your powers to command your way through them. Triumphalism . . . and the stars also seem to be singing together for joy.

INDEX